OBJECTS OF DAILY USE

Illustrated by the Egyptian Collection
in University College, London.

SIR W. M. FLINDERS PETRIE

 OXBOW | books
Oxford & Philadelphia

This edition published in the United Kingdom in 2023 by
OXBOW BOOKS
The Old Music Hall, 106–108 Cowley Road, Oxford, OX4 1JE

and in the United States by
OXBOW BOOKS
1950 Lawrence Road, Havertown, PA 19083

© Oxbow Books 2023

Paperback Edition: ISBN 979-8-88857-012-8
Digital Edition: ISBN 979-8-88857-013-5 (epub)

First published by the British School of Archaeology in Egypt, 1927
Facsimile edition published in 1974 by Aris & Phillips Ltd

Oxbow Books is grateful to the Petrie Museum for their collaboration in bringing out these new editions

Printed in the United Kingdom by CMP Digital Print Solutions

For a complete list of Oxbow titles, please contact:

UNITED KINGDOM
Oxbow Books
Telephone (0)1226 734350
Email: oxbow@oxbowbooks.com
www.oxbowbooks.com

UNITED STATES OF AMERICA
Oxbow Books
Telephone (610) 853-9131, Fax (610) 853-9146
Email: queries@casemateacademic.com
www.casemateacademic.com/oxbow

Oxbow Books is part of the Casemate Group

Front cover: Wooden comb carved in the form of a seated cat. Provenance unknown, likely Dynasty 18 (*c.* 1550–1069 BC).
Petrie Museum UC40667. Image courtesy of the Petrie Museum of Egyptian and Sudanese Archaeology, UCL.

CONTENTS

CHAPTER VII
KOHL TUBES AND STICKS

CHAPTER VIII
MIRRORS

CHAPTER IX
HEAD RESTS

CHAPTER X
BOXES, SPOONS, AND TOILET TRAYS

CHAPTER XI
IVORY AND BONE CARVING

CHAPTER XII
FURNITURE AND WOODWORK

CHAPTER XIII
METAL FITTINGS

CHAPTER XIV
GAMES

CHAPTER XV
TOYS

CHAPTER XVI

WRITING

CHAPTER XVII

STAMPS

LIST OF PLATES

Groups of numbers	plates	listed	figured	Groups of numbers	plates	listed	figured
Jewellery	i–x	252	251	Head rests	xxx–xxxii	40	32
Engraved stones	xi–xvi	354	354	Boxes, spoons	xxxiii	17	17
Hair- and ear-rings . .	xvii	60	60	Toilet trays	xxxiv	18	18
Buckles, fibulae	xviii	37	37	Ivory, wands	xxxv–xxxix	114	119
Hair pins	xix	78	78	Furniture	xl–xlii	179	40
Combs	xx, xxi	55	39	Metal work	xliii–xlvi	149	98
Kohl-holders	xxii	38	38	Games, music, toys .	xlvii–lv	607	366
Kohl-sticks	xxiii	69	69	Writing	lvi–lxii	300	152
Mirrors	xxiv–xxix	65	51	Totals . . .		2432	1819

vi

PREFACE TO THE 2023 EDITION

In the 1970s, a much-anticipated new series of publications illustrated objects and themes related to the excavations of the archaeologist William Matthew Flinders Petrie (1853–1942) in Egypt, and aspects of the collection of University College London's Petrie Museum of Egyptian and Sudanese Archaeology. A young couple setting up in business in the early 1970s, Aris and Phillips published these works, written by members of the UCL Egyptology Department, in their *Modern Egyptology* series. Building on Petrie's own observations, the authors of these volumes aimed to complete the great task of publishing the Petrie Museum of Egyptian and Sudanese Archaeology's vast collection, and to present some of the research that Petrie himself was not able to address in his own published works during his lifetime. As the current Curator of the Petrie Museum, it is a great privilege for me to support Oxbow Books in their mission to republish the series, which remains a key source of information for all those interested in object-based approaches to the study of the ancient world.

The Petrie Museum, part of University College London (UCL), is home to one of the largest and most significant collections of Egyptian and Sudanese archaeology in the world. Free to visit, this extraordinary collection tells stories about the lives of ordinary people who lived along the Nile Valley thousands of years ago. Originally set up as a teaching collection, the Petrie Museum comprises over 80,000 objects housed together with an internationally important archaeological archive. It is a collection of world firsts and 'oldests': the oldest woven garment; the oldest worked iron objects; the first known depiction of loom weaving; the oldest known written document about women's health; the earliest veterinary treatise; the oldest will on paper. The Museum has Designated Status from Arts Council England, meaning that it is considered to have outstanding resonance and national cultural significance. The collection has a substantial, visible international reputation for research, supporting hundreds of researchers every year, both remotely and in person.

The Petrie Museum is named after Flinders Petrie, who was appointed in 1892 as the first Professor of Egyptian Archaeology and Philology in the UK at UCL. Over three-quarters of the material in the Museum comes from excavations directed or funded by Petrie, or from purchases he made for university teaching. In 1880 at the age of 26, Petrie travelled to Egypt to survey the Great Pyramid. For the next five decades he was at the forefront of the development of archaeology in Egypt and later in Palestine, and his detailed methodological approach continues to shape the discipline today.

Petrie worked at more sites, with greater speed, than any modern archaeologist: seeing his life as a mission of rescue archaeology, Petrie aimed to retrieve as much information as possible from sites that were shrinking dramatically in size as Egypt modernised during the late 19th and early 20th centuries. He published a large part, but not all, of the finds from his excavations in his illustrated typological volumes, arranged according to object types and themes. Today, much of the Petrie Museum's collection is displayed and stored in a way which reflects these publications: for example, several storage cupboards are dedicated to the material illustrated in the 'Objects of Daily Use' volume, and objects in the drawers are arranged according to the order of the published plates. This offers a unique opportunity for researchers to engage with Petrie's typological and methodical approach to archaeology, as well as with the history of museum collections.

The first catalogue to be published in the *Modern Egyptology* series was *Amarna: City of Akhenaten and Nefertiti* in 1972 by Julia Samson, Petrie Museum Honorary Research Assistant. As official publishers to the UCL Egyptology Department the series went on to produce facsimile reprints of eight of Flinders Petrie's most important site reports and many of his object catalogues, originally published through the British School of Archaeology in Egypt. The substantial annual royalties from these reprints were paid into the 'Petrie Fund' at the time, which provided special grants to students in financial need.

In many ways, the new reprints of this classic series can be seen as the latest layer in a vast 'publication stratigraphy' of the thousands of finds from Flinders Petrie's excavations, which now live in museum collections around the world. On reading these volumes, I hope that readers will also be inspired to learn more about the Petrie Museum collection and its fascinating history.

Dr Anna Garnett
Petrie Museum of Egyptian and Sudanese Archaeology,
University College London
January 2023

PUBLISHER'S PREFACE

Oxbow Books is pleased to present this title in our *Classics in Egyptology* series. This series of facsimile re-issues is comprised of two sub-series. The first consists of 16 typological catalogues produced by W.M. Flinders Petrie based on his massive collection of Egyptian artefacts. Mostly excavated by Petrie during many seasons of campaign in the last years of the 19th and early decades of the 20th century, they now reside in the Petrie Museum at University College London. Published between 1898 and 1937 and long out of print, the catalogues were re-issued in facsimile by publishers Aris and Phillips in the 1970s. These were followed in the next 15 years or so by publication of a number of newly commissioned titles, based on more recent examination of elements of the Petrie Collection by contemporary experts, under the name *Modern Egyptology*. A selection of these additional titles forms the second component of our own series.

The archaeology of Egypt continues to fascinate. Multi-disciplinary investigation and research continues unabated, encompassing methodologies, scientific and data processing techniques, theoretical approaches, and even whole paradigms that were unheard of in the 1970s and undreamt of when Petrie was working in Egypt. Yet all the titles included in this series continue to be invaluable sources of basic data, providing an unparalleled resource that can easily be cross-referenced with the actual materials they describe and discuss. They remain within the Petrie Collection where they may be accessed and re-examined as new research flourishes. As historic documents, the Petrie catalogues stand as exemplars of the craft of typological classification, the backbone of modern archaeology – much of which, though refined by absolute dating and another 100 years of research, still stands the test of time.

A note on presentation

The facsimile titles of Petrie's catalogues re-issued in the 1970s were produced from scans of the original publications. Scanning technology at that time was not of the standard or resolution of today. The scans are no longer available, nor has it been possible to obtain, and in doing so destroy, original copies of the Petrie catalogues. These titles have therefore, of necessity, been rescanned from the 1970s re-issues. Where necessary the pages have been digitally enhanced for clarity of reading and to ensure the good quality of the plates, though inevitably a few are not of the standard we might wish, because of the quality of the previous scan, and occasional blocks of text are not precisely 'straight' or evenly situated on the page. However, some pages in the 1970s re-issues had been inserted in the wrong order and this has been corrected. The originals were produced at a folio size. The pages have been reduced slightly to standard A4 for ease of shelving and because this has the effect of slightly improving the scanned images. In some cases, illustrations were presented to scale and the original scale is given on the plate. There were also no digital files available for titles included in the *Modern Egyptology* series, so these too have been scanned from printed copies.

OBJECTS OF DAILY USE.

INTRODUCTION

1. THIS volume of the University College catalogue of Egyptian objects includes references to other sources, in order to trace the historical changes. On reaching the Graeco-Roman period, however, it would be too wide for treatment in a catalogue. The arrangement of the plates follows the order of the subjects as far as practicable, and the occasional inversions will cause no difficulty, as the numbering is continuous in each subject. The methods of manufacture have been described, so far as they can be traced, as that is justly recognized now as a necessary part of any catalogue. This amount of material might have been spread over three times the number of plates, with much advantage as a matter of mere book-making; but as it would then have taken three times as long to refer to it, and cost three times as much, the advantages to archaeology seem to be all in favour of compact publication. To sacrifice the use of a book to the entirely different desire of bibliophile display, is like sacrificing the subject of a museum to the desire of displaying fanciful architecture.

2. In the collection here published there are some unique objects, but the main purpose has been to show the varieties of Egyptian products, and the extension of Greek and Roman influence in Egypt. Much always depends on the opportunities and chances of acquisition, but material which can be dated has been gathered when possible. Such dating depends mostly on groups found together, where one object may fix the age of others; for instance, the silver necklaces which include coins (figs. 2, 3) or were found with coins (5); or groups in tombs, where one or more objects are dated by a name, or by similar objects elsewhere. The exact period is sometimes shown by style, obviously later or earlier than some dated examples, or intermediate between fixed points. The reason for each dating here assigned is stated; where no precise comparison can be made, and only a personal impression can be given, it still may be of some use to state it, but a note of interrogation is placed after it. For the sake of reference, the date is placed last of all in each description.

3. All the dated examples of objects should be brought together, as has been well done in publishing series of examples of dated manuscripts. Here only a beginning has been made, on very scattered material, which needs much addition of fresh discoveries, fully recorded. The published catalogues of museums give but little help; comparisons are seldom made, and only the obvious is stated. The most valuable exceptions to this banality are in the works coming from the prehistoric and mediaeval department of the British Museum. Most museum material has been severed from its connections and origin, and cannot be dated except by its internal evidence. Earlier publications are seldom of use, because of the neglect of preserving evidence and groups. In one of the latest publications the same fault is seen, the show pieces are issued on a grand scale, "and what is omitted is of minor interest except for the specialist"; thus the evidence which would help to fix the ages of methods and styles is held back, and the scientific value of discoveries suffers. A large part of Schliemann's objects from Mykenae have never been published, and cauldrons full of minor antiquities lay under the tables in the store house there. Gold seems to blind the eyes of excavators to everything else, and is as detrimental to publication—whether of Mykenae, Cyprus, or Egypt—as it is demoralising to the workmen who find it.

This volume is but a tentative contribution to the material for a general *corpus* of all varieties of form and style in these subjects, each to be

1

dated with their limits of period. Such a *corpus* for each class of antiquities is what is needed as a foundation for the science of archaeology; and on such a basis future generations will map out the whole past of the varied activities and endeavours of man.

CHAPTER I

NECK AND HEAD ORNAMENTS

Neck ornaments. Pls. i and ii.

4. IN this class we only deal with metal ornaments, leaving aside the enormous subject of beads of all other material, which will be dealt with under the catalogue of beads. The plates cannot be arranged completely in order of period, as various conditions interfere; but the description here will be according to date, with cross-references.

The earliest metal beads are the prehistoric examples of silver at S.D. 42, and small ones of gold, used for anklets, at about S.D. 50. By S.D. 60, the prehistoric Egyptian had attained the art of burnishing out the gold very thin, over a core of limestone or stony paste. Cylindrical beads of this nature were found alternating with iron beads, at about S.D. 60. Of the early dynasties, metal beads or ornaments are scarcely known, very few examples (such as those of king Zer) having escaped the general plundering of graves.

The great period of jewellery is in the xiith dynasty; the necklaces of gold lions' heads, of cowries, and of pendants are the most magnificent of any age. The treasures of Dahshur and Lahun have rendered these familiar to us. Here, there is one example. Fig. 7. Gold. A necklace of 20 hollow ball beads, made by soldering two hemispheres together; a slight puckering, round the edges, shows that they were pressed in a die. Through the poles of the hemispheres a tube is inserted, to carry the thread. This tube is made of a coil of sheet gold, and is soldered in at each pole. Weight 82 grains. A necklace of larger silver beads, of similar form, is in the bead section.

The period of the xviiith dynasty and Ramessides is illustrated by the Aoh-hetep jewellery, that of Tutonkhamen, and of Tausert, and the Zagazig find; but necklaces of metal are unusual at that period, carnelian beads with gold pendants being the general design.

5. Coming to Greek times, the next necklace here is:—

1. Gold and coral. Memphis 1910. 8 hollow ball beads of gold, made by rolling thin sheet gold into a tube, soldering down the joint, and burnishing in the ends over a globular core of soft paste. With these were 32 beads of red coral, mostly faded; also three earrings of gold, burnished over a body of paste like fig. 163, with holes for thread suspension. From these it seems that this necklace may be dated to about the close of the xxvith dynasty.

2. Silver and stones. Memphis. 6 silver beads, 2 coins, 17 beads of varied stones and red coral. With this string were silver figures of Neferatmu, 2 of Horus (small), and 2 small silver rings (like one figured). Also two gold earrings, with a small pearl set at the end of each. The curved hexagonal silver beads, and the polysphere beads are well known types elsewhere. The agate beads with two holes, and a groove outside, are like those of Nesi-tehuti from Saqqara (xxvith dynasty). The legible coin is of Abydos, with Gorgon's face, attributed to the vth cent. B.C. From the depth of the incuse, it is not long after 500 B.C.; so the group may best be placed at about 450 B.C. The hexagonal beads begin in the xxiiird dynasty or earlier (*Hyksos and Isr. Cities*, xxxiv A).

3. Large group, of which a selection is figured here. The silver beads are so choked with corrosion that only a few could be threaded. In all, there are, of silver, 83 curved hexagon beads, 13 polysphere beads, 9 polysphere cylinders (which began as early as the xixth dynasty), 4 net work spheres, 8 coins of Aradus, 4 others illegible, a spherical bead, two squares, an oval with grainwork, and a rough scarab (not figured). Of stone, there are globular beads of green quartz (13), agate (3), lazuli (3) and green glass (3), also 50 beads of red coral; altogether 126 beads of silver and 72 of stone and coral. Weight of silver 4466 grains after cleaning. The small flat bead built up of globules (top right in middle) is a Persian type, see DE MORGAN, *Suse*. The various types of silver beads here are good examples for dating, as the coins of Aradus (which seem to be of the latest style) would fix this group at about 350 B.C.

4. Large group of silver beads of which a selection is figured here, as they cannot be threaded. There are 22 curved hexagon beads, (no circular beads), 14 imitation polysphere cylinders, (no poly-

sphere beads), 31 net-work spheres, 1 spring catch (?), 2 heavy pyramidal pendants, 1 square, 1 frog. The latter figure and the net-work spheres are fairly well made, but the polysphere cylinders are merely a piece of sheet silver coiled round, and imitation spheres made by filing and punching. Owing to their complete corrosion, many of the net-work spheres crumbled away in cleaning. The group still weighs 3077 grains, with also a lump of rough silver of 296 grains. The large pendant in perfect condition is 339 grains, and one a little corroded, 327. They might be intended for the weight of double Persian shekel of 170 grains. From the polysphere cylinders being of a degraded style, this group might be dated to about 300 B.C. or later.

The fashion of wearing such masses of silver for necklaces seems to be a strange custom of the xxixth dynasty. When complete, these necklaces must have weighed from half a pound to nearly one pound. The net-work spheres are formed of two polar circles, around each of which are from 6 to 8 lesser circles of wire, the two groups joining round the equator, either with or without a band. Such beads of silver are known from the xixth dynasty (Tausert), and reach here down to the xxxth. Glazed pottery imitations of this type occur as early as the close of the xviiith dynasty.

6. In 5, an entirely new fashion arises, with Ptolemaic times. In place of the net-work bead, there are hollow gold balls, with wire patterns soldered on to the surface. The necklace 5 is of 8 such beads, with two spotted beads, 23 hexagonal beads, and 4 small ribbed beads, all of gold; and 51 beads of fine garnet. With it were found several Soemmerring (?) gazelle heads in silver, beaten hollow, (as in the centre here), and many tetradrachms of Ptolemy Philadelphus. Thus this group may be dated to about 250 B.C.

6. A gold bead of the same style as the previous, but of better work, with rings of twisted wire upon it, was bought with three beads of clear quartz. The latter look as if they were bi-terminal crystals ground cylindrical and polished. For fig. 7, see above.

The standard form of gold chain is made by looping together rings of wire; each ring is pressed together from opposite sides until it forms two ovals, and then bent at right angles until the ovals are parallel, see pl. xxviii, 54. In the simplest form, it is seen in the vth dynasty (*Mahasna*, xxxvii),

or with eyes at right angles in the 1st cent. A.D. (*Naukratis* I, xxvii). In fig. 8 there are three such chains, joined together by weaving them with an independent gold wire, which zigzags like a weft thread through the middle of the strands. Weight 326 grains. The style of the uraei in the terminals suggests a late Ptolemaic or early Roman date. For fig. 9, see further, section 12.

7. Hollow gold beads, no. 10; made by stamping each side in a die, soldering two together, head to tail, and putting a ring of twisted wire round each end to strengthen the bead. The smaller beads are all made by lapping down one side. This was found with the much worn gold ring, viii, 114, probably of about the close of the 1st cent. A.D., judging by the dress. Also with it were two alabastra, two bone hair pins, and a stone bead in silver wire sling, in an undisturbed tomb. See *Kafr Ammar*, xxxix. From the ring, the tomb may probably be dated about 150 A.D.

23. Silver necklace, made by loops of wire (as fig. xxviii, 61) passing from side to side of the chain; two such chains of loops cross one another in the middle, and thus there are two complete chains of the single loop type, like no. 8, intersecting. Each loop, as in no. 8, passes through two successive loops of its own series. The two separate series are held close together, in alternate rows, by the breadth of the loops each taking a full quarter of the circumference, and crowding on the next row. Where strained, a knife edge can pass between the rows. The chain can be coiled pretty closely, as seen in the bends shown; but it has very little free torsion, only a single turn in either way. This form of chain is at least as old as the Aoh-hetep jewellery of the xviiith dynasty. The chain passes into a socket at either end, where it is secured by a cross-pin. The clasp is formed by a ring with an outer edge of beading. In the ring are 8 C-shaped pieces, and at their junctions 8 bars touching in the centre. The junctions are all capped with studs. A little loop of silver wire is attached loosely. The pendant is a growth upon the crescent pendant. Within the crescent are two circles of rope-pattern, then a circle of 18 studs, then a raised circle of rope-pattern enclosing 4 compartments round a centre. In the compartments are bits of coloured enamel, set in, but not fused in. The top, centre, and base are dark blue; the two sides, red. The crescent pendant is known to be always accompanied by the ball earring on the

portraits, and the ball earring may be dated to about 100 to 140 A.D. (*Roman Portraits*, 12, 14). As this pendant is a later development from the crescent, it might be put to about 200 A.D. The system of the chain occurs in the Meroe jewellery, assigned to the 1st cent. A.D. and apparently also at Curium of the vth cent. B.C. (Brit. Mus.). The style of the clasp, with 8 radii, shows a leaning to the device of much later times on the Ravenna sarcophagi, beginning by 430 at S. Agatha. The crescent pendant and the 8 radii occur as pendants to a neck chain like this, at Naples. The system of C-pieces round the radii is that seen on the earrings with the pattern of an unquestionably Christian cross (nos. 246–9). About 250 A.D. seems to be a likely date between the various connections, or it might be later, but not earlier. Weight 840 grains.

8. The necklet of a single stout wire of metal belongs almost entirely to the xiith dynasty, and the Ptolemaic to Coptic period. 28. Silver wire with curled ends (as of xiith dynasty, Kahun, see *Illahun*, xiii); on it an electrum shell. That such shell pendants were usual in the xiith dynasty is proved by the Dahshur jewellery; see also a shell with amethyst and garnet beads, recorded in *Naqada*, 67. The making of such shells extended to the xviith dynasty, as shown by the gold one of Ta-aa (*Amulets*, 112 d). Figs. 29, 31 are shells of electrum, and 30 of silver.

32. Two silver wires, bent double, and linked together, with silver shell. This could only go round the neck of an infant; but it might be widened by a length of thread in tying the ends together. The loosely hanging shell would make it impossible to wear this on the wrist; it might perhaps be put on the upper arm, but there is no authority for such a position.

33, iron; 34, 35, silver (35 from Lahun). These are made by each end of the wire being flattened into a band, and then the tip being coiled round the neck of the band on the other end of the wire. The boss is attached to the neck of the band, and serves as a stop to prevent the coil sliding to open the ring further. Thus these necklets could not be opened wider; and, if they were pushed narrower, then the polysphere ornament would not be in the middle. Hence the whole appearance of sliding is merely decorative, and could not be of use. The polysphere ornament is of 6 globules on each side, 21 in all. This form is connected with the triangular pyramid of polysphere work of the xxvith dynasty, as dated by *Defenneh*, xli, 13, and the Cypriote earring of the same age (*Cyp. Mus. Cat.* VII, 4005). Curiously, there is no trace of polysphere work in the jewellery of the Roman portraits; yet it was used by Teutonic goldsmiths certainly after the reign of Valens (BALDWIN BROWN, *Arts in E.E.* IV, cxliii) and down to the vith century.

9. Necklet, 36. Gurob. Iron, with plain double hook.

37. Bronze, twisted, with plain double hook.

38. Bronze. The ends are squared up, and then formed into a coiled wire. On the square ends is a herring-bone pattern incised along the edges, and a row of circles stamped on each face (xxviii, 51). In the middle, a swelling with notches cut all round it, raised rings on either side, and a pattern of birds and branches, in late Roman style. This was the commonest form, of which there are 5 duplicates, some larger up to $8 \times 7\frac{1}{2}$ inches. Of these, three have a band of chevron pattern, with dots at the ends and the middles of the triangles, one is square in section, and one has a spiral graved all round it, imitating a true torque of twisted wires. ivth or vth cent. A.D.?

39. Bronze. Hook fastening beneath central disc. The disc is made by stamping a thin brass plate in a die, copied from the usual head of Focas. This stamped plate is soldered on to a back, surrounded with C-shaped wires, much curled at the ends, and filled in with coloured paste. On either side of the disc is a dome of brass, with a small knob upon it. There is an absolute dating by the head of Focas, who was detested after his fall; this necklet must have been made between 602 and 610 A.D. These domed pieces, on each side of 39 and 42, suggest that the necklet had dwindled from a much larger type, with bosses covering the breasts, and a disc on the chest.

40. Bronze, Lahun. Double hook fastening. Also a duplicate, larger, and one of iron.

41. Bronze, Lahun. Slide fastening. Also two duplicates, one larger.

42. Bronze. Hook fastening beneath middle disc. On the disc, four circles of wire, each containing a scrap of glass, backed with red paste, to imitate garnet. On either side, a high dome with knob on the top. Also a duplicate of this.

This class of neck rings does not seem to have any Egyptian source. They rather belong to the northern family, and probably passed into Egypt with the many northern troops of the Roman occupation. In Europe, the earlier type have Etruscan design, as one figured in LINDENSCHMIDT, *Mainz Mus.* II, ii, 1. The taste for large discs on the ring appears in the north during the late Celtic style, see L., *M. M.* I, vi, 3. They are familiar in Gallo-Roman graves with late Celtic ornament (II, v, 1; II, xii, 4), but in no case is a sliding joint found. That feature seems to be copied from the usual type of Ptolemaic bracelet (as fig. 27); which in turn is from the earlier Egyptian method of joining the ends of a finger ring, through a scarab, with each end coiled round the other shank. This is as old as the xviiith dynasty. The type of the massive neck ring, with its bands of ornament, and bosses, is therefore northern; but the slide with coiled ends is a development after it became fixed in Egypt. Then, later, two which directly copy a northern style, figs. 39, 42, have the plain hook without the slide.

In general, the presence of many examples of northern work in Egypt, as crystal fibulae, garnet inlays, &c., is of some value for dating such work in Europe. Down to the partition of the empire in 395, northern troops were constantly drafted into Egypt, and the supply of northern objects would be frequent. After that, it is doubtful if the Eastern Empire could draw on western troops; certainly after 480, or so, there would be no imperial troops to be had in the west. Further, after the Arab conquest in 640 there would be no European influence of any kind. The northern objects in Egypt are therefore probably before 395, and certainly before 640 A.D.

43. *See* section 11.

10. Three bullae of bronze, 44, from a necklace; hollow, back plate flat. Also six, rather larger, with beads from a necklace.

45. Convex discs of copper (?). 6 large, with a ring soldered on the inside of each. 58 small, with a cross bar on the back of each, cast by *cire perdue*. These were certainly for attaching to some dress or harness; from the small size of most, they may have been for some collar. They suggest stud- or rivet-heads; and, if so, they were probably upon leather.

46. Bronze. Lahun. A scrap of chain, with circular pendants hanging from each link.

47. Bronze. Rosettes and bosses, with an eye soldered on the back of each; still attached to leather. With them, a pendant coin of the elder Licinius, rev. *Iovi Conservatori*; this set is thus dated to about 320 A.D.

48. Bronze. Gurob. Three bosses joined by wire links.

49. Bronze. A complete chain of two-eye links, probably for the neck.

50. 9 Athenian drachmae, much worn; punched, with loops of copper wire, to hang on a necklace. With them was found a lump of silver scraps, including the setting of a ring scarab, a figure of Nebhat (phot.), and a small silver ring.

51. Brass. 4 square and 3 round plaques, stamped in dies, of thin sheet metal. Subjects: (1) a helmeted bust, with spear in front; (2) a gryphon seated with a wheel beneath an upraised paw, the letter Π in front, probably copied from a coin or device of Panticapaeum; (3) an emperor standing, holding a globe surmounted by a cross, and the labarum, ЄVAVШСТШРОVТI around ("well invoke the cross"?), in exergue T?..A; from the coin types, this appears to be about 470 A.D.; (4) an eagle, spread, holding a serpent. The work is about as good as that of coinage, but the plaques have been roughly punched, and linked by copper rings. Each plaque also had a hole below (or two holes) from which pendants were hung. This was probably brought south by some Gothic soldier from the Crimea.

Head ornaments. Pl. iv.

11. Gurob, 43. A false front of plaited hair, in which 62 bronze pins have been inserted. This is probably the only example surviving of the well-known hair-dressing of the period of Trajan. Perhaps it would be rather later, 130 or 140 A.D., in the Fayum province. 8 pins below have been detached.

52. This brass band may have been from a head-dress, or from a belt. It was punched with a die, and afterwards tooled over. The work is very barbarous, but northern rather than Coptic. Along the top are, a monogram of AШ or AΠШ, two spread eagles and palm branches, a saint on horse-back with nimbus and cross, three more spread eagles, and a monogram of ΠAP, sideways. In the lower band are 9 busts alternate with palm branches, of extreme rudeness. From the style of the monograms, they may be of the vith century, hardly later; equestrian saints are familiar on weights, &c., from the vth century onwards. This may have

belonged to one of the northern Greek soldiers of Justinian.

Miscellaneous.

12. We now turn to a few objects of jewellery that have been passed over, in describing the plates.

Pl. ii. 9. Gold amulet case, Harageh. Grave 211. xiith dynasty. Around it are 7 rows of 4 triangles each, of polysphere work; each triangle has 11 spheres on the side, or 66 in it; total 1848 spheres. Normally, the globules are 0·020 inch each, but a few are rather larger, about 0·025. The ground is thin sheet gold, quite flexible, over a core of copper. The rusting of the copper has burst the sheet gold down one side. The globules were clearly all separate, and are held down by a rather paler gold solder. The heating was not done from under the sheet gold, as the solder only just joins the globule to the sheet, leaving hollow spaces between, but it has run freely between the globules. This shows that the heating was done by blow pipe on the top. How the globules could be held in position, on the curved surface, is hard to see. The caps at the end are of stout sheet gold, with sides coiled, and soldered to the ends. Such cases as this were of course only for show, and could not contain any charm, or be opened. xiith dynasty.

11. Gold. Uraeus pendant, of sheet and wire work. The soldering is of exactly the same colour as the wire. The coils at the base are kept together by radial pieces of sheet soldered to them. The soldering is precise, having no excess at any point. Weight 180 grains. xiith dynasty.

12. Gold, and inlay of greenish grey paste. The base is a single piece of sheet gold, coiled at the end for the suspending loop, and burnished into grooves to produce the ribbing. The body of the fish is soldered on to the base plate. This, and other examples, were found together in Nubia. Roman?

13, 14. Toggle pins of gold and bronze. The gold one from Gurob dates this type to the xviiith or xixth dynasties. Those found at Enkomi were with a ring of the same period. The gold pin weighs 49·4 grains, probably $\frac{1}{4}$ of the gold unit, or beqa, of 197·6 grains. Such pins occur as early as the Hyksos (*Hyksos and Isr. Cities* VI, 11–15), pointing to an Asiatic origin; they are also found in Palestine and Hissarlik, but not in Hungary (MYRES, *Cyp. Cat.* 54).

15, 16. Two copper pins of the prehistoric style, with a loop head turned over, see *Tools*, p. 52.

17. Gurob. Pale red coral, apparently cut to imitate a worn lower canine human tooth of large size. It is drilled through vertically, and cut with a deep concave seat at the lower end. It seems as if intended for a false tooth, to be pegged on to a stump. Coral would be an excellent material, as it is fairly hard and tough without being too harsh for the opposing teeth. It was found loose, so it is uncertain whether it belongs to the xviiith dynasty or the Graeco-Roman age, both of which left remains at Gurob.

18–22. Sard and agate studs. Four are circular and one oval. The groove around is roughly sawn, but the faces are highly polished. Each one has a hole drilled through the neck of the stud. This proves that they were attached by a string, and served as a form of button, probably only passing through one loop or eyelet. They were bought at different times, but without any clue to their age. From the use of agate, they are probably not before the xxvith dynasty, but they might be as late as Roman times.

24. Gold heart, hollow. Memphis. Made of two similar plates soldered together round the edge. Top open, with a cross bar of wire put through for suspension. A loose plate of gold, found with it, exactly fits the top and an oval ring fits the neck and may have formed a lid, but, if thus closed, the cross bar would be useless. Other scraps of gold with it are not distinctive; but part of a carnelian pendant of lotus seed, found with it, is probably of the xixth dynasty.

25. Gold pendant, with amethyst inset. Made of twisted wire soldered on to a gold plate. On the back two vertical rings, one over the other. Roman?

CHAPTER II

BRACELETS.

Pls. v to vii.

13. FROM the early ages, bangles of ivory, horn, tortoise shell, slate, flint, copper, and glazed ware are found; and on a carved figure of an arm, made for a spoon handle, there are ten bangles represented as worn close together above the wrist. These early forms are described in *Prehistoric Egypt*, p. 31.

In the royal tombs, pieces of bangles were common in the tomb of Zer, of ivory, shell, limestone, slate, marble, chert and chalcedony; and some others occurred in the tombs of Zet and of Khose-khemui. After that, the use of bangles seems to have died out, until after the xiith dynasty. Bracelets of beads and figures were evidently familiar in the 1st dynasty, judging by the variety made for the four bracelets found in the tomb of Zer. (*Roy. Tombs* II.) In the Old Kingdom, the women wore bands of bead work round the ankles, successors of the strings of gold and carnelian beads found as anklets in prehistoric graves.

Pl. v. 53. Slate. Rifeh. From the surroundings, this is believed to be of the xvth dynasty, but it was not part of a group of objects. A similar bracelet, slightly thinner, was in grave 278 Tarkhan, of the 1st dynasty.

54. Silver. Qurneh. This is a group of 5 hollow silver bangles, which were separate, as shown by their skew relation on the arm. This was found with three stone vases, and one of paste, in a burial under the store rooms of Sety I; by these objects, the bangles are certainly of the xviiith dynasty. (*Qurneh*, 12; xxxi, 16.) Four gold bangles were found with a burial of the xviith dynasty; these weighed so closely the same, that they were certainly made to a standard, varying between 80·7 and 81·4 grains, half of the necef weights usual in Syria. (*Qurneh*, xxix.)

55. Bronze. Tell Amarna. As this was bought, after some modern use, there is no connection to show the age. It has hard red oxide upon it, as well as green carbonate, so it cannot be recent. It is unlike any Roman or Coptic pattern, so there is a presumption that it may be of the same age as almost everything at Amarna, the end of the xviiith dynasty.

56. Gold and lazuli. Bubastis. In this portion of a bracelet, the discs of lazuli are sawn into notches at the edge, so as to give a zigzag outline; they are united by a stout copper wire through them. The gold is a zigzag band, soldered around a disc of gold. Probably there was originally some organic paste, to fill up the hollows on either side of the disc and hold the parts in position. The cutting of the gold and of the lazuli was done quite independently, and so irregularly that there is much misfit in some parts. This was found with the large group of jewellery of Ramessu II at Bubastis. xixth dynasty.

57. Bracelet cut from a large cone shell. On the inside is scratched an inscription (see pl. xxviii, 57), which is certainly ancient, as it is caked with the embalming material. The signs are mixed with some hieroglyphs, apparently; the general nature seems much like the ostraka of the xviiith–xixth dynasties, namely a mixture of old pot-mark signs and hieroglyphs, used at that time for continuous inscriptions. xixth dynasty?

58. Gold. Part of a serpent bracelet, made hollow, of fairly stout gold. Traces of a solder joint run along one side. Ptolemaic?

59. Bronze. Pair of heavy bangles; flat on one side, to be worn together. Rather like 55, but closed at the ends. Date uncertain.

14. Pl. ii, 26. Gold. Pair of bracelets of wavy wire soldered to two strips, which are edged with a ribbed wire, like that on a pendant of *Naukratis* I, xxvii. The weights are 149·5 and 151 grains, one qedet. As the ribbed wire at Naukratis is dated to the 1st cent. A.D. by the name found with it (Tiberios Klaudios Artemidoros), these bracelets are probably of about the same date.

27. Gold. Pair of bracelets, of stout construction, made by bending thick sheet gold, and soldering it along one side. The tube is hammered up into thick wire at the ends, which are coiled round each shank, and easily slide further open for passing the hand. Weight 457 and 462 grains (2 sela). Ptolemaic?

Pl. iii. 60. Gold, over a white paste core. The normal ends of the bracelet are linked together, and a second joint provided, to be fastened with a pin. The sheet gold has probably been joined along the inside of the ring, but there are very slight traces of any joint. Roman?

61. Gold. Bracelet of similar work to the previous, but smaller; probably one was for the wrist, the other for the upper arm. That bracelets were worn just above the elbow, is shown by the cartonnage busts of the 1st cent. A.D. The hinge of this has the ends closed by flat plates; a loop, fitting a socket, fastened by a pin, serves for the joint. Roman?

62, 63. Gold, over a core. About an inch of the length is hatched with crossing lines, made by pressure, three ring lines come at the ends of those, then chevrons and lines of dots. There is no trace of joint along the length, but a lapping joint around the core at the crossing lines. The gold is obviously very thin, and there are a few rucks around the rod. Apparently it was made by a tube of gold, continuously burnished out lengthways upon a plaster core until it joined. It is a very skilful piece of economic jewellery. A similar pattern occurs on silver bracelets of the xixth dynasty, but it extends to late Roman work also. Probably Roman.

64. Silver. This form is derived from the serpent bracelets which were worn in the 1st cent. A.D., as shown on the cartonnage busts, and the earliest of the canvas portraits. As the ends have been modified to rosette knobs, this is later, probably about 150 A.D. Weight 582 grains, 4 qedets.

65. Bronze. Stout bangle of circular section.

66. Bronze. Made of twisted wire, still flexible and elastic. This system was familiar in Roman gold work, and this is probably of the same period.

15. The following are all of bronze unless specified, and are probably of Coptic period. See also broad decorated bracelets with late Coptic bead necklaces.

Pl. vii. 67. Ending with large knobs.

68, 69. Ending with debased figures of fish.

70. Twisted pattern ending in cubic knobs, truncated. Lahun. Also plain ring with similar knobs, 2 Lahun, 2 Gurob.

71. Square ends notched.

72. Ending with small square knob, and rings on shank. Lahun.

73. Plain square cut ends, circular rod; also 3 others much corroded.

74. Ends bulbous. Lahun. Also 2 Lahun, and one with slighter ends, Gurob.

75. A thin band, with cross-hatched pattern around, hook and eye fastening.

76. Ends twisted round shank, as 27, Lahun. Also others from Lahun and Gurob.

77. Iron, with rough pattern of stamped circles, and filed crossing lines.

78. Ends pointed, and lapping one over the other. Also smaller, Lahun.

79. Slight ring, with bulbous ends, Lahun; also from Gurob.

Other plain rings, with simple ends slightly lapping, are from Gurob and (3) Lahun. A broad plain band is from Gurob. A large quantity of duplicates of bronze bracelets have been rejected, selecting only the above types.

80. Ivory; 81. Horn, Hawara; 82. Horn, Lahun; 83. Ivory, Gurob, perhaps xixth dynasty; 84. Ivory, made in two halves; 85. Ivory, Gurob; 86. Bone, Lahun.

Pl. vii. 87. Iron, three crosses alternating with two discs: found with another having two large discs, and square and ovals between. (Also 3 others having discs of concentric circles, discs surrounded by 8 lesser discs, and disc with a saint galloping on horseback with a banner. Also a pair of iron, and one bronze, with alternate squares and ovals, and one with alternate notches on the edges.)

88. Iron, thin bangle, ribbed. (Also same size, plain, lapped ends.)

89. Iron, pair, loop and hook fastening, flattened by the loop.

90. Iron, wavy band, with double zigzag line. Lahun.

91. Iron, band of ovals with four ties at intervals. (xxviii, 56.) Set upright by it, a twisted iron ring with bezel, cut with diagonal cross pattern.

92. Iron, pair of rings, ending in dogs' heads, also two links. Lahun.

93. Base silver, pair, of twisted wire; two separate twists, joined together only at the ends; there, hammered flat, and a triangular plate soldered over them. The end plates ornamented with twisted wire and globules. The fastening is by a spring pin. Roman or late Arab.

94. Iron, pair, of plain bar twisted, with end rings.

95. Silver, hollow V section, punched zigzag line patterns.

96. Silver, pair, solid D section, punched herringbone and cross patterns.

97. Base silver, hollow O section, with imitation fastening, really continuous. The spiral patterns have been punched by hand, and the edges of the band brought together and joined along the inner side.

Unfigured. Two iron wire bracelets, and one of beaded wire. Lahun. Also 10 small iron bracelets or rings, and one of bronze.

98, 99. Two bracelets of vegetable fibre. Apparently strips of rush stem wound around twisted rushes. Lahun.

100, 101. Bangles of black glass, ribbed outside.

102, 103. Pieces of jet bangles, notched. Lahun. (Also piece of a thin ivory bangle.)

104. Pair of bangles of palm leaf fibre, wrapped round with thread, which binds on,—glass balls made with a loop,—glass balls blown in a lozenge mould,—and black glass beads. Also a similar pair with glass beads, green, amber colour and black with white zigzag. Probably late Arab.

105. Pair of bangles of palm fibre bound with thread, with glass beads, blue, orange, green, and white, also red coral beads. Arab. Gurob.

106. Blue and white twisted glass bangle. Arab.

107. Red glass bangle, with green and yellow band, zigzag. Arab.

108. Green and brown glass bangle. Arab.

109. Pair of yellow and brown glass bangles. Arab.

Pendants. Pl. viii.

16. Pl. viii. 110. Silver. Two hawk-headed sphinxes of Mentu, facing, wearing the crown of Lower Egypt. The bases on which they stand are not clear, they look like boats. At the back was a horizontal tube at the top, and another at the base, for threading. The tails of the sphinxes curl like a dog's tail, a form which is very unusual. This pendant is made by impressing a sheet of silver in a die, and then soldering it to a flat sheet for the back. It is thus very thin and hollow; and the amount of corrosion that it has suffered prevents it being cleaned. xiith dynasty.

111. Electrum outlines, silver back and inner lines, inlay of carnelian and soft green and blue-green stones. Two rings at the top for hanging. The subject is a round-topped shrine, or sarcophagus, flanked by two uraei. The uraeus to the right has lost the setting, roughly replaced later. xiith dynasty.

Finger Rings. Pl. viii.

17. Pl. viii. 112. Gold. Of Amenhetep I. The placing of feathers over a cartouche begins about the xivth dynasty (scroll scarab of Ra-ne-ka), and recurs in the xviith (Kames). The form of the name is unusual, see remarks in *Scarabs*. The thumbs turned outward on the *ka* arms occur just after this, under Tehutmes I. The work has the boldness and crudity generally seen at the beginning of the xviiith dynasty. The surface has been burnished, and had a slight amount of knocking wear on the sides. It has in the hollows, and inside, a good deal of brown matter, remains of embalming oils, &c., showing that it has been buried on a mummy, and not lost in the soil. It was probably on the king's mummy, which was broken up by plunderers, and twice rewrapped anciently. This source is the more likely as the ring was brought by a Luqsor dealer to Cairo immediately after the tomb of Amenhetep had been cleared in 1914. Weight 250 grains. xviiith dynasty.

113. Electrum. *Hat(hor) nehati, neb pet, ar kh(et)*. "Hathor of the sycomores, mistress of heaven, performing things." The metal is only slightly paler than gold. It has been beaten out with half the ring at each end of the bezel, and the ring then bent up and soldered at the back. In the inside is left a good deal of the red coating slowly formed on the surface of the ancient metal. Weight 75 grains. From the crude cutting, this must be either early xviiith dynasty or after the xixth: and as the rhomboid outline is found in the xiith, but not after the middle xviiith, this should be placed to the early xviiith dynasty. Flat square bezels were made under Tehutmes III (Maket tomb) and Heremheb (Leiden).

18. Pl. viii. 114. Gold. Female, draped, offering at an altar. The bezel is large and circular, and the ring wrought by hammer work. Weight 238 grains. This was found in an untouched tomb at Kafr Ammar, with a string of gold beads, fig. 10, two alabastra, two hair pins, and a white limestone bead in a silver sling. (*Heliopolis and Kafr Ammar*, xxxix, 18–24.) The style of robe, and the careful work, would indicate probably about 100 A.D. for the date; as the ring has seen long service, and been much worn and bruised, the grave and other objects may be about 150 A.D.

115. Gold. Of Antoninus Pius, with his cartouche. The ring has been cast, having small blow holes inside the bezel and the hoop. The finish was done by scraping and burnishing. The signs were entirely cut with a graver, and not punched. It has had but little wear. Weight 353 grains. As the gold ring was officially limited to the equestrian class and higher ranks, and the Prefect of Egypt of equestrian rank was the highest person allowed in the country, there can be little doubt that this was the official seal of the Prefect. 138–161 A.D. This may have gone astray when a prefect was murdered by the mob, in this reign.

116. Gold. Sistrum between two uraei. Beaten out, with half the ring at each end of the bezel; the ends bent up, but not soldered together, being left cut off clean by a chisel. Design punched, not graved. Weight 21 grains. xviiith dynasty.

117. Electrum. A pair of open-work wire rings with *uzat* eyes. The hoop is formed of two wires, which curve back at the ends. To the curved ends

are soldered three rectangular wires, forming the *uzat*. Weight 12 and 13 grains. xviiith dynasty?

118. Gold, set with green glass. Double finger rings. The hoops made hollow; probably soldered at the outer edge, as they have cracked there when crushed. Bezels hollow, of sheet gold. Eight-leaved flower in the middle, a *cire perdue* casting, chiselled on the top, rough below. The setting of the green paste is fixed by a ring of twisted wire and 4 globules, soldered in the flower. 150–250 A.D.?

119. Gold, set with two beryl beads, and one of grey stone. Double finger rings. The hoops made hollow. The holders for the beads secure them by pins, so that they can rotate. These double finger rings are rare. 150–250 A.D.?

120. Gold, set with beryl bead. The hoop made hollow. The form of setting the beryl as in the last, but a leaf on either side masks the junction of the setting with the ring. 150–250 A.D.?

121. Gold, with plain red sard, cut domed. The hoop is of two wires twisted, and two globules at the junction of the wires with the setting of the stone. 200 A.D.?

122. Gold. Two thin rings, soldered side by side, with a twisted wire and globules between the bezels. On each bezel, a female figure leaning on a staff with one hand, and holding an object in the other. Rude work. Weight 24 grains. 250 A.D.? Multiple rings begin in the xviiith dynasty. (*Illahun*, xxii.)

123. Gold. A ring forking into two bezels. Subject as last. 38 grains. 250 A.D.?

124. Gold. Ring with head on the bezel, apparently chased out of the solid. From the style of this work, it seems to belong to the Hellenistic age. The fillet suggests a ruler, perhaps one of the lesser dynasts of Asia Minor. The beard and fillet without a tie appear on Prusias. Weight 104 grains. 200 B.C.?

125. Gold. **EIC ZEYC CAPAΠIC**. Solid hoop soldered to oval bezel, two globules at each junction. Weight 40 grains. 200 A.D.?

126. Gold. Serpent ring of wire, roughly beaten to a head at the end. Weight 19 grains. 100 A.D.?

127. Gold, set with dark paste. Joint on one side of the hoop, cut out of sheet gold. Zigzag line and dots around the hoop. 200 A.D.?

128. Gold. Twisted wire, with the ends coiled round the shanks, so as to slide. Late Ptolemaic?

129. Gold. Polygonal ring, surfaces quite plain. Beaten out of one piece. Weight 44 grains. 200–400 A.D.?

CHAPTER III

EARRINGS.

Pls. viii to x.

19. EARRINGS are not found, or represented, before the xiith dynasty. At that time they were occasionally used by both men and women; the ears of Akhenaten are represented as pierced for rings. Also scribes as Auta and Moyă (Leiden, Mon. II, vi, vii). Some early rings were suspended by thread, as 164, and that suggests that closed rings or close spirals (132, 136) may have been thus used. The well-formed hook for passing through the ear (207, 208) is of late development.

130. Gurob. Bronze. Ring fluted in the direction of the length. Perhaps from furniture. Roman?

131. Bronze. Heavy ring, gap closed.

132. Gold plating on bronze. Heavy rings, gap closed. The purpose of these closed rings is unknown. The stout Cypriote rings are always an open spiral into which tresses of hair could be passed, as xvii, 60. These closed rings would be difficult to use for hair. They might be forgeries of value rings for exchange, as used in Egypt in the xviiith dynasty. Another ring, not figured, is worked with six lines of rope pattern along it, and the gold has been pressed in to the pattern; the plating has mostly fallen away.

133. Gold plating on bronze. Also a similar ring, but with a gap.

134. Bronze. Band with six ribs externally, cut down to two at one end, in order to pass through the ear. Such begin in the xiith dynasty (*Riqqeh*, i, li); similar to ribbed bracelets of xiith (*Arabeh*, i).

135. Bronze. Band of four ribs, cut down to two (see *Amrah and Abydos*, liii). xviiith dynasty?

136. Gold plating on bronze. Spirals of $3\frac{1}{2}$ turns of wire, ribbed over half a turn at each end.

137. Bronze. Gurob. Elastic spirals of $2\frac{1}{2}$ and of 4 turns (*Amrah and Abydos*, liii). xviiith dynasty.

138. Two earrings. Gold, hollow. Abydos, grave D 116. There is no trace of a joint, but the gold has been much rucked up on the inner side by bending, showing that it was worked in a V-form to begin with. These are well dated by a scarab of Hatshepsut, as well as others of Tehutmes III (MACE, *El Amrah and Abydos*, liii), and other things agree with this date (pl. xlvi).

An exactly similar earring was found at Tell Amarna; so this type may be dated to middle and end of xviiith dynasty. Fig. 139 similar, without locality.

140. Gold, hollow. Joint along outer edge. Found with Ptah-seker and crocodile of green glaze, of xviiith or xixth dynasty, as a reburial in the xith dynasty cemetery, grave B 26, at Qurneh. Long ends were retained in the xxvth dynasty (*Hyksos and Isr. Cities*, xixc) though the lower point was lost.

141. Silver. Rifeh, grave 135. Two pairs of these are dated, by accompanying beads, to early xixth dynasty. Similar plain earrings occur with the Ramesside jewellery at Cairo. (*Le Musée Egyptien* II, pl. l.) xixth dynasty.

142. Gold. Like the previous, with a well worked gold *Mitra* shell as a pendant. xixth dynasty.

A pair of bronze earrings seem to be rough copies of this form; and a pair of silver rings from Lahun are of this form, but closed.

143. Bronze. Hawara. These plain rings with a hook seem to be a later form of the previous, but are undated. Round earrings without a hook are dated to the Bronze Age in Cyprus (MYRES, *Cyp. Cat.*, 4003).

20. 144—7. Silver. The family of boat-shaped earrings is well marked; it may be derived from the fullest form of the crescent gold earrings, as figs. 163—4, but as that family certainly descends later, it is here described below. This almost globular type does not seem to occur in Cyprus. xxvith dynasty?

148—9. Bronze. The longer boat form is known in Cyprus, vith to ivth cents. B.C.; these simplest forms without long loops may be put to the xxvith dynasty.

150. From the influence of the boat form comes the strange type of this earring, made to hang on over the ear, with a plug of a soft paste in it, which passed behind the lobe of the ear, and so helped to keep the earring in place.

The long form, to be hung over the ear, dates back to the xviiith dynasty. In MURRAY's *Excavations in Cyprus* it will be seen (pl. x) that the long earrings were found with some bull's head earrings in tomb 75; and exactly the same bull's head earrings were found in tomb 84 (xii, 452) which is dated to the middle of the xviiith dynasty by the pottery, p. 38. In accord with this, there was, in tomb 75, the Egyptian ivory figure of a girl swimming, holding a dish, which type is regularly of the xviiith dynasty. These earlier long earrings

were however closed; and the open form, seen here, suggests the influence of the boat type. As to the date of this, the boat form belongs to the xxvith dynasty. The pile of spheres in lines below the boat is of the family of the polysphere cylinders, which begin in the xixth dynasty (*Mus. Eg.* III, pl. l), and we have seen it in the necklaces fig. 3, dated to about 350 B.C. Perhaps 600 B.C. may be the date of this.

151—2. Gold. This pair of earrings (without a history, from the Price collection) is of the same form as the last. The pile of spheres is more like the polysphere cylinders of necklace 3. On the other hand we shall see that pile, in the next group, going back to about 600 B.C.; and the little group of spheres at the bottom is like the larger pyramid groups of Defenneh. The cylindrical pile is made here by beating over a mould, not by aggregation of actual spheres as at Defenneh. Probably these may be dated to about 500 B.C.

21. Pl. viii. 153—162. These twelve objects were found together at Memphis. The large lobed earrings, 161—2, are the most striking forms, especially as having a late Mykenaean trace of design, in the lines wound around bosses. The material is gold, backed with a white paste. Such lobed earrings are in the Cairo Museum, with various patterns of rope, circles, ribbed bars, and globules. They are merely termed, there, Graeco-Roman. The earrings, 160, with pile of spheres below, are like the work of the large earrings 151—2, just described. They are also akin to the earrings with pendants, each bearing a pearl, with necklace 1, which is dated to about 450 B.C. The forms 159, 160 are of about 600 B.C. (*Defenneh*, xli, 2). The *uzat* eyes, 153—6, are of very fine work, thick and well engraved; they may be as early as the renascence under the xxvth dynasty 700 B.C., and cannot be after the decadence of about 550 B.C. These *uzats* are, 153 of sard, 154 of brown haematite, 155 of grey syenite (not engraved), 156 of jade. The two eyes 157—8 are of gold, as also all the earrings. The trace of late Mykenaean design takes this group back early in the renascence, and, with the *uzat* eyes, it seems most likely that this should be put at 600 B.C., within 50 years either way.

163—4. The lesser of these is dated by the last group. The fuller form is probably later, as it has threading holes for a separate hook to the ear, perhaps 500 B.C.

22. Saft 165–6. Two ball pendants of gold, with groups of three globules soldered on, and six globules below each handle on the lesser pendant. These were found with a pair of earrings, fig. 167, in grave 663 at Saft (*H. and Isr. Cities*), dated by pottery to the Ptolemaic age. An almost similar vase pendant, with globules on it, was found at Curium (MURRAY, *Exc. Cyp.*, xiii, 8) in tomb 73, dated about 400–300 B.C. (see vase 73, p. 76, and coin of Alexander, p. 83). These may, then, be dated about 300 B.C.

168–171. The plain gold crescent earrings are not yet well dated. Some are as late as 300 B.C. in the last group; others seem to belong to a much earlier period, and those with a pointed base (fig. 138) are of the xviiith dynasty. Probably the discrimination must be made by the form of the ends, plain, hooked, twisted together, or pierced for a separate wire. The plain ends are of the xviiith dynasty (ENKOMI, *Exc. Cyp.*, viii), the twisted ends are of 300 B.C.

172. Silver. Ring with a hook and eye fastening, and a boss attached below the eye. Grave 669. Saft.

173. Gold. Twisted ends forming a sliding joint. (600 B.C. See *Defenneh*, xli, 4.) Saft.

174–5. Bronze. Bull's head earrings. These are dated to the ivth and iiird cents. B.C. in Cyprus. (Also three single earrings, one with spiral twist.) HADACZEK dates them vth and ivth cent. (*Ohrschmuck, Abh. Arch. Univers. Wien*, 1903.)

176. Bronze. Bull's head earrings, cut out of flat sheet, and soldered on the end of the wire. Hawara. Edw. coll.

177. Silver. Rings of wire are put around the earring; then a fine wire is twisted round, zigzagged, and fastened down with slight soldering. Ptolemaic?

178. Silver. As last, but only one wire is twisted, without separate rings.

23. Pl. ix. 179. Pile of gold globules, soldered as a three-sided pyramid. Such a pendant of an earring is dated to 660–560 B.C. *Defenneh*, xli, 13, and classed to viith–vith cent. in Cyprus.

180. Earring of sheet copper, hollow; with pendant formed of four triangles of sheet copper, punched to resemble globules. Cheap degradation of previous. Hawara.

181. Copper wire ring, and pendant cone punched to imitate globules.

182. Gilded copper ring, and pendant cone, smooth; the last degradation of the polysphere ornament.

183. Silver. Ring with 9 globules (see *Mus. Eg.* III, pl. l). About xxvth dynasty? Gurob.

184. Silver. Square wire ring with single ball. About xxth dynasty? Of the xxiiird in *Hyksos and Isr. Cities*, xxxiv A.

185. Silver. Ring with twisted ends, pendant of 4 globules.

186. Silver. Pair of similar rings. Lahun.

187. Copper. Pendant of earring of stamped metal, with opaque green glass balls inserted. Gurob.

188. Cast pewter earring. This form is also found in N. Syria about 600 B.C. (see *Annals Arch. and Anth.*, Liverpool, vii, 119, tomb 17).

189. Gold. Pair of S-earrings, with pearls threaded on. These never occur on the portraits of the 1st to iiird cents. A.D., and are probably of Ptolemaic age.

190–1. Gold. S-earrings with silver beads.

192. Lead wire, with glass beads; these still remain on the ears of the mummy, showing how they were attached. Dated by a papyrus and jar, to about iind cent. A.D.; Hawara. They illustrate the transition from the S-earring to the hoop earring with beads, which was usual about 100–160 A.D.

193. Pair of brass wire earrings, with hollow pewter pendants, cast in a double mould. Probably cast by chilling in the mould, as there is a hole on each side, by which the liquid metal could be poured out, and air enter.

194. Two gold beads; made on an equator band, with twisted wire borders, to each edge of which six loops of gold are fixed, joining together in a polar ring. A very small ring is put over each junction of the loops. It seems probable that these beads were for fitting on S-earrings. Ptolemaic.

195. Silver. Large bead, with equator of twisted wire, and on either side five circles of twisted wire, each circle containing five lesser circles. Knobs in the centre of each circle, and between circles. This system of circles of twisted wire on hollow metal beads is that of the gold necklace fig. 5, which is dated by coins to about 250 B.C. This bead was probably for an earring.

196. Pair of silver earrings, with coarser forms of the preceding 194. Probably late Ptolemaic. (Also another, and a smaller one, similar.)

197. Pair of copper earrings, degraded from the preceding type. Late Ptolemaic.

198. Bronze ring with three imitation pendants cast on it, open point behind.

199. Pendant of earring, or necklace; made of sheet gold and twisted wire. Set in it is a polished translucent green stone.

200. Pottery earring, stuccoed and gilt.

201—5. Bronze earrings with terminal knob degraded from the form of 196. 202 Lahun. 203—4 Gurob. 205 with blue glass beads threaded on it. As none of this form appear on the Roman portraits or the gilt cartonnage of the 1st cent. A.D., it seems that they end with the close of the Ptolemaic age.

24. *Roman earrings.*

206. Gold ring, hollow, lapped on inner side, with wire pendant for a pearl, now lost. For an exaggeration of this type, see *Hyksos and Isr. Cities,* xl, xlvi.

207. Gold framing, hook, and pendants, with square of green glass, over it a pearl, pendants of beryl and pearl. This form of hook is classed as the latest of the Hellenic types of ivth cent. B.C. onwards; examples of the iiird and iind cent. occurred at Curium with single pearls. The square setting seems late Ptolemaic, or more probably Roman, and this may probably be put to the 1st cent. A.D.

208. All of gold. Plate with two strips of plaited wire soldered across it. Top hemisphere surrounded by a ringed wire, like that from Naukratis of the late 1st cent. (*Naukratis* I, xxvii), but carelessly copied, probably early iind cent. The bar with three drops is of 140—160 A.D. (*Portfolio,* xvii, xix). The gold balls below are of two hemispheres, soldered round the equator; compare *Cyprus Catalogue* 4093.

209. Bronze frame and wire; glass set in square; silver-in-glass beads below. A cheap imitation of 207, probably iind or iiird cent. A.D. The bar with two drops is of 160 A.D. (*Hawara Portfolio,* xxiv).

210. Gold wire, S-loop, with two pearls and beryl. iind cent. A.D.? The ring with a single pearl is of 170 A.D. (*Portfolio,* xxv).

211. Hollow ring of gold, with amethyst pendant. iind cent. A.D.?

212. Silver, cast in one piece. Later form of figs. 185, 186, and see 197. B.C.? (Also a similar form in silver, but with no globules below the small ring. Also a pair in silver as last, but made of soldered wire. Lahun.)

213. Gilt brass, with beaded rim and small ring. Lahun, probably Ptolemaic. (Also a pair with longer beaded edge, and no small ring. Lahun.)

214. Silver. The melon pendant and two notched rings revolving on the pin. iind cent. A.D.? The drop pendant is seen in Assyria, and came into Egypt in the xxvth dynasty (*Hyksos and Isr. Cities,* xixc).

215. Brass. Pendant cast over twisted wire. iiird cent. A.D.?

216. Carved bone pendant, brass loop and two yellow glass beads. (Also two other pairs with yellow and with red beads; and one with silver-in-glass bead.) ivth cent. A.D.?

217. Brass ring with two pendants; one, brass bead and gold-in-glass bead; other, brass links with green glass bead and silver-in-glass. iiird cent. A.D.?

218. Brass rings with silver-in-glass pendants. Gurob. iiird cent. A.D.? (Similar from Lahun.)

219. Brass ring with hook and loop, drop of stamped brass, relief on both faces, joined. Lahun.

220. Silver wire with one bead of carnelian and one of silver. See *Hawara Portfolio,* xviii. iind cent. A.D.

221. Silver hoop, and band of zigzag wire work with twisted edge. Beads of carnelian (middle), green glass and silver-in-glass. iiird cent. A.D.?

222. Silver ring, carnelian bead. Lahun. iind cent. A.D.?

223. Brass ring, beads of blue glaze, green glass, silver-in-glass. Gurob.

224. Brass rings, with lead pendants. Lahun. iind cent. A.D.?

225. Brass chain with pendant ball from which hung three beads, one silver-in-glass remains.

Pl. x. 226. Twisted brass wire hoop, with two blue glass beads and two lead (?) beads.

227. Gold wire hoop and four knob beads, gold ball of two hemispheres, four pearls, quartz bead covered with indigo glaze. Shurafa. See *Hawara Portfolio,* xvi. iind cent. A.D.

228. Silver wire and hollow silver bead.

229. Brass wire. Beads of black glass with small white spots; beads of white glass blown hollow. iiird cent. A.D.

230. Brass wire. Beads of blue and green glass, and hollow beads of white glass. iiird cent. A.D.

25. Pl. x. 231. Gold. Twisted wire and plain wire open work. Two sides alike, separated round the edge, by a strip of gold with bosses, and plain along the triangle. 61 grains. See DALTON, *Christian Antiquities,* 268—9.

232—5. Silver. Punched with degraded vine pattern, decaying to mere zigzags. From the tough state of the silver, these are probably Arab, and not early.

236. Lead. Crescent, perhaps from a necklace, with ball top pierced. iind cent. A.D.?

237. Silver. Sheet with soldered wire pattern, pierced for three pendants.

238. Brass. Three chains and discs. vth or vith cent.?

239. Brass. Balls stamped out as two joined cups, and then bent up, with wavy edges which overlap. vth or vith cent.?

240. Brass ring, with three silver-in-glass bead pendants. Lahun. iiird cent. A.D.?

241. Brass ring, with beads of yellow, blue, and black glass, and blown glass balls, joined with coiled and twisted wire.

242. Embossed gold foil with rock crystal plate at back. Fayum.

242 A. Lead cross pendant.

243. Iron rings, with pendant iron crosses. Lahun.

244. Silver. Looped cross with twisted wire circles around. Entirely wire work. vith cent.?

245. Brass. Cross with looped ends.

246. Brass. Looped cross with looped borders.

247. Brass. Looped cross.

248–9. Brass. Looped cross in looped border. viith cent.? See border of no. 39.

250–1. Mother of pearl cross, clear glass beads with white streaks.

Though various types of late earrings are figured in DALTON's *Christian Antiquities of the British Museum*, and STRZYGOWSKI's *Cairo Catalogue*, there is no dating given in centuries, and therefore no help in historical arrangement.

CHAPTER IV

EARLY CUT STONES AND EGYPTIAN RINGS.

Pl. xi.

26. Pl. xi. 1. Translucent green serpentine, pierced, domed back. Tortoise in side view, showing legs and head. Three balls beneath. The Greek figures of the tortoise show the back view, on coins of Aegina. From nos. 1 to 5, scale 4 : 3.

2. Black jasper, pierced, thick, slightly domed back. Ibex standing, seven balls in front. The style of this is like archaic Greek engraving.

3. Black steatite, pierced, coarse scarab back. Bird? 11 balls and 18 grooves.

4. Dark brown limestone, pierced, very rough scarab back. Man striding along, holding a curved line from one hand to the other, 12 balls in the field.

These four stones are obviously all of one family, with strong Egyptian and archaic Greek connections, yet not clearly of either source. The groups of balls upon them are like the uncial marks on the early Italic coinage. This suggested examining the weights of these, which are

		grains			grains
No. 1	3 balls	69·4	÷	3	23·1
2	7 balls	144·0	÷	7	20·6
3	11 balls	250·0	÷	11	22·7
4	12 balls	116·0	÷	12	9·7
	(or 5 balls		÷	5	23·2)

Thus in the first three there is a pretty near agreement between the marks and the weights. The last has the balls in groups of 3, 4 and 5; if these possibly show its value on different standards, the group of 5 would agree with the other stones. If a reference to weight can be accepted here, it must be to the Stater, or Attic standard, as the double obol of that would be from 22·1 to 22·9 grains. It would be most desirable to find the source of this class. A stone from Melos has three balls in the field (FURTWÄNGLER, *Gemmen*, v, 39 a); another from Egypt has seven balls (Brit. Mus., *Gem.* 111). The numbers 3, 5, 7 and 11 are all primes.

5. Steatite; very badly formed scarab. Koptos. The letters seem to read ITEᏏ IᎱᎪIVCSVᎱ with the scarab and *onkh* sign inverted.

27. Pl. xi. 6. Glazed pottery, faded. Two male figures each holding one hind leg of an animal, which is suspended between them. They have similar broad-brimmed caps, but one is nude, the other in a long striped robe. The same group repeated. Cypriote style. Nos. 6–7–8 on scale 5 : 4.

7. Glazed pottery cylinder, gone white. Man with conical cap and bushy hair (Assyrian style), standing in long robe. A tall staff or stand with eight uprights on the top of it, and two rings on each side (a fire altar?). Another man, similar, in robe, holding a tree with seven sloping branches. Facing that, a winged bull standing, and a winged panther(?) couchant. Cypriote style.

8. Glazed pottery, green. Hunter holding bow; before him a scorpion and two serpents. Probably Horus conquering evil.

8 A. One purely Egyptian subject must be noted here, a haematite seal engraved with the scene of

reaping the tall corn of the paradise of Aaru. The reaper has a conical cap, a beard, and is covered with a short tunic; a tree rises behind him; around the whole is the serpent, meeting head to tail, to show that the scene is in the future world of the Duat. This is the latest instance of the representation of the fields of Aaru. On the back ƎƐⲤⅩⅠⲰNՆϽ, "about to avert" as a protective charm. Actual size, as also the succeeding figures.

28. 9. Black limestone. Four sides shown, A to D; base flat, with four lines of inscription (see *Amulets*, 130). A. Nude man standing, holding a branch in one hand, and a bow with everted ends in the other hand. In front of him is an ox couchant. B. Branching tree, with three sprays rising from the ground, and two more above, on each side; below are two lines of inscription. C. Palm tree, with young ones springing from the stem on each side. D. Mountain like Mt. Argaeus, with head of ibex (?) near the top; on one side six sprays or trees up the side of the mountain, on the other side three. Two lines of inscription below. This unique seal cannot yet be read, but the 58 signs upon it, separated into words by dots between, give a wide base for comparison. The fashion of a god standing on, or over, an animal is Hittite; the trees growing up the mountain show a moist climate; yet the palms prevent assigning this to Asia Minor. Probably North Syria, or perhaps the Cilician coast, is the most likely source.

10. Light blue-green glaze. Octagonal conoid seal. Man holding a papyrus staff. xxvith dynasty.

11. Brown steatite. Scarab. Indistinct markings.

12. Fragment of carved ivory, rough back. Cyprus. Guilloche pattern, below it a head with a pointed ribbed cap. Presented by Col. Massey.

13. Chlorite, decomposed brown surface. Carved on all sides, except the narrow end. Pierced. Carved similarly on both the wide faces, symmetrically opposite. On the wide end a palm branch pattern. On the base, five pairs of balls. The style of the signs is more like Hittite hieroglyphs than like anything known elsewhere.

14. Pendant of black clay, with incised lines, and possibly four Cufic letters in an oval.

29. *Finger rings.* Pl. xi.

15. Large finger ring, cast, of clear white glass, with hollow for setting an engraved stone.

16. Bronze ring with bust of Serapis. 1657 grains, nearly $\frac{1}{4}$ lb.

17. Iron finger ring. Busts of Serapis and Isis.

18. Glass finger ring.

19. Bronze ring, with shrine and cross on the top of it.

20. Bronze ring, with a cross for a bezel.

21-4. Five pierced lifting key rings. One pronged lifting key ring.

25-6. Eight barrel-and-ward key rings.

27. White glass, clear. Gryphon walking, much decayed.

30. *Egyptian finger rings.* Pl. xii.

28. Bes dancing; blue glaze. Late xviiith dynasty, as the following.

29. Bes dancing, with tambourine; blue glaze.

30. Ape eating fruit, lotus in front; violet.

31. Ibex between lotus flowers; blue.

32. Two ibexes; red glaze.

33. Cow among papyri; green.

34. Bird flying over papyrus clump; light blue.

35. Four uraei; green.

36. Fish; bright yellow.

37. Flying scarabaeus; blue.

38. Lotus and buds; light blue. (Also from Gurob.)

39. Artificial lotus group; green.

40. Same, incised; violet.

41. Imitation jewellery, one blue between two red ovals, in yellow glaze to resemble gold.

42. Similar, two red ovals in a green basis.

43. Four *onkh* signs; violet, double ring.

44. Horus on the lotus flower; silver.

45. Hathor seated in a boat; silver.

46. Bird on nest of eggs over papyrus clump; carnelian.

47. Bird over papyrus clump; violet glass.

48. Bird over papyrus clump; violet glass, double ring.

49. *Mut neb pet taui,* "Mut, mistress of heaven and earth;" sard.

50. Uazet serpent on papyrus clump; rich blue glass.

51. Plant; black steatite.

52. Lotus flower and buds, incused; dull green.

53. Ra falcon (?) in boat; bronze.

54. *Hes men,* probably "praise Amen"; silver. Gurob.

55. Two cartouches of the Aten; carnelian, double ring.

56–57. *Aăkhet neb neheh*; blue.

58. *Amen neheh neb*; blue.

59. *Zetta neheh*; blue. "Time and eternity."

60. *Amen-ra neb*; blue.

61. *Amen-ra zetta*; blue.

62. *Amen-ra mer neb*; blue.

63. *Amen-ra nezem nef neb*, "lord of the sweet wind;" blue.

64. *Uzat neferui neb*; blue.

65. Queen playing lyre, ape walking before, lotus bud above; in relief; blue.

66. Scarabaeus; bronze.

67–8. *Uzat* eyes; blue. (Also others, two violet, one yellow.)

69. Scarab flying; dull green.

70. A god seated; blue. (Also Taurt and 3 others.)

71. Cat; blue.

72–74. Perforated ring; Ra seated; blue. About xxiind dynasty.

75. Perforated *uzat* between two scarabs, 3 seated gods; green.

76. Perforated, Ra in boat; blue.

77. Perforated, goddess seated; blue. (Also two rings, ribbed.)

78. Wire scroll on gold scarab, body crushed. Gurob.

79. Glazed setting for a bezel, perforated; blue.

80. *Ra mentu . . .*; large ring, xxiind dynasty; blue.

Beside the objects figured, there are the following which will not photograph distinctly. Bezels:—

Taurt; blue.

Ra Sebek neb; dark violet, in silver setting and ring of Roman or Arab age.

Ra user maot, setep ne ra; blue.

Rannut nefer neb kau; blue.

Nefer onkh neb; violet. Amarna.

Uast em heb se neb "Thebes in festival for all men"; blue.

Sistrum between uraei; blue.

Amen-ra standing; blue.

Uzat eye in square; green.

Aăkhet nefer ka neb; blue.

Two illegible, and fragments.

Group from Gurob; triple ring of silver, plain silver scarab in gold mount, two electrum and one silver *uzat*, blue glazed frog with scorpion on base, blue glazed plain ring. (*Illahun*, xxii, 11–14.)

Hathor head?; white glazed ring.

12 rings plain or illegible; blue.

31. *New Year presents.*

81. "Bastet, open a good year for her lord." Bezel, light blue. This shows that these rings were for presents to the master of the house, like the inscribed pilgrim bottles.

82–83. "Ptah open a good year"; olive. Rings.

84. "Ba of Mendes open a good year"; blue, burnt. Ring.

85. "Amen open a good year every day." Steatite scarab.

86. Same. Green glaze ovoid; Ra seated, in relief on back.

87. "Amen open a good year"; blue pottery scarab. Lahun.

88. Same; olive pottery scarab.

89. Same; blue pottery scarab.

90. Same, but confused with Up-taui the god. Green glazed ring.

91. Same; light green jasper scarab.

92. "Amen open a year (?) of good protection." Scarab, gone white.

93. "Amen open a good year"; blue-green glaze, ovoid.

94. "Isis open a good year"; olive pottery scarab.

95. "Isis open a good year for her lord"; green, bezel.

96–97. "Bastet open a good year"; light blue, bezel.

98. "Bastet open a good year for her lord." White limestone, cat.

99. "Bastet open every day . . ."; blue paste plaque.

100. "Bastet open a good year"; green, bezel.

101. "Open a year . . . Isis"; blue burnt brown, plaque.

102–7. "Open a good year"; light blue rings and seals. (Also three others.)

108. "Open a good year every day." Papyrus group on back. Blue paste.

109. "A good year in peace." Pottery scarab, faded.

110. "Open a good year." Head of Bes on back. Green.

111. "Open all good years" (blundered). Blue, pottery scarab.

112. Same. Blue-green, pottery ring.

113. "Open a good year"; light blue, pottery seal.

114. "Open a good year all days"; blue paste, ovoid.

115. "Isis open a good year"; durite, flat back.

116. "Open every day most excellently"; green, pottery scarab.

117. "A good year, venerating (*nini*) Ra, for all things." "Ra lord of good year"; rough green ring (not figured).

32. *Metal rings*. Pl. xiii.

(Of bronze unless specified. For those with names, see the catalogue of scarabs.)

118. Two bulls facing, a spray of a plant over each, a house sign between. xviii.

119. Cow in a boat in the marshes. xviii. Green jasper.

120. Gazelle galloping past a tree. xviii. Opaque blue glass.

121. Horse running towards a man, mountain sign below, bird above. xviii.

122. Ibex head. *Ra-nefer-kheper*, Amenhetep IV. xviii.

123. Silver. *Uzat* eye. xviii.

124. Nondescript cartouche. Ra, Amen and Ptah, *mer taui neb*. xviii.

125. "Ra is the king of Egypt who is over all." xviii.

126–7. *Aten-nefer-kheper, ua-ne-aten*. Akhenaten. xviii.

128. *Aten hes*, "Praiser of the Aten." xviii.

129. *Aten hesu nub*. "Praises to the golden Aten." xviii.

130. "The Aten adored by all peoples." xviii.

131. "Rennut give all good food." xviii.

132. *Ra ne onkh neferui neb*.

133. *Amenra oku neb*, "Amenra (gives) all food." xviii.

134. *Ra nefer kheper* (winged), Akhenaten and Măot facing, *Aten peh*. xviii.

135. Isis and Horus standing.

136. Mut seated, signs illegible. xxvi.

137. Scorpion. xviii.

138. Silver. *Per Bastet*, with a branch behind the seated goddess. xviii.

139. "Mut give good life to her servant." Silver-gilt. xxvi.

33. 140. Ptah. Graeco-Roman, as also the following.

141. Head of Serapis and uraeus.

142. Serapis standing.

143. Uraeus with head of Serapis, in relief.

144. Isis and Horus.

145. Anubis, tree behind.

146. Sacred ram and head.

147. Sacred ram.

148. Two hawks of Koptos.

149. Hawk on standard, before Min of Koptos.

150. Baboon of Thoth.

151. Baboon of Thoth.

152. Ibis of Thoth, and caduceus of Hermes.

153. Crocodile. Gurob.

154. Bust of Isis.

34. 155. Heads of Dioscuri.

156. Male head, filleted; Juba?

157. Male head, TO; perhaps the initials of an official. Iron ring.

158. Male head.

159. Helmeted head. Ethiopian work?

160. Blue glass paste in iron ring. Diomedes with the Palladion; a rather usual subject, see FÜRTWÄNGLER, *Gemmen*, 49, 1, 2; 50, 10, 12. The paste appears ancient, and the iron ring, though in good state, is not likely to be recent.

161. Standing female. Probably of iind cent., as also the following.

162. Female in flounced robe, kneeling over a basin on a stem. Another robed female is pouring a vase of water over the back of the kneeler. A stand of the group is apparently shown below. This has a trace of Cretan style in the design.

163. Female seated on a scroll. Iron ring.

164. Biga, full face. Iron ring.

165. Victory standing.

166. Female leaning on cippus.

35. 167. Victory (?). Probably of iiird cent., as also the following.

168. Hermes holding a bag, and caduceus (?).

169. Anubis (?) standing.

170. Head of Isis, crowned with four ears of corn. A key ring.

171. Heads of Serapis and Isis facing. A key ring, wards broken.

172. Head of Harpocrates.

173. Head of Serapis.

174. Apis bull.

175. ΜΕΜΦΙϹ.

176. Three circles.

177. Seated ape.

36. 178. Man standing, holding two branches. Probably of ivth cent., as also the following.

179. Silver ring. Eagle displayed. Monogram of ΦΟΧΟⅬ.

180. Bird.

181. Swan? Iron.

182. Bird? Iron.

183. Panther.

184. Cross, with shorter cross between the arms. Cross with double lines (not figured).

185. Η ΒΟΗΘΙ ΜΑΚΑΡΙ.

186. ĪС ΙΟϹΙϕ, Iesus, Ioseph.

187. ĪС ΒΘΙ ΑΑΕΞ+.

188. ΓΕѠΡΓΕ.

     ΑΝΔΡΕΟϹ (not figured).

189. ϹΑΡΠΙѠΝ.

190. Man standing with staff and basket (?), under a vine (?).

191. Bird and cross. vth cent. or later, as also the following.

192. Lion seated.

193. Female head, with hair dressing of vth cent., see the diptych of Aetius.

194. Virgin and Child seated, the adoration of the magi.

195. Head with long beard and nimbus, ĪС X̄С, Iesous Christos.

196-7. Figure with nimbus, upright figure, portions of others below. Resurrection?, or raising of Lazarus?

198. Saint on horseback, with cross.

199. Cross pattern.

37. 200. Dark grey jasper. Flat back.

201. Red jasper. Flat back.

202. White glass ring.

203. *Allah Allah.* Bronze.

204. Bronze.

205. *Allah.* Brown jasper, in cast silver ring.

206. Spread eagle in rays. Cut in horn, relief design stamped. Also 36 other metal rings, plain or illegible.

CHAPTER V

38. ENGRAVED STONES.

Pl. xiv.

Semitic. 207. Cobalt-blue glass, opaque; thick, with domed back. Apparently reading (on impression) לעברי בנפתרא, "belonging to Obri son of Petra." The name Obri is in 1 Chron. 24, 27. I have to thank Prof. Hirschfeld for suggestions on this and other inscriptions.

208. White quartz, thick, with domed back. Reading לארכיו חלדי, "belonging to Arky and Khaldy," perhaps a partnership, or a double name. These

names are found in the Archite, Jos. 16, 2 and 2 Sam. 15, 32; also Heldai in 1 Chron. 27, 15 and Zech. 6, 10 (Hirschfeld). M. Clermont Ganneau read the first name אדניהו "Adonya(h)ou," Adonijah in 1 Kings, 1 and elsewhere. The letters however seem to be clearly ארניו, "Arnyu," possibly connected with Aren, Gen. 36, 28, or Oren 1 Chron. 2, 25.

209. Green quartz, thick, with domed back. Winged sea monster. Below מתבעל "Mat baal," a known abbreviation of Matan-baal, "the gift of Baal."

210. White quartz, burnt(?) grey in parts. Back cut as a scarab. Subject, a hero bearded, holding up two horned animals by the tails. This is strongly Babylonian in the subject.

39. *Egyptian, &c.* 211. Black steatite, rough back, not bored. Sarapis seated, front face, and the bull-headed Mnevis (?) seated, side face; between them the heart of Osiris with human head, crowned with horns (*Amulets*, 158), and the jackal of Anubis. It is remarkable to see Serapis and Mnevis as separate gods in conclave.

212. Burnt carnelian, back flat, unpierced. Isis seated on a throne, holding Horus. Roman age.

213. Brown jasper, scarab, back broken away. A god with bulbous crown, seated before a fire altar, winged disc above a star in the field. This type appears in FÜRTWÄNGLER, *Gemmen*, xv, 4, and similar designs in vii, 12; xv, 2, 3.

214. Brown and white onyx. Man standing, with a sword, holding a wreath. Behind him four letters, approximating to square Hebrew, חתר, "besought," a personal name.

215. Carnelian, gone white at one end. Bead, pierced. A quadruped, possibly the front view of a goat capering. From Aden, presented by Major L. L. G. Thorpe.

216. Brown steatite. Back roughly copied from a scarab. Letters of unknown character.

217. Haematite. Upper part of a cylinder. Bearded god with horned hat. Facing him, a goddess with similar hat. Between them the sun and moon and serpent sign. Also Ishtar, or one of her maidens with hands joined below breast. "Anida... handmaid of the deity... and the deity..." About 2000 B.C. (I have to thank Prof. Pinches for this account.)

218. Haematite. Lower part of a cylinder. Top row of 7 lions; next of 12 hares; next of 12 ibex heads; at the base, 22 fishes(?). Remembering the hare in the Egyptian word *unnut*, "hour," and the connection with the hours (RENOUF, *Essays*, ii, 413),

it seems not improbable that the 7 lions are the days of the week, the 12 hares the hours of day, and the 12 ibex heads the hours of night. The worn state of the cylinder makes the number of fish uncertain, at least 22, perhaps 23 or 24. They may refer to short intervals of 24 to the hour, $2\frac{1}{2}$ minutes each.

40. *Archaic Greek.* 219. Black steatite, thick, domed back. Warrior goddess (Athena Promachos?) with round shield and spear. From the long flounced skirt, the flying cape, and the prominent breast, this is certainly a female figure; only the absence of a helmet hinders the attribution to Athena. But as the style of this belongs to the vith, if not the viith, cent. B.C.—the age of the early mercenaries—the usage of the helmet may not yet have been fixed for the goddess.

220. Sard; back, a scarab, of deep and foreign form. Man holding a branch, on which he kneels with the right knee. The left leg is awkwardly bent in the opposite direction. This peculiar style of work appears in FÜRTWÄNGLER, *Gemmen*, vi, 20, 21, and also can be traced in xii, 17 (see the parted knees), and xix, 63, 71.

221. Turquoise, much worn. Back slightly domed, unpierced. Two men, front view, details lost.

222. Calcite. Back domed, unpierced. Stag browsing. Fine work.

223. Brown limestone. Tall conoid seal, with four faces, and edges bevelled. Ibex grazing. Star and *ka* arms(?) above.

224. Deep Prussian blue glass, of Persian period. Domed back, pierced. Wild ox, roughly cut.

41. *Graeco-Roman.* 225. Sard. Flat back for a ring. Head of Alexander as Herakles. The fine gem, accepted as Alexander in the lion's skin, in FÜRT-WÄNGLER, *Gemmen*, 37, 23, is obviously the source of the face in this, which is probably a Roman copy. Though coarsely cut, the sense of weight and shagginess of the lion's skin is well rendered.

226. Paste imitation of sard, skilfully made. Head of a Roman of the late Republican age, of good work.

227. Paste imitation of aquamarine. Surface partly decomposed. The original gem seems—from coin types—to have been about 450–400 B.C. and probably Syracusan. It was a very charming work, but this replica is imperfect in the full outline of the profile. The curved masses below appear not to be flaws, but to represent a dolphin across the neck, and a crescent in front.

228. Cameo, white agate on a blue-grey ground, which is now mostly broken away. There can be no doubt that this is of the same empress as a cameo in Florence, *Gori* 22, 6; *Reinach*, pl. 12. There, this is attributed, with doubt, to Julia Paula, first wife of Elagabalus. There can be no question by the hair, and the style, that it must be between 200 and 250 A.D. The notable details are the natural flowing hair, the fall of it in a loop at the neck, the end plaited up to the top of the head, but not over, and the ear bare. No heads on the coins comprise all of these points. Many empresses were too old at accession, for this portrait; Domna, Soemias, Maesa, and Mammaea are all impossible. The flowing hair is occasionally seen in Aquilia Severa and Annia Faustina. Rarely, the plait is carried upward in Domna, and then not again till it goes over the head, in Tranquillina and Otacilia; but the flowing hair excludes those. Orbiana had too aquiline a nose, and too severe a face. We seem to be limited to the three wives of Elagabalus, yet none of them show this type of face on the coins.

229. Red jasper, back flat. Serapis seated, before him a temple of Cypriote Aphrodite. In front of it is a paved courtyard; in the shrine is a conical stone with a double cap, and two side projections; above the roof is a star; on either side is a column with a bird upon it. The doubling of the upright sides of the shrine suggests that the front and back corner posts are shown, or else a pair of columns before the temple, as well as the temple front. A similar temple is published in FÜRTWÄNGLER, *Gemmen*, 64, 81; and the coin type in DONALDSON's *Architectura Numismata.*

230. Orange sard, flat back. Warrior helmeted, with spear and parazonium, leading a horse.

231. Red jasper, flat back. Greyhound chasing two hares. ΔΙΝΔΟΥΠΟΛΙ, "the city of Dindyme," perhaps on Mt. Dindymos in Phrygia, sacred to Cybele.

232. Sard. Two fighting ants on the back of a stone; the same on the front, polished, but chipped.

233. Black and blue-white onyx; flat back. Female with cornucopia, and another with basket; child with round shield and spear between them. SΛLO below. Perhaps Abundantia and Providentia —or other genii—joining hands over the young Saloninus. 253 A.D.

234. Brown-on-white onyx. Head of Herakles. This is a coarser version of the head on brown sard in FÜRTWÄNGLER, *Gemmen*, 26, 32.

235. Black jasper. Head of Serapis. ΔIΛIVΛΛCCE.

236. Green glass, clear. Orpheus seated on a rock; from a cave in it appears a wolf (?); on the other side, a sheep under a tree and a bird upon it; from the rock a large tree rises, round which a serpent is coiled. A fragment of an Orpheus gem in FÜRTWÄNGLER, *Gemmen*, 14, 40, is quite different from this group. Clumsy work, about 250 A.D.

237. Sapphire. Monogram of φ ΔHMHT XA.

42. *Impressions of gems in clay.*

238. Head of a Ptolemaic queen. 239. Head of Medusa. 240. Female head. 241. Female head. 242. Head of Pallas?. 243 and 244. Portrait heads of the iiird cent. B.C. 245. Roman head.

Pl. xv. 246. Cartouche of ... *men kheper*, behind a kneeling figure with hands raised. 247. "The adorer Hap-onkh-uaz son of Her-nez-(at)f." 248. "The guardian of the house Her (son of) Henu-tehuti" ("Thoth provides"). 249. "The prophet Mor-hap" ("Hapi defends," or covers). 250. "The prophet ... Sebek-ra." 251. "Ra-kheper ...." 252. "Amen-ra-n" and lotus bud. 253. "Men-măot." 254. Figures of gods.

255. "Onkh-neter-kheper." 256. Sphinx holding *onkh*. 257. "Onkh Hes Anpu neb," or Set? 258. Sistrum of Hathor and uraei. 259. "Nefer măot neb." 260. Un-nefer. 261. Harpocrates under a bush (?), *nub* below. 262. "Onkh-măot." 263. Zed between degraded uraei.

264. Ptah. 265. Isis seated. 266. Isis and Horus under a bush, surrounded by seven uraei. 267. Isis and Horus, busts. 268. Harpocrates on a cippus. 269. Harpocrates on a lotus flower. 270. Same. 271. Harpocrates, *onkh* in front.

272. Amen seated. 273. Anubis seated. 274. Upuat of the north and of the south. 275. Baboon of Tehuti seated, disc on head. 276. Quadruped on a standard. 277. Ichneumon. 278. Uraeus and illegible signs. 279. Circles and lines, debased scroll pattern.

280. Apollo. 281. Priest with patera. 282. Same? 283. Herakles with club. 284. Man standing, torch holder (?) at side. 285. Female holding short staff 286. Victory.

287. Indistinct figure. 288. Male figure (god?) with three ears of corn on the head. 289. Old man dressed in a skin, leaning on a staff. 290. Priestess offering with patera and oenochoe. 291. Priestess offering. 292. Seated female. 293. Man leaning back

on a staff. 294. Man resting on staff (only upper part).

295. Isis and Horus, column behind. 296. Worshipper and Măot. 297. Male and female figures. 298. Eros following Psyche. 299. Worshipper before helmet (?) on an altar. 300. Herakles and the stag. 301. Man in pointed cap. 302. Man running, like the hunter on the coins of Segesta.

303. Runner. 304. Man seated, hands in lap. 305. Man seated on altar. 306. Sheep. 307. Horse galloping. 308. Pegasus. 309. Eagle on wreathed altar, star behind, serpent in front.

310. Dog. 311. Dog. 312. Owl (?) on altar. 313. Amphora. 314. Kantharos and grapes. 315. Fly. 316. Sacred stone in an enclosure, with the solar disc and lunar crescent upon it; on each side, a tree with five pairs of branches. See the engraved gems with figures of sacred stones, 350, 351. 317. Lotus flower. 318. Bunch of grapes. 319. Cornucopiae. 320. Key. 321. Cuttle fish?. The value of such impressions lies in the assured age of the various types, which serve to guarantee the authenticity of such on engraved stones.

43. *Large rings and stones.* Pl. xvi.

322. Ivory finger ring. The portrait appears to be that of Arsinoe Philopator. The mode of the hair is more like that of her predecessor Berenike II, but such a fashion might well last over one reign. Back of the ring broken.

322 A. Ivory ring of smaller size, apparently of the above queen.

323. Bronze finger ring. The head is of the Ptolemaic style of hair dressing, but the features prevent it being identified with any of the queens on the Alexandrian coinage. Dr. G. F. Hill suggests that it is not unlike the head of Arsinoe (wife of Soter) on the coinage of Ephesos 288–280 B.C. She was born in 315, so would be 27 to 35 years old at that time.

324. Bronze, flat back for setting. Unknown portrait head.

325. Disc of brown chalcedony, engraved on both sides, casts also here shown. Helios, in a quadriga, holds a globe in the right hand. On the reverse is the sacred ram of Ammon on a stand, Zeus Ammon standing before it, and, behind it, Aphrodite holding her tresses. The disc has been roughly pierced, to be suspended from a riband. Probably due to the sun worship of Aurelian, 275 A.D.

326. Glass paste imitating onyx, white on purple. Youthful head.

327. Burnt carnelian, flat back. Helmeted head.

328. Iron finger ring. Heads of Severus, Caracalla, and traces of Geta, ... VP·CE B·Λ·CEΠΤΙ CEVH/////CI·CEB KAI M ANT ....

329. Bronze seal, handle at back. Half length figure of St. Basil, ΑΓΙΟC ΒΑCΙΛ. Around ✠ ΤΟΥ ΑΓΙΟΥ ΠΑΤΡΟC ΜΟΥ ΕΠΙCΚΟΠΟΥ ΒΛΑCΙΟΥ ΤΟΥ ΙΕΡΟ ΜΑΡΤΙΡΟC ΙCΧΟΡΙΘΟ ΤΟΙΚΑΛ.. ΙΖΕ (?). "Of the holy one, my Father, Bishop Blasios, of the holy martyr, I should be strong (?) ...." On the back is a maker's stamp of four letters, illegible.

44. Gnostic stones and pastes.

Most of these were published in *Amulets*, whitened to show the inscription. They are repeated here, clear of filling, to show the detail of the art.

330. Light blue glass, thin. Isis Pharia on a couch. On the flat back, VHΛ.

331. Opaque black glass, thin. Serapis seated, Isis behind, Nephthys in front. On the flat back, NIKA H EICIC.

332. Durite. Aphrodite spreading her tresses. On back, blundered cartouches of Ramessu II and Merneptah.

333. Durite. Tell Yehudiyeh. Serpent-headed god on legs, bandaged as a mummy.

334. Durite. Uraeus on human legs, with waist cloth. The inscriptions, on the previous stone and this, are from the same source, and are here put parallel.

PIMYAVCIAⲰΙ   ΘΕΡΝΕΜΙΝⲰ   ΠΙCΙΔΑΟΟΘΙΒ
ΙΡΜ AVC   ΛΕΡ ΘΕΡΜΙΝΘΙΝⲰ ΠΙCΙΔΑ   ΘΙΒ

335. Durite. Half-length of Harpocrates radiated and crowned, with cornucopiae, over a galloping lion. Star in front. On flat back, ΕΥΚΑΙΡΙΑΝ.

336. Durite, rounded back, suspension hole at top. Set standing, holding scourge and *onkh*. ΙⲰ CHT ΙⲰΙⲰ. On back, ΙΑΕⲰ ΒΑ ΦΡΕΝ ΕΜΟΥΝ ΙⲰ ΕΡΒΗΤΙ ΠΑΚΕΡΒΠΙ.

337. Greenish chalcedony. Lion-headed serpent, radiated; behind it three S serpents across a staff. On lentoid back, ΟΘΜΟΥΗΡ ΧΝΟΥΜΙC ΖΜΧ.

338. Brown steatite. Isis seated with Horus, ΑΘΛΘΑΘΘΑΒ. On flat back, Bes standing. ΤΑC ΒΕΡΒΕΡΕΤΕ.

339. Green jasper bloodstone, flat back. Harpocrates radiated with disc on head, holding scourge,

seated on lotus flower, between two crowned hawks. Sun and moon in field.

340. Lazuli. Isis seated, crowned, holding phiale; within a circle of a serpent with tail in mouth.

341. Black steatite. Bennu bird by an altar with a plant upon it. Below it two serpents across a bar. On the similarly curved back, ΕΥΠΕΠΤΙ.

342. Black steatite. Lion-headed serpent, with radiate disc behind. Below it two serpents across a bar. On similarly curved back, bennu and plant as above, ΙΑⲰ; below, SS at sides. This lion-serpent and barred serpents are on fig. 334 also. For other examples of the bennu and altar, see *Amulets*, xxi.

343. Blue glass. Around, lion, Set, Anubis, scorpion; lion ... opposite. Harpocrates on the lotus flower; three khepers over him (Trinity); three goats and three serpents (evil souls) behind him. On flat back, ΦΡΗΘ, BAINY WWI .., and parts of three lines of foreign letters. For the complete subject, see *Amulets*, xlix.

344. Lazuli-blue glass. Horus seated in a reed boat, arms outstretched, radiated, with disc and feather on head. On either side, a winged figure (Isis and Nephthys?) guarding him. On flat back, ΣΑΒΑⲰΘ ΑΔⲰΝΑΙ.

345. Blue-green glass, thin. Two hearts of Osiris on ring stands. On the flat back, H ΧΑΡΙC.

346. Haematite. Serpent-headed figure, holding spear and basket (?); sun and moon in field. On flat back, ΜΙΧΑΗΛ.

347. Haematite, rough irregular back. Two figures and altar (?) very roughly cut.

348. Brown jasper. Anubis holding bow and arrow. On flat back, ΕΡΖΕ VΑΡΘΟΥΡ ΚΑΡΟΦΡΗCⲰΡ.

349. Red and green jasper. Anubis with arms raised, over a mummy placed on the back of a lion. On flat back, ΑΒΡΑCΑΖ.

350. Haematite. A sacred stone in an enclosure, or upon a stand; two serpents on each side of it. Above, mummiform Anubis and Isis with cornucopiae. ΙΑⲰ ΟΡⲰΡΙ ΟVΘ. The whole enclosed by a serpent, with tail in mouth. Back inscription, see *Amulets*, 135 j.

351. Black steatite. Sacred stone in enclosure, or upon a stand. Lion-headed serpent above it, two rampant animals (?) at the sides. Back flat. See fig. 316.

352. Haematite. Falcon .... ΑΘΑ, and five foreign letters.

CHAPTER VI

HAIR RINGS, EAR STUDS, BUCKLES, HAIR PINS, COMBS.

Hair rings. Pl. xvii.

45. A LARGE class of rings have been supposed to be intended for the ear, or for retaining locks of hair. Unfortunately there is little or no direct evidence as to the position. On some mummy cases the rings are shewn projecting from the wig, vertically, edge forward, in a way which could only result from wearing them on the lower lobe of the ear. Also in Cairo are rings of this style without any cross cut, but only a recess and a pin to hang them from; these must have been hung, and probably from the ear. On the other hand, there are a large number of rings which have a cross cut too narrow to admit any cartilage of the ear, such as a gold ring with a gap of $\frac{1}{50}$th inch, jasper with gap $\frac{1}{30}$th, alabaster with gap $\frac{1}{20}$th. As the actual thickness of the edge of the ear is $\frac{1}{10}$th inch, and of the thinnest double skin (between fingers) $\frac{1}{16}$th, it is evident that gaps of a half or a third of that amount could not clip on the ear, and must be for inserting hair, to hold tresses together. A pair here, fig. 4, must have been hung on the upper lobe of the ear, and as the gap is $\frac{1}{16}$th inch, there is no difficulty about it. This position is like that of the silver earring worn by Nubian boys at present. None of these forms of ring appear before the xviiith dynasty. Whether the earring starts from the Nubian influence of the xiith dynasty kings, or was restarted by the Syrianising of the Hyksos and the xviiith dynasty conquests, is not yet clear.

46. Cut rings. 1. Alabaster, broken. 2, 3. Alabaster. Also a pair rather smaller than 2, with blue wafer beads of xviiith dynasty; Gerzeh, grave 50. 4. Pair, of alabaster, with pendants in one piece, to go on upper lobe of ear. 5. White glazed pottery. Also a ring of blue paste of the same size, without any gap. 6. Pair of shell rings. 7, 8. Rings cut from cone shell. 9. Pair of red jasper rings, with raised line around, notched as rope pattern. A rope edging is in the xviiith dynasty (*Illahun*, xxvi). 10. Pair of red jasper rings. 11, 12, 13. Sard rings. 14, 15. Carnelian. 16. Piece of carnelian ring with a knob, perhaps a degraded duck. There is also a ring cut out of cone shell; and an alabaster ring with lobe pierced with two holes for pendants. 17. Red jasper ring, pierced to carry a pendant. 18. Red glass imitation of jasper, changed to green. 19. Red glass ring. 20. Red glazed pottery ring, with raised edge line. 21. Red pottery ring. In making the red glass rings, a flat strip of glass was drawn out lengthways to the required thickness; it was then turned round a metal rod, and chopped off to the required length; the sides of the gap were then ground, so as to make the opening smooth. The red pottery ring was made continuous in red paste, a gap was cut in it when dried, and then it was glazed over the outside, and a little over the edges, but not over the inside. The glaze cannot have been applied by dipping, and the spread over the edge is probably only due to creeping, when melted.

47. Another kind of glass ring was made of small round rods of glass, which had been drawn out lengthways. A piece of rod was snapped off to the right length, softened in the furnace, and then bent round a rod (which has left a faint flattening inside); but the ends were not ground, having been softened and slightly rounded by the heating. Of this pattern are the following:— 22, clear white glass; 23, translucent white; 24, 25, translucent white; 26, black, with three white ribs, earliest colouring; 27, transparent dark blue, with opaque yellow band; 28, see below; 29, transparent dark blue; 30, black; 31, amber glass; 32, dark brown with satin sheen; 33, translucent violet; 34, blue glazed pottery; 35, violet glaze; 36, violet pottery, glaze perished. Over 60 various hair rings have been set aside as duplicates. 28, gold ring, hollow, with joint round the inside, and two lines of twisted wire around the outside. The ends of the hollow are capped with gold plates soldered on, each with a small central hole. Weight 136 grains.

Ear studs.

48. During the xviiith–xxth dynasties, large discs attached to the ear lobe were a favourite ornament, culminating in the huge embossed gold discs of late Ramesside times. The usual form in the xviiith dynasty was a stud in two halves, with a peg on one, and a socket on the other, to hold it. These are shown as attached and as separated in fig. 37. The materials are:— 37, ivory; 38, alabaster.

49. A simpler form was the solid stud; but as that involved stretching an opening in the lobe to pass one side of it, the groove in the stud could not be much less than the outside. The stretch of the lobe was monstrous in some cases; 39 is 1·3 inches on the narrow face, and 1·12 in the groove; 43 is 2·14 on the face, and 2·0 in the groove. The materials are:— 39, alabaster; 40, green glaze; 41, blue glaze; 42, limestone; 43, dark brown jasper, weight 1408 grains, beside some loss by chipping; 44, ivory; 45, 46, 47, limestone with caps of ostrich egg-shell; 48, calcite, clear; 49, limestone; 50, 51, alabaster.

50. The stud form being so injurious to the lobe of the ear, a better type was adopted, of the mushroom form, 52 to 57. Fig. 51 is an intermediate form. The mushroom ear studs are 52, of glazed pottery, white body, with violet and red inlay; 53, ivory; 54, 55, 56, 57, alabaster. Over 50 various ear studs have been set aside as duplicates.

Pendants.

51. 58. A set of 25 conventional flower pendants of stamped gold foil, bought in Egypt by Greville Chester, for Miss Edwards; apparently from the same die as 23 pendants in the Cairo Museum.

Greek Hair-rings (?).

59. A pair of rings of copper, plated with gold, probably Cypriote.

60. A spiral, ending in a lion's head, of copper plated with gold. See MURRAY, *Excav. Cyp.*, p. 101, no. 8, and MYRES, *Cyp. Cat.*, 4115. ivth cent. B.C.

52. Buckles. Pl. xviii.

(The whole of this material needs to be studied with the Continental graves, and in relation to the northern tribes known to have been stationed in Egypt, see *Notitia Dign.*)

1. Bronze scarab, heavy casting. Legs joined below to form two loops, the hinder one of which is broken away. By the hollow in the back of the scarab, and depression of head and tail, a thick cord would be sharply bent on being drawn through this. It probably served as a friction buckle. Pre-Greek.

2. Foreparts of two dogs joined. Between them, below, is a hinge with a tongue which has been broken off; other attachments were behind the heads, so that this was probably a form of brooch or buckle. Roman?

3. Bronze ring, with oval stud below to button into a leather belt, and duck's head hook above to fasten the other end of a belt. Roman.

4. Similar bronze ring, but with a plain round stud in place of the duck's head. Roman.

5. Bronze fibula; as found at Tell Yehudiyeh of about the xxvith dynasty (*Hyksos and Isr. Cities* xx A); also known in N. Syria, with scarab of Menkara of xxvth dynasty, 710 B.C., so perhaps 650 B.C. (*Annals Arch. and Anth.*, Liverpool, vii, 117, 128).

6, 7. Bronze buckles. Roman.

8. Bronze buckle, with thickened bow. Late Roman.

9. Green glass buckle, with bronze tongue (see 20). Alamannic (Mainz, v, 181).

10. Bronze buckle plate, with hinge below. Ring ornament. Late Roman.

11. Bronze belt-hook, with one side attachment; the hook ending in dragons' heads. Late Roman.

12. Bronze plate, with three iron rivets for attachment to a base. Roman.

13. Bronze ring, with cross bar. Set with glass balls of green and light blue colour, four at each end, one in the middle. Roman.

14. Iron buckle and attachment plate, originally gilt. Lahun. Roman.

15. Bronze buckle and attachment plate. Roman.

16. Iron buckle and attachment plate, with two loops below, to pass through the belt, and a bolt through them to secure the belt. Lahun. Roman.

53. *Fibulae.* 17. Bronze fibula, pin lost. A loop at the hinge, fastened on by the hinge pin. The end of the point-holder closed with a knob.

18. Bronze fibula or brooch, pin lost. Inlaid with orange, red, and green glass. Roman. iiird or ivth cent. A.D. (*Greek and Roman Life*, 145).

19. Bronze fibula, with ribbed bow. End of point-holder closed with large knob.

20. Crystal buckle, with bronze pin. Frankish.

21-5. Cruciform bronze fibulae. The broken end in 24 shows that it has an iron wire in the core to strengthen it. 21 has an iron pin, 22 a bronze pin. Those in the Mainz Museum are assigned by LINDENSCHMIDT to mid iiird to mid vth cent. A.D. (III, ii, 4), or to late iiird or early ivth cent. (IV, pl. 57). In the British Museum they are dated to late ivth cent. (DALTON, *Early Christian Antiquities*, nos. 227, 256); or to vith cent. (BALDWIN BROWN, iii, 261).

54. *Inlaid buckles.* Most of the above forms on this plate are of northern origin, and doubtless due to the numerous Gothic and Germanic troops employed by Rome. The following examples of the north Asiatic art of garnet inlay are further evidences of these importations by the northern soldiery.

26. Gilt bronze, with inlays of glass; attachment plate for a buckle, with three eyes projecting on back. This is like fibula-discs dated to the earlier part of the vith cent. (BALDWIN BROWN, *Arts in E. E.,* cxlv).

27. Gilt bronze, with three garnet plates in gold setting; attachment plate for a buckle, with three rivets.

28. Bronze open work, made of soldered strip, inlaid with garnet plates and malachite, backed with plaster. Attachment plate for a buckle.

29. Disc of bronze, inlaid with sixteen sectors of red, green, and grey glass. No sign of attachment on the back.

30. Bronze pendant, with carnelian bead in a setting.

31. Gilt bronze side piece of a buckle, inlaid with green glass.

32. Gilt bronze attachment plate of a buckle; three eyes on back.

55. *Bells.*

33. Bronze bell, on bronze bracelet for an infant.

34. Bronze bell, on iron bracelet.

35. Bronze bell, on iron bracelet with a disc, bearing three crossing lines.

36. Bronze bell, on iron bracelet.

37. Bronze bell, with pattern of cross lines, on iron bracelet.

All these are from late Roman or Coptic burials. The use of such bells however began by the xxiiird dynasty (*Hyksos and Isr. Cities,* xix A), the origin probably being to track infants by the tinkle.

Hair pins. Pl. xix.

56. *Egyptian.* Both round and flat hair pins of ivory were usual in the first prehistoric age, and the hair was also retained by combs with long teeth, and usually surmounted by figures of animals. The hair pins of this first period, and also the round hair pins usual down to the dynastic period, generally bear the figure of a bird on the top. This feeling for artistic design disappeared in the

historic times, and it is not till the Roman age that figures are again usually found upon hair pins. The prehistoric forms are described in the Catalogue of *Prehistoric Egypt,* p. 30.

The earliest dynastic hair pins here are of the xiith dynasty. The simplest example (fig. 1) is a bit of fine reed with a head of clay pinched upon it. 2 is a bone pin with uraeus. 3, bone pin with hand. 4, bone pin, flattened at head. 5, ivory pin. 6, bone pin. 7, wooden pin head?, used as knob for a box. All these are of the xiith dynasty from Kahun. In the section of the small figures is a wooden pin with a dog's head, apparently from the set of gaming pieces in the Cairo Museum. 9 and 10 are wooden pins of xiith or of xviiith dynasty.

The pins from Gurob of the xviiith dynasty are:— 8, bone pin with ebony head. 11—16, bone pins, 16 is the top half of 11. 17, wooden pin with rude hand. 18 and 21, wooden pins of xviiith dynasty from Lahun. 19, 20, 22, 24, 25, wooden pins of xviiith dynasty from Gurob. 23, wooden pin perhaps of xviiith dynasty, but condition seems later.

26, ivory pin carved with a hand, fingers bent, a uraeus bracelet on the wrist. Ptolemaic. Gurob. 27, 28, two plain bone pins, late dynastic? Gurob.

57. *Roman.* The following are Roman hair pins of bone. 29, with hand holding a ball. 30, with Aphrodite. 31, with seated cat?. 32, with cock, these four from Gurob. 33, with vase, Lahun. 34, with Taurt, eyes, nostrils and navel deeply drilled, arms fitted in; Hawara. 35—41, with round heads. 42, 43, with vases. 44, with diagonal line pattern, Gizeh. 45, plain. 46—51, with multiple globular heads. 52, with triangular head, no point, but a hole near the flat end. 53, iron pin with the upper half square, the lower half round. Also two plain bronze pins without heads. 54, with hand holding wreath. 55, with cock. 56, with hand holding a ball. 57—64, from Shurafa. 57, head with hair dressed to a peak. 58, with hand holding a fruit? 59, 60, with vases. 61 as 57. 62, with female head wearing hair dressed high. 63, bronze pin with globular bone head. 64, unknown object, with figure of Aphrodite.

The following are bronze pins, probably all of Roman age. 65, with fluted head. 66—72, with plain ball heads (compare iind cent. pins in IV, 43). 69, from Gurob. 73, ebony pin, pierced work with cross, Christian period. 74, with open frame head, enclosing a loose ball. 75, iron pin, plain head.

76, cast bronze pin, crescent and wheel. 77, 78, pins of clear white glass; 78, from Hawara.

Combs. Pl. xx.

58. The comb with long teeth, to retain coils of hair, was developed very early, in the Badarian beginning of the prehistoric civilisation. It usually had figures of animals in the round, carved on the top of the comb, and was always cut in bone or ivory. These combs are usual from S.D. 32, and are commonly found until S.D. 44, when the ideas of that civilisation were much subdued by the later invasion about 40–42. A later type had only a notching without long separate teeth, apparently for scratching the head. Such combs were brought in by the civilisation at 40 S.D., and became commonest in the middle of that age, about 57–60. A third type was the notched comb on a hair pin, which was used through the first half of this civilisation, S.D. 39–60. After that, from 60–80 S.D. combs are not found. That was, no doubt, a time of decadence; but the decline in skill would hardly account for the disappearance of the comb. Possibly shaving the head may have then become usual; certainly, prehistoric statuettes have loose wigs modelled, suggesting that shaving and wigs were customary. These prehistoric combs are catalogued in *Prehistoric Egypt*, p. 29.

The earliest dynastic combs have short teeth (as *Royal Tombs* II, iii, 20), or are mere scratch combs, like the late prehistoric; see one of obsidian and one of ivory from the Menite tombs (*R.T.* II, xxxii, 10, 11). A well made flat-topped comb of king Zet was found at Abydos (*Tombs of Courtiers*, ii, 6; xii, 5), and another of the reign of Zet (1st dynasty) was found at Gizeh (*Gizeh and Rifeh*, iv, v, 8); this has a round back, characteristic of prehistoric European combs, and not found elsewhere in Egypt.

During the early dynasties and pyramid age, few combs are found. We know that the men clipped the hair very short, or shaved it off, and wore thick wigs. The women also had thick and long wigs, but their own hair is seen beneath the wig, as on the statue of Nefert. Probably it was cut short, so as not to require much combing.

Of the vith dynasty, there is a piece of a thin ivory comb from Zaraby (Univ. Coll.) drawn in pl. xxviii, 55. This has a tall plain body above the teeth, like a comb from Meyr, 44320 at Cairo, of the xiith dynasty.

The usual proportions were reached in the xiith dynasty, as no. 16; but generally with more detail than in later time, such as the curved band of open work on 16, and the lotus handle on 1. Later, in the xviiith dynasty, projecting bands or knobs on the back were usual.

59. *Egyptian.* No. 1 may be dated by the style of work, so similar to the spoon handles of the time. It had a long handle, which is now lost, like that at Leyden (*Aeg. Mon. Nederl. Mus.* II, xxxi, 6). For others of the xiith dynasty, see *Kahun*, viii.

Nos. 2, 3. These are not dated; but, from the state of the wood and the style of cutting, they are not later than the xviiith, and may be of the xiith dynasty or earlier.

No. 4. Rifeh, grave 161. This is of the early part of the xviiith dynasty, before Hatshepsut.

No. 5. Lahun. This comb, with a horse on the back, is dated to Ramessu II by a similar example (*Illahun*, xviii). With it was the bronze group of a cat and *onkh*, and the bronze kohl stick, besides some beads. xixth dynasty.

Nos. 6, 7. Gurob. These were found with the bone hair pin, with cris-cross pattern, and ushabtis of Hora and Ta-ur-shed.

No. 8. Gurob. This has traces of the ridges on the back; xixth dynasty. A similar form, no. 9, but without any back ridges, is of Coptic age.

Nos. 10, 11, with deep back ridges, are probably of the xviiith dynasty. See *Kahun*, xviii, 2.

No. 12 is probably of the xixth dynasty.

Nos. 13, 14 were bought together, and are probably of the xviiith dynasty, by the style.

No. 15 is the only example of a bronze comb, probably of Roman age.

No. 16. Kahun. The same pattern of back occurs on another example (*Kahun*, viii, 31); and the spot and circle decoration occurs also for the eyes of ram-heads on a wooden bowl (*Kahun*, viii, 3). This appears therefore, both by form and pattern, to be of the xiith dynasty.

No. 17. Kahun. This comb has the spot and two circle decoration, used in the New Kingdom and later. The early date of it is indicated by the woolly and rounded cutting at the roots of the teeth, due to a bronze saw; this entirely differs from the sharp cutting by a steel saw on the Roman and Arab combs.

60. *Roman.* No. 18. Lahun (18 A, Wushym). This and the following combs are all of Roman or

Arab times. Much Coptic material came from native plundering of the cemetery at Lahun.

No. 19. Wushym. This is of late Roman age, but before the Arab conquest.

Nos. 20, 21 (21 A Wushym), 22, (23–5), 26, (27–8), 29, (30), 31, 32 are probably all of Roman and Coptic period. Those numbers in parenthesis are not figured here, but are duplicates of the preceding number; they are left in the Coptic section.

Pl. xxi. Nos. 33, (34–9), 40, 41, 42, 43, (44–5), 46 are probably all of Arab period.

No. 43 is from Lahun. No. 33 has inlaid discs of ebony with a little plug of bone in the middle, on both sides. No. 40 has foliage pattern on each side, probably about the xivth century. No. 41 has two bands of pierced pattern. No. 42 has a broad band of pierced pattern, and a disc with letters in relief, on each side. It appears to read *M n* (or *b* or *t*) *a l* on one side, *A l q* (or *f*) *l* on the other. Lettering about 1250 A.D. There are also two combs like 43 in the group of doll's furniture (*Hawara*, xix).

It is singular how various details of the comb continue through long ages, such as the spot and circle decoration, the concave sides, sometimes ending in a spur, or the slight saw line along the roots of the teeth. There are wide differences, however, to be observed—the knobs or animal figures of the New Kingdom, and the fine and coarse comb united, in Roman and later times.

A special class are the long combs 47 to 55 (49 in Coptic case). These are clearly all late Roman; 52, 53 have little looking glasses inlaid, like those in the plaster mirror frames of Gheyta; 54, 55 have animal figures cut in open work. The breaks are probably due to burial, and only one of these, 53, shows any signs of actual wear. From the awkward size of these, and the decoration, it seems likely that they were show pieces of the bridal trousseau, seldom or never taken into real use.

The early European combs, of bronze age and onward, differ entirely from the Egyptian examples, being always single edged, and round backed. See *Verh. d. Berl. G. f. Anthrop.*, 1899, p. 169.

CHAPTER VII

KOHL POTS AND STICKS.

Pls. xxii, xxiii.

61. THE earliest eye paint was the green malachite, *uaz*, so commonly found in the prehistoric graves, along with the slate palettes and brown flint pebbles which were used for grinding it, and which sometimes still retain the paint upon them. In the close of the prehistoric age, galena was also used, perhaps rather more commonly than the malachite. The dynastic people began to use covers for the grinding slabs, to prevent grit being mixed with the paint. (*Gizeh and Rifeh*, v, 9–12; *Royal Tombs*, ii, xxxiv, 23.) By the iiird dynasty, we find the ground malachite kept in shells (also Chessylite, *Medum*, xxix, 12). No special pot was used apparently in the Old Kingdom; but just after, about the viith dynasty, a blue-glazed pot (Univ. Coll.) was used for kohl (*Diospolis*, xxviii, viith dynasty group); and similar forms in drab pottery were used for it in the xith dynasty, such as *Qurneh*, xvi, 268, 272–3, 278, 281–2, which often contain grey kohl. For a study of the various minerals used for eye paint, see WIEDEMANN in *Medum*, pp. 41–4.

The forms of kohl pots are necessarily a part of the subject of stone vases, and must be dealt with under that class. As Prof. Hamada of Kyoto has already drawn all of those with the kohl-tubes, it is not desirable to divide that series, and it will appear in my Catalogue of the Stone Vases. Here, therefore, we shall omit the usual vases, and only give the tubes in photograph, to show their style. Beside these with toilet objects, some will appear in other volumes. With Figures, (A) ebony Bes statuette, pierced as a tube; (B) limestone tube with dancing Bes in relief. With Vases, (C) ape holding tube; (D) Taurt pierced as a tube; (E) usual kohl-pot form with fish on the vase; (F) lid with fish engraved; (G) standing female figure with kohl-pot at her back. With Architecture; (H) a bone model of plain octagonal column; (I) five bone models of lotus column.

62. Pl. xxii, 1. Limestone vase lid with figure having uraei proceeding from the elbows and toes, also on the top of the head. A similar figure, holding two serpents in each hand, appears on the ivory wands.

2. Piece of a limestone kohl-pot, with figure of Taurt. Gurob. xviiith dynasty.

3. Black steatite figure of Bes (broken), holding a vase with an ape on each side of it; this will appear with figures. xviiith dynasty.

4. Limestone figure of ape seated, holding a tube. xviiith dynasty.

5. Limestone figure of ape standing, holding a tube. These figures were usually stained dark

brown, and had the incised lines coloured bright yellow, to imitate ebony with gold wire inlay. They appear to be Theban, of the early part of the xviiith dynasty.

6. Hard grey limestone figure of a woman seated, holding a tube. The hair hangs in ringlets down each side, and is plaited at the back in five tails. Early in xviiith dynasty.

7. Green glazed schist lid of kohl-pot, with eight-leaved flower. Early in xviiith dynasty.

8. Black steatite lid, with lotus pattern, and central flat dome of red limestone. xviiith dynasty.

9. Ivory double tube; one containing resinous material, the other brown earthy matter. On the front, a nude figure in thick wig, holding her left hand on the middle of the body. xviiith dynasty.

10. Wooden triple tube, empty. On front, kneeling ibex, neck and head too slender for body. On reverse, the same, indistinct. Above and below the scenes, a zig-zag line between rows of triangular dots. Two wavy lines down each edge. xviiith dynasty?

11. Limestone block with two tubes, widening downward from the mouth; empty. Scratched on the side in a cursive hieroglyphic inscription:— "Divine father, priest of Ptah, cleanser of the temple of Memphis, Auf-hensi, chief engraver." (See pl. xxviii, 53.) On the reverse, a figure of a falcon wearing the crown of Lower Egypt. xxist dynasty?

Also a similar limestone double tube, rather more tapering and taller; empty.

12. Grey steatite triple tube; tubes in half relief on front. Contents, grey kohl (galena), decomposed to white. On back, cross-hatched bands and two birds. xxth–xxvth dynasty?

13. Grey steatite double tube; tubes in half relief on front. Grey kohl (galena), decomposed to white. On back, line patterns, diagonal and crossed. Koptos. Roman?

14. Black steatite double tube; tubes showing on three sides in a framing outline. Empty. A lion couchant, at the bottom of each narrow side. On back, Harpocrates standing in a shrine with pediment. On each side, a couchant sphinx on a base. Below, two altars, with Roman mouldings. On the base, a plough scratched, pl. xxviii, 52. Roman.

15. Grey veined serpentine, sextuple tube; empty. Groove down end of block, for kohl-stick.

63. *Wood.* 16. Quadruple tube. One with green powder, plugged with a roll of cloth; one with black kohl, one empty, one cut clean through the bottom. Between two of the tubes, a bronze wire loop, one above that lost (see figure); for holding the kohl-stick. Gurob. xixth dynasty.

17. Blue-glazed, quintuple tube. Brown powder in one (manganese?). Kom Afryn, western Delta. xxth dynasty?

Also a square block of wood with four tubes cut in it. Empty. This has a central hole for the kohl-stick, a pin for a hingeing lid, and a knob for tying down the lid. The corners of the block are recessed to hold inlays of other wood. Kahun. xiith dynasty? Also two wooden triple tubes; grouped as three joined tubes, a groove between two of them for the kohl-stick. Tubes pierced halfway down in one, two thirds down in the other. A separate base-piece pegged on to the base of one group.

18. Wooden double tube; one containing grey kohl, plugged with linen. Kohl-stick in groove between tubes. Lid missing.

Also another of similar form, no contents or stick.

19. Wooden tube, lid missing, kohl-stick in groove on side.

20. Wooden tube, lid and stick missing. Corners recessed. Gurob. xviiith dynasty.

Also dark-green serpentine double tube, as 18. Green and white kohl in one tube. Also alabaster double tube, as 18; empty.

21. Wooden tube in form of lotus column, swivel lid missing. Contains brown powder, manganese? xviiith dynasty.

22. Bone tube in form of lotus column. Swivel lid missing; xviiith dynasty. For others see *Architecture*.

23. Ebony tube, in form of palm column. Swivel lid broken away, pin remaining. Has been used for black kohl, but empty. xviiith dynasty.

24. Bone tube with traces of white decomposed kohl (split, no bottom). Three lotus flowers engraved on the side. xixth dynasty?

Also alabaster tube, plain, no lid or stick; with traces of black kohl. Gurob.

25. Ebony tube, cut in form of reed, with leaf-bract at base joint. Brown powder inside.

26. Wooden tube, with two bands of cross-hatching, originally filled with blue. Gurob. xixth dynasty?

27. Wooden tube, with two bands of cross-hatching, between two bands of vandykes, filled with blue. Grey kohl; traces of linen plugging.

28. Wooden tube with four bands of cross-hatching, and leaf-bracts at base. Split by oxydizing of galena kohl, decomposed white.

29. Ebony tube, with two bands of cross-hatching, and three of diagonal lines.

30. Bone tube, with cross-hatching and rings. Part of bronze kohl-stick in it.

64. *Reeds.* 31. Natural reed, with brown powder. Gurob. xixth dynasty.

32. Reed, with white powder, plugged with linen. Gurob. xixth dynasty.

33. Reed, empty. Gurob.

34. Reed, with dark grey kohl. Kahun. Coptic.

35. Reed, with dark grey kohl.

36. Reed, empty. Gurob.

37. Wooden tube, cap lost, empty. Wushym. Late Roman.

38. Wooden case, tube $\frac{1}{3}$ of diameter; traces of black kohl. Outside, black top and bottom, yellow in middle. Cap black. Turned wood. Coptic.

The small glazed pots are of the vith dynasty; the same forms in drab pottery succeeded in the xith; alabaster and blue marble pots began in the xiith and continued to the reign of Tahutmes III, but not later. Within that reign the tube or reed came into use from Asia, and continued till Coptic times. The name of Job's daughter, Keren-ha-puk ("the horn of eye paint") refers to this custom.

65. *Kohl-sticks, unguent spoons.* Pl. xxiii.

1–12 from Kahun, probably xiith dynasty. 1–5 of wood; 6–11, haematite; 12, haematite with copper tube handle; 13, copper, with bent ear-pick end.

14. Ebony dish of shell form, probably for kohl-stick and hair pins; inscribed, "A royal offering given to Min lord of Apu (Ekhmim); that he may give incense, and ointment, for the *ka* of the prophet Antef." xith or xiith dynasty.

15, 16, 17. Copper kohl-sticks with squared shanks, to fit in a handle (?).

18, 19. Wooden kohl-sticks, from Tell Amarna. xviiith dynasty.

20–5. Wooden kohl-sticks, from Gurob. xviiith to xixth dynasties.

26–9. Haematite kohl-sticks, from Gurob. Same date. 29 with remains of bronze handle.

30–5. Bronze kohl-sticks, from Gurob. Same date.

36–40. Bronze kohl-sticks with spatula end for mixing the paint. These are of the xviiith dynasty,

as in the groups in *El Amrah and Abydos*, xlvi, D 116, and li, D 77: *Cemeteries of Abydos* III, xi.

41–3. Double-ended kohl-sticks of bronze, undated.

44. Bronze kohl-stick. Wushym. Roman.

45–50. All bronze, double-ended. 45 plain. 46–50 more or less squared up in the middle, with a notched pattern, to give a grip. Roman.

51–6. Unguent spoons of bronze. Roman.

57–60. Ear picks, bronze. Roman.

61. Spatula, bronze. Roman.

62. Wooden spoon, shell form, supported by uraeus, duck head with ivory beak at top of handle (*Kahun*, viii, 17).

63–5. Hawk, horse, and lion-headed handles.

66. Ivory shell-spoon, with hawk-head handle.

67. Unknown utensil in bone. Roman.

68–9. Ear picks, ivory.

CHAPTER VIII

MIRRORS.

Pls. xxiv to xxix.

66. THE invention of mirrors has yet to be traced, and two examples that have recently come to light suggest the earlier stages. On pl. xxviii, the first object, marked 26, seems to be the beginning of the idea in Egypt, preceding the dynastic series of metal mirrors. This is a disc of slate, half-an-inch thick, with a hole for suspension, and a personal mark incised at the lower edge. The surfaces are fairly flat, and not rounded like nearly all the slate palettes; there is no trace of a grinding hollow, as on the palettes. When the surface is wetted, this is an efficient reflector, probably as good as most of the metal mirrors when new. It serves that purpose well, and could not serve any other use that we can imagine. There is another early stage of the mirror in prehistoric Greece, in the very shallow, flat, dishes of black ware, either plain, or with relief designs; these with a little water in them, would be good mirrors, but not so convenient as the slate disc hung up by the Egyptian.

The earliest dated metal mirror (xxviii, 27) is an historical puzzle. It was found in an entirely undisturbed tomb (no. 315, *Sedment* I, p. 2). The entrance was regularly bricked up, with the small bricks used in the 1st dynasty; the body was contracted in the manner of the earliest dynasties;

the stone vases are of forms belonging to the reign of Den, in the middle of the 1st dynasty; there was nothing of any later date in the tomb. The evidence of age is as strong as possible, and we have to consider how to reconcile this with the absence of any mirrors otherwise known before the ivth dynasty. Another matter enforces this divergence; the outline is drawn downward to the handle, and not regularly elliptical like the early mirrors. This pear-shape is not dated before the xviiith dynasty. To account for a late type of mirror being dated as the earliest, there seems no recourse except to suppose that the pear-form belonged to a distant centre—probably Asiatic— far earlier than in Egypt, and that, rarely, examples were traded to Egypt in the earliest dynasties, while the Egyptian did not make mirrors till the ivth dynasty. The common use of the pear-form mirror in Egypt belonged to the xviiith dynasty, as being the period of a vast invasion of Asiatic products, due to Egyptian conquest in Asia. The case would thus be parallel to the history of glass. It should be noted (xxviii, 47. 48) that the mirror is repeatedly shown on Hittite monuments, and seems to have been familiar in lands beyond Egyptian control. The mirror xxviii, 28 may be another of the earliest, as it is closely like no. 27, and is of pure copper. The date of the xviiith dynasty, which is otherwise indicated by the pear-shape, is contradicted by the use of beaten copper, for, in the xviiith dynasty, castings of bronze were usual.

The forms made in the Old Kingdom are known from the tombs of Qau, see xxviii, 29–35. The shape is almost elliptical, but slightly slopes to the tang. There is no perceptible difference between the examples of form 31 from the vth dynasty and from the xith dynasty tomb of Emsaht at Asyut. The tang is usually hammered out in one piece, but in 32 it is separately rivetted on. The tall form 34 is not very flat, and might possibly be a razor; it is not far from the Italian form (*Tools and Weapons*, lx, 42). Large mirrors of the vith dynasty are of the form of 33, but with a parallel-sided tang.

The form of the mirrors seems to have remained within the same variations throughout the Old and Middle Kingdoms. The ellipticity of it in the vith dynasty varies from $\frac{1}{40}$ (BEBETTA, *Diospolis*, xxxi, N. 19) to $\frac{1}{7}$ (*Denderah*, xx, 524). In the xith to xiiith dynasties the ellipticity is from $\frac{1}{30}$ (*Dios-*

polis, xxxi, W. 32) to $\frac{1}{7}$ (in many instances). No distinction therefore can be made in the proportion. In form, there is also no difference; the curve is not at all elongated toward the handle, but is the same below as above. These are the *circulaire* and *solaire* forms of Bénédite (*Cairo Cat.*). The length of the tang varies from $\frac{1}{4}$ to $\frac{1}{9}$ of the height in the Old Kingdom, and $\frac{1}{4}$ to $\frac{1}{12}$ in the Middle Kingdom.

With the xviiith dynasty a new style arose. The outline is drawn down toward the handle, more or less in a pear-form, and often the top curve is much flattened, tending toward a triangular outline (the *cordiforme* of Bénédite). The ellipticity also is greater, being between $\frac{1}{9}$ and $\frac{1}{5}$. The extent of overlap of the two styles is shown by a tendency to the triangular form as early as the xiiith dynasty (*Arabah*, xvi, E. 251, from tomb of Nekhta, 252). The example of the early form, Cairo 44024, though found with the xviiith dynasty mummy of Meshent-tamehu, only belongs to the "assemblage qui constituait la fausse momie de la princesse" (*Cairo Cat.*), and hence is merely some robber's loot of unknown age. Another example (*El Amrah and Abydos*, li, D 77) has the wire pattern handle, which is there of early xviiith dynasty, and the knife with duck-head handle, as found by Reisner in the tomb of Hepzefa of the xiith dynasty. It seems therefore that the forms were mixed, from the xiiith to the beginning of the xviiith dynasty. In the New Kingdom, the tang became much longer, from $\frac{1}{6}$ to $\frac{2}{5}$ of the height. This change was due to using bronze. In earlier times, the mirror was beaten out, and as it was difficult to provide a long tang, it was often (1 in 5) rivetted on. But when bronze came, and the mirror could be easily cast, then a long tang was as easy to make as a short one, and better for fixing the handle.

In the xxvth dynasty, the loot from Thebes (*Cairo Cat.* 44078–80) shows the pear-form 78, lessened in 79, and becoming almost circular in 80. These are all clearly Ethiopian in the fashion of the figure-engraving. On reaching the xxvith dynasty, the circular form was established as the sole shape. The date is given by the examples in *Hyksos and Isr. Cities*, xx A, xxviii, 44, here of the vth cent. B.C., *Naukratis* I, xxviii of the 1st cent. A.D., and *Hawara*, xx, 21 of about the iiird cent. A.D. The regular Roman mirror, without a handle, was always turned circular. The tang in these late times was from $\frac{1}{4}$ to $\frac{1}{2}$ of the height, and narrow.

In one instance (fig. 42), a socket was cast in one with the mirror.

67. It should be noted that there are often associated with mirrors, shallow concave pans with handles, which have sometimes been called mirrors. That such pans are not mirrors seems shown by their occurrence along with ordinary mirrors (*Abydos* III, xvii; *Cemeteries of Abydos* III, xi). These examples show that they were made as early as the xviiith dynasty, and they continued in use till the xxvith dynasty (*Defenneh*, xxxix, in *Tanis* II). They are cast much thicker than mirrors, and about half the size. Being apparently for toilet use, they may have been to hold oil for the hair; perhaps such oil was heated with incense, to perfume it.

Another class of objects outside of the ordinary mirrors is that of the ceremonial mirrors set on angle-stands, such as support the emblems of nomes and of gods (xxviii, 49, 50). These are found along with ordinary mirrors (Tombs of Ament and Emsaht, *Cairo Cat.* 44048–9), and figured on coffins with ordinary mirrors. They are not therefore a substitute, but a distinct class with a religious or ceremonial meaning.

68. The handles of mirrors are mainly of the lotus or Hathor types. The earlier examples, of the vith dynasty, have not been preserved, probably owing to being of wood. The lotus type was probably the first used (as figs. xxiv, 1, 2, 4, 5, 6, 7, 8) because the earliest Hathor head (xith dynasty, *Cairo Cat.* 44035) has the splay of the lotus combined with it; and all the mirrors upon steles and coffins of the Middle Kingdom are of the lotus type. The Hathor head was certainly well established in the xiith dynasty, for the handle, as on the great silver mirror with gold Hathor head from the Lahun treasure (Cairo), the lesser gold heads from Dahshur (*Cairo Cat.* 44089), and the wooden handle from Kahun (*Illahun*, xiii). It also appears on three out of five handles of the Middle Kingdom from Kerma in the Sudan (Boston Museum, *Bulletin*, Dec. 1915). These latter are important, for the patterns of the stem. They all have stems copied from a plaited wire model, probably by *cire perdue*. Such mirrors are known from Egypt (*Arabah*, xiv, 145), with handles entirely of plaited work; and the forms of the mirrors—equal above and below—show these to be all before the Hyksos age. This same system of handle, with wire waves or coils between the plaits, extends to the xviiith

dynasty, as found in a tomb group (*El Amrah*, li, D 77): and the form here, fig. 1, slightly drawing down to the handle, indicates the early xviiith dynasty. The Kerma mirrors usually have two hawks as supporters, on the curves of the flower— more or less degraded. In Cairo are other examples of such hawks (44027–31), and the stems of these handles have both the plain plaiting and the plaits with waves and spirals. We must conclude, then, that spirals go back to the Middle Kingdom, and also the hawks. The lack of registering the sources of the Cairo Collection prevent our having any indication of the ages of those mirrors. In the xiith dynasty the lotus handle was also of blue or green glaze, see xxviii, 37.

The Hathor-head type (xxviii, 40) was usual in the xviiith dynasty (*Riqqeh*, xi), and into the xixth (Berlin, 2818); but it does not appear in the tomb of Rameses III (ROSELLINI, xc, ii).

In the last the lotus handle is continued, and the conventional lotus with rolled leaves, which was already started late in the xviiith dynasty (*Cairo Cat.* 44016). Probably of the xviiith dynasty is the handle with Bes head on the lotus (*Cairo Cat.* 44017). Though stated to come from the tomb of Gem-ne-onkh, its history is confused with reference to the Serapeum, and the form of the disc is clearly of the xviiith dynasty type.

The figure handle appears to belong to the xviiith dynasty, as fig. 9. It occurs dated by locality (Gurob, in *Kahun*, xviii), and by a tomb (*Arabah*, xiv, D. 166). One in Cairo (44044) has the hair in the style of the Middle Kingdom, but the same fashion appears to have been continued to early in the xviiith dynasty (Univ. Coll., kohl-pot 6, and figure). The attitude is with the hands down the sides (*Cairo Cat.* 44044, 45; *Arabah*, xiv), or with the left arm across the body (*Cairo Cat.* 44038, 39, 41, 42; Univ. Coll. ivories), or with the right hand up holding a dove (*Kahun*, xviii), or with both hands raised up to the tips of the lotus flower (fig. 9 here, *Cairo Cat.* 44046).

One example might be supposed to show an earlier figure, *Cairo Cat.* 14038, as the disc there is evidently of the Middle Kingdom or earlier. This seems however to have been put with a wrong handle, like fig. 9 here. The junction of disc and handle is stated to be soldered, and no solder joint is known in the New Kingdom; moreover the disc is quite disproportionate to the handle. As it comes from Ekhmim, a place notoriously plundered by dealers, these discrepancies indicate that the combination is modern.

The *hen* handle seems to be solely of the New Kingdom, see figs. xxvii, 20, 23, 24. The dated examples are a model from the tomb of Amenhetep II (*Cairo Cat.* 44010); another, late in the xviiith, or early in the xixth dynasty, in *Abydos* III, xvii; and one of the xviiith in *Cemeteries of Abydos* III, xi. The handle fig. 24 is of the same age, being from Gurob. Fig. 23 is of the xixth dynasty by the light blue glaze and clumsy work. The decoration on fig. 20 is probably late in the xviiith dynasty. Thus all these agree closely in period.

69. *List of metal mirrors.*

All are figured in pls. xxiv to xxviii except the numbers with curve (prefixed. Those numbers with curve following), are in other collections.

No.	plane p. concave v. convex x.	width ins.	ellipticity 1 in	thickness 100 to inch	tang in height	
1	p. x.	4·0	6	3–6		Beaten. Handle plaited wires, wavy line or spirals between, moulded and *cire perdue* casting. Early dyn. xviii
2	p.	4·8	11	3	6	Beaten. Wood handle.
(2 A	p.	6·4	12	4–5		Beaten, like 2; plain handle of horn.
3	p.	5·5	14	3–4	6	Beaten. Handle pinkish limestone, Hathor cow head each side.
4						Ivory handle, square tenon fitting lotus, slit for tang. Kahun. xii
5						Dark serpentine handle, circular tenon, slit for tang. Kahun. xii
6	x. x.	3·6	14	8–15	5	Probably cast; handle cast and rivetted. ? xviii
7	p.	4·5	8	3		Beaten, handle cast, no rivet. xviii
8	p.	2·5	8	3		Beaten, handle cast, rivetted.
(8 A	p.	2·0	100	1·5	10	No handle.
9	p. ?	5·3	7	10		Cast, mirror xii? Soldered to figure of xviiith with four neck strings and three waist strings.
10	p.	4·3	5	6		Beaten? Handle an offerer, wrongly joined on.
11	p.	5·2	10	6	2	Cast. Hair rings, beads, ivory duck dish together. Gurob. xviii
12						Wooden handle, split by groove of tang. Kahun. xii
13						Wooden handle, rough oval hole for tang. Kahun. ? xii
14						Wooden handle, square tenon for lotus; slit for tang. Kahun. xii
15						Ivory handle, triangular papyrus form with sepals. xii
16						Alabaster handle, in top a tang set in resin; not for mirror?
17						Ebony handle, squared tenon for lotus.
18						Blue paste handle, bronze pin; perhaps pendant of a flail.
19						Blue stone ware, for mirror or sistrum. xxvi
20	x. x.	5·0	10	8–12	4	Cast? Loose in wooden handle. xviii
21	p.	4·7	9	5–6	2	Cast, inscribed *Ran set hayt* "the great hall names her"; perhaps used in official naming. Ebony handle of fish form. xxii
22	p. x.	6·8		4–8		Beaten: handle cast. Form of leaf of blue lotus (*Nymphaea caerulea*). A bud proceeding from the flower has the mirror rivetted in it. ? xxvi
23						Blue glazed handle, slit for mirror. xix
24						Wooden handle, oval hole 2·5 deep in top. Gurob. xix
25	p.	5·4		4–5		Beaten? Leaf of white lotus (*N. lotus*); tang original, not cut or broken recently.

No.	plane p. concave v. convex x.	width ins.	ellipticity 1 in	thickness 100 to inch	tang in height		
26	p.	10·7	33		0	Slate. Prehistoric?	
27)		8·3	—11		7	Copper. Sedment 315, Sydney Mus.	1st
28	p. x.	6·1	0	4—9	5	Copper, beaten, see *Arabah*, xvi, E 251.	1st?
29	p.	5·3	10		9	Copper. Qau. 1089 in group.	iv
30	p.	5·3	14		5	„ „ 7366 in group.	iv
31	p.	4·3	12		7	„ „ 3191 and Emsaht, Asyut.	v, xi?
32	p.	5·6	17		6	„ „ 7329	vi
33	p.	2·7	13		6	„ „ 1030	vi
34	x. x.	2·6	—4		3	„ „ 2040, perhaps razor.	vi
35	p.	6·7	15		7	„ „ 5004	vii
36	p.	2·1	16	2	5	xxviii. Wood handle as 15; blue ring beads. Abydos 1922.	xii
37	p.	4·6	11		?	Green glazed handle. Harageh 275, with scarabs.	xii
38	p. x.	8·9	10	3—6	4	Copper, beaten.	xii
(38 A	v. x.	8·4	9	6—10	7	Beaten. Concavity 0·06, tang rivetted over stump. Kahun. xii	
39	p.	3·5	13		7	Copper, beaten. Qau 494, with long axe as T. W., vii, 150. xvii?	
40)		6·2	9			Wooden handle. Brit. Mus. 24632.	xviii?
41	p.	4·8	12	4—5	4	Yellow bronze, cast.	xviii?
42	x. x.	5·7	6	15—32	3	Cast bronze.	
43	v. v.	4·5	0	7—18	3	Cast.	
44	p.	5·1	0	13	5	Cast; as from Amathus, about 500 B.C. (MURRAY, *Exc. Cyp.*, pp. 102, 108).	xxvii
45	v. v.	5·0	0	7—17	2	Cast.	
46	p.	4·6	22	2—3	9	Beaten.	
47	v. x.	7·4	8	6—9	8	Cast. Concavity 0·07 inch.	
48	v. x.	7·0	10	4—10	7	Beaten, bronze? Concavity 0·22 inch.	
49	v. x.	6·8		6—8	10	Cast. Leaf of *Nymphaea caerulea*, tang with 2 rivets.	xxvi?
50		5·7				Mirror cover, cast, turned. Circular, no handle.	Roman
51	x.	5·8				Bronze mirror, tinned: turned.	
52	x.	5·7				Cast bronze mirror, tinned: turned. Traces of back handles.	
53						Cover of 52.	
54						Cover of mirror?	

70. *Roman glass mirrors.* Pl. xxix. 55. Plaster disc with 6 pieces of thin glass, around a central glass mirror, centre now lost. Grave 202, Gheyta. This and the following plaster mirrors are of the iv th or v th cent. A.D., as a cross occurs on one, and the associated pottery is of about this age.

56. Plaster disc with glass mirror; border black with four knobs and red spots. Grave 200, Gheyta.

57. Plaster tablet with central disc of glass and five squares around. Shurafa.

Various pieces of glass from graves 254, 475, 494 and 569 at Gheyta.

58. Turned wood frame with glass mirror, fixed with red wax; wood, red polished. Two knobs at sides, one lost.

So far, all of these glass mirrors were not backed, except with white plaster; hence the diffused light made it very difficult to see a reflection.

In 59 the better system of a dark backing was used, the glass being backed with resin (?), and fixed in the turned wooden case by bees' wax. The mirror sinks entirely into the cover, evidently to be carried in the pocket.

60. Lastly a metallic backing of the glass was obtained, and the piece here is set in a turned wood case.

61. The best example of the metal and glass mirror is this pocket pair to fold together, framed in red leather with a border of papyrus put round the glass. The papyrus proves that it is not mediaeval or recent. On the back of the pieces of mirror is seen a surface crystallisation of the alloy, apparently in the cubic system.

All of these glass mirrors were blown as large bubbles, and then cut up. The size of the glass bubbles was from 10 to 28 inches diameter. Those with metal backing were the smallest. The backing was put on before cutting up the bubble. It seems probable that when the bubble was blown, and had cooled down stiff to near the melting point of pewter, a small quantity of melted pewter was poured in and swirled round the inside of the bubble until it set. Such a method was followed at Nuremberg in the xvth century.

CHAPTER IX

HEAD RESTS.

Pls. xxx, xxxi, xxxii.

71. THE head-rest is so unfamiliar in Europe that its purpose is often misunderstood. It is not to rest the neck upon, in order to leave the hair untouched; such a position would cause an impossible strain. It is entirely to take the weight of the head, being placed immediately above the ear, under the centre of gravity of the head. The edge of the top curve is always made thin, in order to pass between the top lobe of the ear and the head, as the support is needed as near the ear as possible. This quite precludes the idea of any pillow or softening being placed over the support, nor is any such cover needed. The sense of hardness is due to excess of pressure on a small area, such as the curves of bones,—especially the skull,—touching a plane. If the surface fits the body, and so spreads the pressure, there is no sense of hardness. A wooden pillow that fits the curve of the head, and so supports a large surface, is quite comfortable for sleeping on. The reason for adopting this form is the heat, and the need of allowing of free evaporation around the neck. In prehistoric times flock pillows were used, and they must have been unpleasant in the summer.

The earliest head rest known is a small one (pillar lost) of S.D. 78, or just before the 1st dynasty (Tarkhan 1608); when complete it was most like no. 8. A single pillar, like no. 5 without abacus, and small, was of S.D. 80, or early in the 1st dynasty (Tarkhan 2051).

The earliest dated figures are of the beginning of the iiird dynasty (QUIBELL, *Tomb of Hesy*, xiv, xxi). At that date two different forms were in use, those here shown as figs. 1 and 5. It is unlikely that so much variety would be made in the first stage, and the plain single pillar is the form during the 1st dynasty. It is a familiar object in Central African life; but whether it was invented in Egypt, or introduced from some earlier source, is not likely to be settled, in the absence of early dating elsewhere. The dating of the types in the Old Kingdom has been studied by Mr. MACKAY, from the Kafr Ammar cemetery, in *Heliopolis, Kafr Ammar, and Shurafa*, pp. 20–22, pls. xviii–xxi.

72. Though the earliest examples are simple, we here take the double-column type first, as it disappeared before the pyramid age.

No. 1. Kafr Ammar, grave 235. This is made in four pieces, the base, the two columns, and the abacus and curve in one. The column shafts have oblong tenons fitting in the abacus and the base. On the base board are carved two circular raised bases, with a sinking in the middle of each to receive the foot of the shaft. Similarly, very slight hollows in the abaci receive the heads of the shafts. Between the two raised bases two holes are drilled, and a groove connects them below. This seems to show that at one time a cord was passed through them, to retain the top in some way. If so, it must have been a patchwork fitting, with the cord looping over the ends of the abacus below the curve. Height of hollow, 6.3 inches. As the natural height for the head above the shoulder, lying on the side, is $4\frac{1}{2}$ or 5 inches, there must have been about $1\frac{1}{2}$ inches of mattress under the body, beyond which stood the head rest.

The architectural source of this and other forms is important, in the absence of remains of buildings as early. The round base, shaft, and square abacus are fully developed; the tapering of the shaft was also adopted. These columns are decorated with true flutings, not the channelling commonly misnamed fluting. There are ten flutings in relief around each column; the smooth spaces between are about three times the breadth of a fluting. In the figures of the tomb of Hesy there are no flutings or channels shown; the abaci are separated, and support a top slab, a detail almost suppressed in no. 1. iind dynasty.

No. 2. Kafr Ammar, grave 468. This was made in the same number of pieces as no. 1, but is rougher, and debased in detail. The column is a slip, flat on one side, slightly convex on the other, roughly and irregularly grooved. There are no circular bases and no abaci. The base slab is almost bevelled away on both sides. Through the base and the under-plate of the top, a hole is cut, in order to lash top and base together. Height of hollow, 5·7 inches. iiird dynasty.

No. 3. Bought. This is a coarse form of the previous type. The base-block bevelled on sides and ends. Pillars oval and smooth. Holes in base and top block, for lashing together. Height of hollow, 6·4 inches. The under side of the base is so much rounded that it will not stand; this was probably in order to tilt it, in use, so as to fit the position of the head. iiird–ivth dynasty?

No. 4. Meydum. Not figured. Of the form of no. 5, but channelled with 20 grooves on the column. In three pieces; circular raised base 3·6 wide; column, base 2·8 wide, height 4·65. The diameters are rather less from side to side. Height of hollow, 7·2 inches. End of iiird dynasty. (See pottery case.)

73. No. 5. Bought. In three pieces; with two tenons, side by side, on the column foot, fitting into mortises in the base. A single thick tenon on the top of the shaft. The shaft trimmed into 16 faint planes at the foot, the result of successive halving; the upper part with traces of whittling down into a circular form. This form, but with straight converging sides of the column, is shown in the tomb of Hesy, so must be as old as the beginning of the iiird dynasty. By the bold form and fine cutting, this may be of the ivth dynasty.

No. 6. Not figured. Similar to last, but the shaft octagonal. (Funerary section.)

No. 7. Not figured. Square abacus as last, but sloping base as no. 8. (Funerary section.)

No. 8. Bought. This is cut out of a single block, but with obvious remembrance of compound forms. The foot stands as a ridge on the base slab; the column has no abacus, but spreads out to the ends as a raised ridge on the curve. The single block forms, when dated, belong to the vth dynasty. Height of hollow, 6·1 inches.

No. 9. Bought. In two parts; a tenon on the top of the shaft coming through the curved part. The form of this is much like one of those of Hesy, especially in the fineness of the shaft, which is more slender than that of Shepses in the vth dynasty. (Kafr Ammar, xviii, 10.) Under side of base rounded, for enabling it to tilt to the head.

No. 10. Bought. Hard white limestone with shells. Around the shaft are 23 flutings, and a wide band, equal to 6 flutings, which was intended for an inscription. The work is clumsy, and it was evidently merely a funeral object, the parts being stuck together without any tenons. Height of hollow, 7·0 inches. ivth dynasty?

No. 11. Bought. Hard white shelly limestone. Around the shaft are 12 flutings, and a band equal to 4 flutings; thus it was divided by repeated halving. This is also a funerary object, without tenons. On the base slab is a slightly raised circular base to the shaft. Height of hollow, 6·0 inches. ivth dynasty?

No. 12. Bought. Not figured. Alabaster. In four pieces originally, but separate abacus lost. Around the shaft, 19 flutings. A slight circular base with faint dome tenon under the shaft. Of coarse work, but the curved piece thin and regular. Only for funerary purpose. Height of hollow originally, about 5·0 inches. vith dynasty?

No. 13. Gizeh. (Gizeh and Rifeh, vii B.) Limestone. This form has a reminiscence of the early two columns, in the groove down the shaft. There is no trace of a circular base, but the square abacus remains, bent upwards. Height of hollow, 6·2 inches. vth dynasty.

No. 14. Tarkhan, no. 1939. No. 15. Rifeh. These light splayed forms are of an entirely different family to all the others. From the example found at Zowyeh, they are of the late vth or early vith dynasty. In both of these examples the grain of the wood is continuous from one leg into the other, showing that a branch must have been trained into the required form when young, and left to grow for about a generation before it was thick enough to be trimmed into shape. It is a more elaborate work than the training of right-angle bends for the Egyptian furniture. Height of hollow, 6·9, and 6·5, inches. vith dynasty.

No. 16. Meydum, grave 136. (Meydum and M. III, p. 29.) This is a simple round piece of a branch, with a flat side cut for a base, and hollowed on the upper side for the head. The height of the hollow slopes from 1·7 to 2·1, from side to side. This must have been placed on a support, probably on a brick, to bring it up to shoulder depth. The curve is too wide for the back of the head, so it was not for sleeping on the back. It is the simplest of all types, but far from the earliest, as it is probably near the beginning of the ivth dynasty.

No. 17. Tehneh. Plain upright block, with curve on upper side; 9·5 long, 3·2 thick to 2·7 at top. Hollow 5·1 high, end 6·7 high. This comes from a tomb of about the vth dynasty at Tehneh, found by Mr. Frazer. (With group of pottery.)

No. 18. Rough pottery, reddish buff. Qau, no. 3262. Probably Old Kingdom. See no. 30 with four pillars.

No. 19. Limestone, painted red. Edge projecting, to fit over ear.

No. 20. Limestone, block form model, roughly cut. Late?

74. No. 21. Wood. Sedment, no. 383. ixth dynasty.

No. 22. Wood. Sedment, no. 298 A naturally forking branch for a tripod stem, with a top fixed on by a square tenon. ixth–xth dynasty.

No. 23. Wood. Sedment, no. 275. xth dynasty. Top supported by two pillars, resting on a raised ridge on the base plate. This is in Edinburgh, but is figured here as the latest example of the two-pillar form.

No. 24. Wood. Sedment, no. 630. A doubly wide top, with very projecting side flange, and ribbing beneath, and down the stem. vith–xth dynasty.

No. 25. Wood. Solid block, with figure of a pillar head rest in relief on each side. Probably ixth–xth dynasty. Sedment, no. 1805. For the types of the ixth and xth dynasties in general, see Sedment, pls. xiv, xv, xxi.

No. 26. Wood. Made of three pieces with thick dowels, a thinner variety of the xith dynasty type, no. 31. Bought.

No. 27. Bought. Block carved, with curve projecting at the top. Height of curve, 6·0 inches. The solid block head rests are of the vth dynasty when dated, as at Deshasheh, and this may be of that age.

No. 28. Bought. This type is formed of a base and a curve, connected by six separate sticks. The different angle of one stick is due to part of the top being broken away, and the repair being anciently made by boring a fresh hole for the stick. Such compound head rests at Kafr Ammar were found with pottery of the xth or xith dynasties. Height of hollow, 6·1 inches.

No. 29. Tarkhan, 2017. Unfortunately this cannot be dated; but, from the clumsy form, it seems likely to be nearer to the Middle Kingdom than to the Old Kingdom. It has a strong slope to fit the head, the hollow being 5·7 on one side and 5·3 on the other, above the base.

No. 30. Not figured. Bought. Red-faced pottery. Four pillars in a row support the curve. The flaking, red-polished, face is most like late Old Kingdom ware, of the vith–xth dynasties. Height of hollow, 5·3 inches. (See pottery case.)

No. 31. Bought. Made of three pieces, with thick tenons. The massive clumsy form is that of a head rest in a burial of the xith dynasty at the Cairo Museum. This has been stuccoed originally. Height of hollow, 6·5 inches. xith dynasty.

75. No. 32. Bought. Long thin base, octagonal column; of three pieces, a short one joining the curve and the base. The length of the base marks the New Empire, as specially seen in the xviith dynasty example from Qurneh (Qurneh, xxv). Height of hollow, 5·4 inches. xviiith dynasty.

No. 33. Bought. Not figured. Similar to last; but shaft oval, rising from a flat board base. Middle piece of shaft missing. Height of hollow originally, about 6 inches. xviiith dynasty.

No. 34. Bought. Shaft a rounded octagon, with long tenon top and bottom, passing through the curve and the base. Height of hollow, slanting from 6·2 to 6·8 inches. xixth dynasty?

No. 35. Bought. In the form of a hare, carved from a single block, with straight grain cut across. Height of hollow, slanting from 5·2 to 5·5 inches.

No. 36. Gurob. Made of wood, with bronze hinge-pin. The upright sticks are let into the top pieces, and fixed with tenons into the foot bars. There must have been a sling of linen fitting over the top pieces. This is an enormous advance on the wooden head rest. The sling would hold the head of any curvature, with uniform ease; the length of it could be varied to give any height of support needed. The whole thing would fold up like a camp stool for carrying about, and be only half the weight of the usual type. xviiith dynasty.

No. 37. Bought. Made in two pieces with a dowel going through from top to base. The dowel ends have been covered with inlayed plates. The shaft is octagonal, deeply channelled. The ridges between the channels are continued out to the edges of the base and of the curve, making a fine piece of decorative structure. On the front is the inscription "Royal scribe, great one over the archers of the lord of the two lands, Amen-em-(ant)." The end is decayed, but it seems to read more like *ant* than *heb* or *apt*. Height of hollow, 5·6 inches. xviiith dynasty.

No. 38. Not figured. Gurob. Made in two pieces, with long dowel through both. Shaft octagonal. Like 21, but base flatter. Height of hollow, 4·6 inches. xviiith dynasty.

No. 39. Bought. Not figured. As last, but coarser. Pieces of original cord around the shaft. Height of hollow, 4·6 inches. xixth dynasty?

No. 40. Gurob. Complete, in two pieces; here shown apart for the sake of the inscription. It is only partly legible, "For the *ka* of (title) ... *no-shănna, măot kheru.*" At the ends of the base are figures of Bes holding serpents, and with knives at his feet. Height of hollow, 4·3 inches. xixth dynasty.

Here the series of head rests, so abundant in the Old and the New Kingdoms, comes to an end. From no tomb after the xixth dynasty have I ever found one, or heard of one: in no museum are any reported of a later date. It is also remarkable that none appear to have been found of the xiith dynasty, though the tombs are perhaps more numerous then than in most other periods. There seem to have been two introductions of the idea into Egypt, one in the iind–iiird dynasties, another in the xviith–xviiith dynasties. In the latter, there is no question of the strong African influence; and, by the portrait of Zeser, the iiird dynasty has been supposed to be of southern origin. It may be that the head rest, so characteristic of Africa at present, was twice introduced into Egypt from African sources, coming in first with the fluted columns of the Step pyramid age.

Another source of dated forms should be noted, the paintings on the coffins of the Middle Kingdom. These are copied in LACAU, *Sarcophages antérieurs au nouvel empire*, pl. xxxv. One, fig. 108, is of the massive xith dynasty type. In fig. 109 the fluted shaft survives. But most of them there, and in *Riqqeh*, xxiii, are of a conventional degradation of the column, base and abacus, quite out of proportion. No help in dating can be obtained from these conventions, based on traditional copies.

76. On coming to the Greek period, head rests of stone, found in towns, are of an entirely different class. The blocks are massive, tapering to the top, and with a hole at each end by which to lift them. They were used until Coptic times, see QUIBELL, *Excavations at Saqqara*, II, xxxv. Sometimes there is a hollow on one side, to give space to the shoulder, as in the models in *Amulets*, xlvi, 34 f, g. One example had a little shrine cut in the side, apparently to hold a sacred figure beneath the head; the idea may have been to influence dreams (*Memphis* III, xxxiii, 14). Another branch of this type was the stone seat, such as is found with a dedication. See DARESSY, *Sièges de Prêtres* (summary in *Ancient Egypt*, 1915, 142). No. 20 is a limestone model of a stone head rest. Models of head rests were often placed as amulets on mummies, from the xxvith dynasty to Ptolemaic times. They are usually of the old column type, and cut in haematite. Rarely, amulets are made in the form of the contemporary stone block type. See *Amulets*, p. 15.

Six other wooden head rests have been rejected as duplicates.

CHAPTER X

BOXES, SPOONS, AND TOILET TRAYS.

Pls. xxxiii, xxxiv.

77. xxxiii, 1. Hard-wood lid of small toilet box, sloping thicker to one end. xiith dynasty?

2. Box of ebony and ivory; parts lost, edges of lid, two edges and bottom of box. Fastened by a peg on cross bar of lid, slipping into hole in end of box, and the other end of the lid secured by tying its handle to the peg on the box. Loop of tying thread still on it. xviiith dynasty?

3. Box of ebony, carved out of a block, with six compartments. Lid sliding in grooves undercut; tapering to the end, so that it only grips at nearly closing. In the compartments are globular, discoid, and bun-shaped pellets of dark brown matter. These are some of mere clay, others mixed with enough resin to burn; apparently they are a much adulterated incense. Late Roman.

4. Hard-wood swivel lid, with two lotus flowers incised, and filled in with blue paste. xviiith dyn.

5. Similar lid, traces of blue filling. Gurob. xviiith dynasty.

6. Similar lid, with middle petal of one lotus rounded. xviiith dynasty.

7. Circular swivel lid, with four lotus flowers incised, and filled in with blue paste.

8. Swivel lid, with lotus flower and seed vessel. Gurob. xviiith dynasty.

9. One of a pair of duck wings, covers of a toilet dish. xviiith dynasty.

Other dishes are classed with the stone vases, sculptured figures, and ivory. See also the duck dish in a group with mirror, fig. 11. Two heads of ducks are from dishes, of limestone painted green and black, one from Gurob.

78. *Spoons.* 10. Wooden spoon with lotus at spring of bowl. From the long thin cylindrical handle, this seems as if of xiith dynasty.

11. Wooden spoon, for food? Handle and bowl cut separately, and badly pegged together. The hole in the end shows that it was hung up, and thus connected with the Arab name for a spoon, *m'alaqa,* a suspended thing. Roman?

12. Carved wood bowl, lashed by leather strip on to a handle now lost. It has been painted with red wax (?) colour. Roman?

13. Bowl of spoon of cowry shell, formerly rivetted to an iron handle. A similar spoon, complete, is in the Turin Museum (phot. 168). Coptic?

14. Bone bowl, very flat, with rough twist pattern on it. Roman?

15. Wooden spoon; handle carved roughly as an animal, holding the butt of the bowl in its mouth. Late Roman.

16. Wooden spoon, with probably a cross on the carved handle. Coptic.

79. *Horn.* 17. A horn of the domestic ox. The smaller end has been moulded into a spout; the larger end is closed with a wooden stopper made in two pieces,—plug and cap,—but not fastened to the horn. The cow's horn found at Qurneh (*Qurneh,* xxv) had an ivory spout fitted on, and the large end closed with a plate of ivory cemented on. A model of such a horn was found in the Maket tomb, about the middle of the xviiith dynasty; it was made of green paste, with the large end closed. It seems as if these horns were intended for sprinkling, by the small hole and splaying mouth. They appear to belong to the early part of the xviiith dynasty.

80. *Egyptian trays.* xxxiv. 18. Wooden tray in the form of the gryphon of Mentu. On the side of the head, a curl extends back from over the eye. It has never had a crest on the top, but below the jaw is a groove, as if to insert a wattle. Early xviiith dynasty?

19. Wooden tray in the form of a gazelle, with the legs tied. Top edge broken. Damaged by salt. xviiith dynasty?

20. Slate tray in form of gazelle with the legs tied. A similar tray is at Turin (phot. 359). xviiith dynasty?

21. Part of green glazed pottery gazelle tray. Colour Ptolemaic.

22. Ivory dish with degraded lotus pattern at ends. Roman.

Portions of ivory dishes, of xviiith dynasty and later, are placed in Ivories. In the collection is also the Hyksos group with a large duck tray. Sedment, xl, 15; xli, 22.

81. *Roman trays.* A considerable class of black steatite dishes, with figures in high relief in the interior, is obviously of one period, perhaps of one locality. The only paper on these is by Sir JOHN EVANS in *Proc. Soc. Ant.,* 13 Feb., 1908, referred to, below, as "Evans." Those published there, in the Cairo Catalogue (BISSING, *Stone Vases*), in Italian Museums, and here, may be summarised as follows:— University College 9, (and 4 fishes) Cairo 6, British Museum 4, Evans Coll. 3, Oxford 3, Bologna 2, Turin 1, total 28. The subjects of these dishes will be described here, regardless of their present position. Dishes of larger size with incised figures of the xviiith dynasty and Roman, will be dealt with under stone vases.

The earliest stage is a bowl with plaiting pattern outside and plain inside, with a real tubular spout, see *Stone Vases,* 960.

Osiris Khentamenti (1). Simple swathed figure, hardly longer than the radius of the bowl. Under side, only a plain rosette within the foot ring. From the unusual subject, and the simplicity of work, this may be the earliest of the class (Evans 9 = Brit. Mus.).

Serapis and Isis busts (4). On a plain bowl, wreath on edge, Bologna. Placed on an inner wreath, Cairo 18754, pl. B; also Evans 2. Placed over a lotus flower (Cairo 18755).

Serapis Isis and Onqet (1). On a wreath, with two cupids and bunches of grapes. The bust of Onqet may perhaps have some connection with Nebhat, but there is little evidence for that. It rather seems to show that this came from Philae or further south, where Onqet was worshipped (Evans 7 = Brit. Mus.).

Serapis Isis and Horus (2). Horus as a small figure between busts of Serapis and Isis. Horus falcon-headed (Cairo 18753), or as Harpocrates (Cairo 18756).

Isis bust (1), in plain bowl, probably early in the series (Evans 1).

Isis seated on dog (1), two cupids below, in rosetted bowl (Brit. Mus. = Evans 6).

Isis and Horus (2); one in a plain bowl (Oxford, Evans 4); the other over a lotus flower and buds (Evans 3); in both, Horus is falcon-headed.

Horus falcon-headed (3), seated between a lion and a falcon (Oxford, Evans 5); on horseback, part of a group; on the back, ten compartments, of which there remain two, with a camel, and a dog couchant regardant, also a fragment of a couchant quadruped (fig. 30); riding on a panther, in a plain bowl (Univ. Coll., fig. 29).

Horus lion-headed (1), standing with upraised arm between two couchant lions, gardant, upon a lotus flower; rosette and wreath border (Bologna, phot. 444).

Harpocrates seated (3), in a plain bowl (Cairo 18757); on a lotus flower in a plain bowl (Univ. Coll., fig. 28); on a goose, surrounded by radiating papyrus plants (Evans 8 = Brit. Mus.).

Pallas bust (1), in bowl with one ring around (Evans 10 = Oxford).

Crocodile (3); two side by side in a plain bowl (Univ. Coll., fig. 24); two side by side, on background a square shrine with curtains flowing down on either side, palm branches outside the crocodiles (Univ. Coll., fig. 25, only the bottom of a large bowl); crocodile in the middle of a plain bowl (Turin, phot. 359).

Scorpion (1), in bowl, ring around, radiate beyond (Univ. Coll., fig. 23).

Shell (3), with palm branch pattern behind it; this evidently had a falcon head at the apex, like the next, but now ground away (Univ. Coll., fig. 31); similar with falcon head (Naukratis, Cairo 18765, pl. B); fragment of a similar shell, about 6 inches across (Univ. Coll., fig. 26).

Gazelles (1). This appears to be a late grouping of three gazelle dishes, like figs. 20, 21 described above (Univ. Coll., fig. 32).

Fish (4). A fragment is very finely worked with scales, and only 0·1 inch thick. In the interior at the mouth it has a human head (Univ. Coll., fig. 27); small fish with scales marked (Univ. Coll., fig. 33); fish, plain outside, on the edge an Arabic inscription, and on the head a figure riding on an animal which looks back (Univ. Coll., fig. 34); an unfinished fish bowl (fig. 35).

Of all these, the group of gazelles is probably the earliest, after that the plain bowls with figures, the bowl with shrine and curtains (fig. 25), then the rosetted bowls, and lastly the fish. As to absolute date, the Horus on a panther (fig. 29), in a plain bowl, seems to recall the equestrian figures of Trajan and Hadrian. The Horus on a lotus (fig. 28) has a back like Evans 8 which is of good work, and, from the whole feeling of these, they seem to belong to the 1st cent. A.D. The florid back patterns of rosette and rope border recall the black moulded ware of Memphis (*Meydum and Memphis* III, xxxvii), which is after the 1st cent. and has affinities with the iiird or ivth cent., in the forms; probably it is about 200 A.D. Perhaps the whole group may be put at 50–200 A.D., except the small fish which must be Arab, unless the inscription was added later.

82. *Outsides.* The patterns of the outsides, and the handles of these bowls, should be noted. The smooth bowl, which appears to be the earliest style (as figs. 24, 29), has on the outside a single rosette (U. C. 28; E. 8, 9), or a central rosette, rope around it, and outer rosette petals (U. C. 24, 29; E. 1, 4), but never has a vine pattern. The bowl with rosette petals inside, around the subject, has, on the outside, rosette, rope line, and petals (U. C. 23; E. 2), and also vine (E. 6). The bowl with wreath around, and a lotus below the figures, has the rosette, rope, and petals (E. 5); but with petals and lotus inside, it has also the vine outside (E. 3, 7). The general result, then, is that the earlier bowls have the simpler outsides; and the bowls that are later, according to style, have the vine outside. With these vine patterns outside is found the motive of the two cupids inside, as E. 6, 7.

Of the bowl handles, the simplest is of a swelled form, ending in a slight turn at each end (E. 10), and this goes with a smooth bowl. The swell broken by two turns in the middle (U. C. 24; E. 4) goes with the smooth bowl inside, and rosette, rope and petals, outside. The handle with a circle and side strokes (E. 1) goes with the same inside and out. The most elaborate handle of two S-curves is once with smooth bowl, once with petals in the bowl, and thrice with a lotus flower and petal border inside (E. 3, 7; Bologna). Thus it belongs to the more elaborate vine group.

There are, therefore, at least three general groups, (1) smooth bowl, simple handles, no vine and sometimes no rope outside; (2) petalled bowl, sometimes with scroll handle and vine; (3) lotus flower in bowl with scroll handle and vine outside. Presumably this is the order of date. Another group seems altogether earlier than these, having a large lotus flower covering the whole outside, sometimes with a central smaller flower. This belongs to the shell-pattern bowl (U. C. 26, 31), and the triple gazelle bowls (U. C. 32). The large simpler style seems to mark that these are earlier, having somewhat of pure Egyptian work apart from classical influence.

83. *Purpose.* The purpose of these dishes has been supposed to be religious by Evans, on the ground of the figures of gods, and from there being spouts,—more or less atrophied,—on the edges. From the Egyptian point of view, the figures of gods do not imply a religious use, as witness the heads of Hathor and figures of Bes on mirror-handles and toilet dishes, or Harpocrates in a shrine on a kohl pot, or the sacred bull on a comb, or Taurt on a hair curler or a chair, or Aphrodite on a pin head. The gods were regarded as presiding over all the intimate sides of life, and their presence on these little dishes only implies their favour being invoked. Such dishes are shown to start from the usual gazelle toilet dish, fig. 20, which passed on to the triple gazelle dish, fig. 32; this on its outside is identical with the shell dishes, figs. 26, 31, which in turn can hardly be separated from the rest of the dishes here. These again link with the fish dishes by the classical example, fig. 27, which lead on to the Arabic dish, fig. 34. Thus the figures of gods do not seem to imply more than on any other toilet object, as already noticed. Perhaps we may regard these as the late substitutes for the sprinkling horns, to receive scents or oil, and pour out drop by drop. Where the spout is entirely atrophied, they may still have been used to dip the fingers in, or may have been mere ornaments of the toilet table, like most of the cut glass bottles and such useless gear made at present.

CHAPTER XI
IVORY AND BONE CARVING.
Pls. xxxv to xxxix.

84. THE earliest carving here (after the prehistoric and 1st dynasty which have been treated elsewhere) is the figure of a girl in open work. xxxv, 1. The style of this could not belong to any times but the Old Kingdom, or the imitation of that in the xxvith dynasty. The simplicity of the work, the good finish in the detail, the naive attitude with the hands protecting the person, all belong to the Old Kingdom. The later imitation, even in a very detailed example here (49) is less finished. From the tongue left above and below, this evidently fitted in to the decoration of a casket, like the open work architectural ivories of the Old Kingdom in the Louvre. Bone. 2·89–2·90 high without tongue. vth dynasty?

2. Figure of a goddess with lioness' head and fore leg (Sekhmet or Mafdet?), broken off at the waist. Kahun. xiith dynasty.

3. Bone, trimmed square; on one side, a lion couchant and crocodile incised; the other side split off. xiith dynasty.

4. Half of similar bone, with lion couchant incised. Kahun. xiith dynasty.

85. *Magic wands.*

The class of ivory wands with incised figures is not yet fully explained. What has been deduced from the nature of the figures and the inscriptions may be seen in *Proc. Soc. Bib. Arch.*, xxvii, 130, 297; xxviii, 33. The remarks here use the principal points of those papers, and some more general connections.

In the prehistoric period, one of the commonest objects in graves is an ornamented tusk. Such are sometimes complete round tusks, with zigzag lines incised; otherwise flat slips of ivory or bone, with a curved outline like a pachyderm tusk. These should be connected with the recognised amulets, such as the half ring with a slight knob for tying on at one end, and a point at the other, cut out of shell, to imitate boars' tusks; note also claw amulets at present recognised as protective amulets in Central Africa, and tusk and horn amulets as protective against the evil eye in Italy. From these, the essential idea of a tusk amulet is protection. The numbers in the College Collection of prehistoric objects is 29 round tusks, and 10 stone imitations; 52 flat tusk forms with 16 stone imitations; and 7 half ring tusks of shell. These tusks belong to the earlier age, 31–55 s.D. When we see that the largest of the prehistoric flat tusks (1419 Naqada) reaches to a length of 6·1 inches, it exceeds the smallest of the wands which is only 5·5 long; the two classes thus overlap one another.

Another prototype of the tusks is an ivory gaming piece found in the Leyden draught-board, which has at the ends of the long slip the heads of lion and jackal (see *Aeg. Mon.... Leyden*, ccxliv, 274–7, and *Descr. Rais. Mon.... Leide*, p. 109).

86. The classification of the wands on the two plates of copies here is by types; on pl. xxxvi are the jackal-head and lion-head terminals, on pl. xxxvii are various terminals, one with a lion head only, K, and L with degraded head. The numbered examples are at University College, the lettered ones A to P are in other collections. The indications of change of style, in the jackal heads, are the detached ears on A; ears drawn free on D; ears adapted to outline, 7, 10, E, of early xiith dynasty (*Ramesseum*, iii); lotus between ears, *Rifeh*, xii; lotus detached, on 15. The entwined serpents are well formed with heads on the relief wand H, but degraded to mere lines on 7 and 8. The winged leopard with bird's head has a human head detached above it on A, B, L; almost joined in 13, E; quite joined on F, K, M; of these, A is an early type, and K is late, judging by the crocodile with two human heads; for these, see no. 12, which is like the style of the xviiith in *Arabeh*, xvii.

It does not appear that the jackal-head type is earlier or later than others. It joins with the plain wands, 5 and 6, which seem early, but the lion head is on the xviiith dynasty example (*Arabeh*, xvii). On the other hand, the wands with names, F, 14, have no heads on the ends, but are likely to be early, as being less formalised. The jackal-head type seems, then, to have been a separate class contemporary with other types.

The absolute dates, that serve to fix the series, are, first, the small jackal-head wand, 5, which was found in cemetery Y at Diospolis (grave 318), ranging from the vith to xiith dynasties; next, the three wands of the style of no. 8, with jackal heads, but no lion heads, dated to the xiith dynasty (*Ramesseum*, iii); later is a wand of Ptah-neferu, daughter of Amenemhat III (Cairo 9438); fragments of two other wands were with beads, of the xiith dynasty types (*El Amrah and Abydos*, xliv). The latest example of a wand is of very debased type, worse than no. 12, found with objects of Tehutmes III (*Arabah*, E 10, p. 12, xvii); this has a debased lion head on one end, and the other may have had a relief jackal head, now broken away beyond the collar lines.

The purpose of the wands is stated by several inscriptions upon them. These are constantly for protection; the phrases are *sa* "protection," "protection by Ra," "Protectors give protection of life to *n*," "Bring protection for *n*"; the gods say "We come as a protection of life daily around *n*"; "Say, We bring this for turning back the enemy on account of *n*"; "May thy name sustain protection for *n*." The wands were therefore to invoke the protection of the gods that are shown on them; and these gods are represented as eating enemies and snakes, and thus subduing evil.

The subjects represented are gods and demons 17, animals 39, monsters 5, hieroglyphic signs 7. In no case is there a repetition of a group of three or more signs together; and it is seldom that any two signs are found repeated together, except the commonest. This absence of repetition of groups is in favour of Miss Murray's view of an astrological meaning; if only protection was intended, a standard formula would be more likely, but if they contained horoscopes referring to the individual life, a repetition would be unlikely.

87. The subjects found and the number of instances are as follows, on 44 different wands.

Gods.

1.	Ram-headed	standing	15.	Bes and snakes standing		
4.	Bull	„	„	3.	Sekhmet standing	
1.	Hawk	„	„	2.	Goddess	„
1.	Set	„	„	24.	Taurt	„
1.	Dog	„	„	9.	„	eating snakes
1.	Ape	„	seated	3.	„	eating captive
1.	Jackal	„	„	1.	Two dog-headed winged genii	
1.	Hare	„	„	1.	Genius holding lizards	
2.	Serpent	„	standing	1.	„	„ hares
1.	„	„	kneeling			

Animals.

1.	Baboon walking	1.	2 lions devouring		
4.	„ with *uzat*	12.	Lion head terminal		
2.	Lion couchant	1.	„ „ on legs		
2.	„ seated	3.	Panther		
2.	„ walking	1.	Cat seated		
1.	„ „ eating snakes	2.	„ „ on *neb*		
1.	Lion on 4 *user*	5.	„ upright		
		4.	Cow mummied		

1. Ram head crowned
1. Deer
1. Set animal
1. Dog standing
1. Ass head
1. Jerboa
1. Hippopotamus head
1. Jackal head in square
1.   „   „   on legs
16.   „   „   terminal
1. Hawk and disc
4. Vulture
4. Crocodile
1.   „   head

3. Crocodile over human heads
6. Turtle
4. Uraeus.
1.   „   on *neb*
10. Wavy serpent
5. Twined serpents
1. Wavy serpent with heads on bends
2. Winged Uraeus
3. Frog
9.   „   on *neb*
4.   „   on stand
3. Scarab.

Monsters.

8. Serpo-leopard
21. Chimaera
1. Mentu sphinx

2. 2 foreparts of bulls
5. 2 foreparts of sphinxes

Hieroglyphs.

3. *Uzat*
9. Ra on legs
16. *User*
3.   „   on legs

1. *Zed*
5. Fire
1. Knife
2. *Sa.*

The most usual subject of all is therefore Taurt, the birth goddess. Next is the chimaera, the frog of Heqt the birth goddess, and the domestic god, Bes, holding snakes. Most of the figures of gods and of animals may hold or devour snakes, and therefore such are beneficent. There is no sign of any evil animal.

88. That these wands were for the benefit of the living, and not of the dead, is shown by the names of the persons never having *maa-kheru* as a suffix. Further there is no mention of the Duat, or of Kher-neter, or of Anup, or Osiris; nothing that relates to the dead appears here. The great amount of wear, on some wands, points to their having been carried as amulets on the person.

The most promising road to interpreting these wands seems to be that of the later Egyptian horoscopes, where the constellations and stars are set out in order; the planetary signs of the epoch are, then, to be sought in connection with the group in which they then were. Apart from Taurt (who is so often repeated that she may be merely protective), the most usual signs are the chimaera and Bes, and they therefore probably represent events. The chimaera is most like the winged quadruped with a beak, *akhekh*, which represents twilight, dawn or even. It would thus mark the division between the signs of the day and of the night. Bes, the domestic god, may well be the sign of the birth; or perhaps the frog of Heqt is the birth sign, and Bes the conception sign (see QUIBELL, *Excavations at Saqqara*, 1905–6, p. 13). In either case, Bes may be taken as the personal sign.

89. Two of the fullest and most helpful examples are the wands with figures on both sides, Brit. Mus. 18175 (F, G, here) and Berlin 14207. On both of these the chimaera only occurs on one side. On F, pl. xxxvii, it has the sun before it and a flame succeeding it; this implies that it is the twilight, succeeded by artificial light. Bes is immediately after this. The signs preceding the evening thus presumably refer to hours of the day, and dominance of planets in those hours. Of the hour signs (*Zeitschr. Aeg. S.* III, 1), there is a goddess, and the only goddess of the hours is Isis of the 9th hour. Before her is an uraeus and a flame, both of the 5th hour of the day. The crocodile sign is over them.

Before these is the falcon, one of the external planets—probably Jupiter—with the disc over it. The *uzat* of the morn is at the beginning. The serpent and Taurt are guardians, as they appear on both sides alike. Thus we gather that Jupiter was about the 4th hour of the day, the crocodile at the 5th hour, and the birth after sunset.

On the similar side of the Berlin wand, the chimaera must stand for the dawn, as behind it, at the end, is the flame of the 5th hour of the day, again accompanied by *user*, as before. The birth sign, Bes, is next before dawn. Next, earlier, is a defaced sign apparently Horus (6th and 7th hours of night) destroyer of evil animals, holding two hares. The falcon sphinx (5th hour?) follows, and the crocodile over three human heads cannot be assigned.

The other sides of these wands have no chimaera, and so do not refer to the day, but rather to the signs of the zodiac in the year. The central group of foreparts of two sphinxes joined, reminds us of the foreparts of two lions joined, referring to past and future, or the double-faced Janus of the same meaning, who opened the new year. This may, then, be the division of the year. It occurs nearly over the sign Cancer; the new year would fall there about 2800–3000 B.C., and so this would agree with the xiiith dynasty epoch. The serpo-leopard does not appear in the later Egyptian signs. The lion being three signs apart from the scarab, cannot be the sign Leo adjoining Cancer, but is probably the large lion with forepaws on water, on the Dendereh zodiac under Libra. The uraeus is, then, the great twisted serpent, between Leo and Virgo, in the portico signs of Dendereh. The head of a ram crowned may be Hershefi, or the 30th dekan (BRUGSCH, *Thesaurus*, 137–174) under Taurt, and the serpent-headed man holding uraei may be the 29th dekan, of four uraei on the Dendereh zodiac (B. T. 152). The sun is represented in the 30th dekan, the birth sign coming there also.

On the Berlin wand there is the serpo-leopard and the uraeus in the same order, and contiguous. Before these is the Set animal, probably Mercury, and the baboon with the *uzat* for the moon. These were between the uraeus and the panther constellation, the latter unidentified. Beyond the serpo-leopard the figures of Anup (?) and Sekhmet are unidentified.

The examination of these two wands, which are the fullest in detail, will serve to show what line the analysis of the group may take. To clear up the whole of the connections would need not only a full study of all Egyptian astronomy, but correlating it with the Babylonian, as these wands come into use after the immigration of the button-badge people, probably from Mesopotamia. This would entail a large separate work, beyond the scope of a catalogue.

90. *Catalogue of wands.*

5. Plain surfaces; jackal head in relief, eyes deeply drilled; five deeply cut bands above it; length 5.5 inches. From Diospolis, Y 318, cemetery of vith–xiith dynasties. From its plainness, small size, and relief cutting, probably the earliest here.

6. Similarly plain, with relief head, and five bands on neck, 10.0 long. Hippopotamus ivory, as also the following, unless described otherwise.

6 A. This has been fully carved with incised figures, like the following; it shows traces of the jackal and lion head terminals; the twilight *akhekh*, Taurt, and a standing lion (?). On the back are two parallel lines, like the borders of inscriptions on other wands, but no trace of signs between them; an animal head is at the end. The enormous amount of wear which this has had, shows that wands might be greatly handled and carried, while kept carefully from breakage.

7. Wand of elephant ivory. Lion head terminal; Taurt; lion goddess eating serpents; cat standing, killing serpent. The *akhekh*. Vulture on stand, 3rd hour of the day (Dendereh); falcon uraeus standing; twined serpents over lion walking; jackal head terminal.

8. Portion of wand. Lion head terminal; Taurt eating serpents; Mehurt mummified cow with flail (see *Book of Dead*, lxxi); Bes with serpents. The *akhekh*. Lion goddess eating serpents; frog on stand, Heqt; part of the *ăker*, double sphinx.

9. Fragment. Lion head terminal; serpo-leopard; sun on legs, over it.

10. Part of wand. Jackal head terminal. Double sphinx, *ăker*. Mehurt cow mummified. Probably of same wand, the *akhekh*; vulture on *neb*; Taurt walking; frog on stand, Heqt; the remainder lost.

11. Two pieces of a wand of lesser size, and more conventional incising. The lion head terminal; Taurt; serpent-headed god... Leg of another god; lion-headed goddess; Set; falcon-headed god. Miss Murray attributes these to the five gods of the planets, Jupiter, Saturn, Mars, Mercury (Set) and Venus.

12. Fragment with frog on *neb*; Taurt; crocodile with two human heads. This is like the style under Tehutmes III (*Arabeh*, xvii).

13. Fragment with *akhekh*; lion eating serpents; twined serpents behind.

14. Half of a wand, engraved on both sides; formerly repaired by drilling holes. Column, "...Pert, born of Kahem." Bes with serpents. "Say, We bring overthrowing of enemies." Lion goddess, devouring an enemy. "On account of the lady of the house Pert born of Kahem." Hather (?) with serpents. "Exercise protection for the lady of the house, Pert." Serpent in four waves.

Other side. Bes standing with serpents. Lion goddess devouring an enemy. Hather (?) with serpents. Serpent in five waves, on three of which are placed female heads. Bought at Thebes for Miss Edwards, 1882.

15. Wand, both ends lost. Apparently a later style than others, and with some influence like prehistoric work. A middle figure with hippopotamus head holds a branch; on either side is Taurt holding knives, beyond her a vulture with wings forward, all protective signs. The lotus at

end recalls the lotus between ears of the jackal head on the wand, *Rifeh,* xii.

16. Later style of wand, with but little trace of old subjects. Crocodile, Taurt, dog, sheep, baboon-headed figure, Taurt, and dog. Burnt black, and very fragile. Bought at Cairo, 1919.

91. *Hand wands.*

A different class of wand, with a hand at the end, is always found in pairs. There is no doubt that some wands with gazelle heads were used to beat time in dancing. They are so figured in the vth dynasty at Deshasheh (*D,* pl. xii); and the usage went back to the 1st dynasty, as shown by the ivory wands with gazelle heads from the reign of Zet (*Gizeh and Rifeh,* iv, v). They continued till the vith dynasty, as figured in the hieroglyphs of the Pyramid Texts (Merenra 468, Pepy 245). After this, wands with gazelle heads continued to the xiith dynasty, see *Kahun,* viii, 13. Then wands with hands came into use; early in the xiith dynasty (*Ramesseum,* iii, 17); of the xiith, *Gizeh and Rifeh,* xi A; *El Amrah,* xlvi; *El Arabeh,* xiv; Kahun and El Harageh in Univ. Coll., of the xviiith from *Riqqeh,* xii, 13; of Tehutmes III, *Hyksos and Isr. Cities,* xii B. As they are found in pairs, never have any designs upon them, and are almost always pierced, they differ from the magic wands already described.

The most elaborate of these wands is that from Rifeh, with a net work in relief over the whole arm, a bracelet on the wrist, and the butt ending in a lotus flower (Cairo; *Gizeh and Rifeh,* xxvii). The latest example dated is of queen Aohmes, wife of Tehutmes I, in Turin Museum (*Stud. Hist.,* ii, fig. 32). The age of these seems to be mainly of the xiith, and extending down to the earlier part of the xviiith dynasty.

18. Pair of wands with hands, and three bands around the wrist. Pierced at the butts. Hippopotamus ivory. From Gebeleyn, obtained for Miss Edwards, by Greville Chester. 8·8 long.

(19.) Fragments of a pair, with triple bands incised across at three places, and joined by diagonal lines. Found at Harageh, tomb 37, of Neakhm (see *Scarabs,* 13 L). xiith dynasty.

20. Pair of small wands, with four bands on wrists; butts pierced. Brown. 6·3 long.

21. Pair of ivory wands of clumsy work, three bands on wrist. 9·9 long.

22. Wand of elephant ivory from Gurob. Two groups of four bands on wrists. Butt pierced. 15·0 long. Gurob. xviiith dynasty.

23. Hand from a wand. Qurneh.

92. *Ivory figures.* Pl. xxxviii.

24. Ivory figure of a girl, nude, right arm bent across body, the left hanging down. Heavy wig. Has been drilled out, 2 inches deep, for a handle, probably of a mirror; socket later broken and mended. Much worn by use. 6·3 long. xixth dynasty?

25. Flat bone figure of a man, wearing a cape adorned with seated figures of two gods. A skirt is also worn. A heavy collar of beads is like those of the close of the xviiith dynasty. 3·4 high. xixth dynasty.

26. Flat bone figure of a youth walking. 3·9 high.

27. Flat bone figure of the same work as the previous; much split by age. 5·0 high. Figures of this class, 25–7, are of one fabric, probably decorations for a casket, of about the xixth dynasty.

28. Ebony figure of a girl, holding a fruit. Bored for a mirror handle. 3·7 long. xviiith dynasty?

29. Flat wood carving, stuccoed and gilt. Probably a daughter of Akhenaten. Qurneh. xviiith dynasty.

30, 31 (32). Parts of 2 figures of girls swimming, with a square toilet spoon. xviiith dynasty.

33. Shell held in the beak of a duck; pierced for long handle, as a toilet spoon. xiith dynasty?

34. Part of a wooden stand (?) with incised bone panels. A gazelle on either side; the bust of a princess in front. Partly burnt. Gurob. xixth dynasty.

35–6. Two ivory busts, flat at the back; probably from the sloping legs of folding stools. xxth dynasty?

37. Part of a hand well carved in ivory, $\frac{2}{5}$ life size.

38–9. Composite vases, carved in oval hippopotamus tusk for the body; in no. 38 the ibex head remains, carved in one piece of ivory, with a roughly cut hole, $\frac{1}{2}$ inch wide, up the axis.

40. Lion in ivory, with paws extended below head; from decoration of furniture? 2·6 long.

(41.) Five fragments of large tusk of hippopotamus, with limbs of animals in relief. Fayum.

42. Two bulls' heads roughly cut in bone. Gurob. xixth dynasty.

43. Large eye of a bull, carved in ivory, and originally painted. With three holes pierced in loops on the back for fixing it. 3·1 high.

(44.) Two falcon heads in ivory, joined together; from tops of steering oars? (with figures).

(45.) Ivory dish in form of a duck, with lid, perfect. 4·1 long. With mirror no. 11, beads, and hair rings. Gurob. xixth dynasty. Pl. xxvi.

46. Ivory dish in form of a duck, head lost.

47. Imitation shell of ivory, 9·6 long, 3·0 wide.

(48.) Part of a similar shell of horn, with six signary marks cut on it.

49. Parts of delicate open work with kneeling gazelle, vulture on *neb*, crowns, &c. Largest piece 1·9 high. Probably from a casket. xxvith dynasty.

93. *Floral forms.*

50. Ivory toilet tray, square broken, with handle, 2·7 × 2·7, ·bearing a group of three lotus flowers and two leaves in relief. xviiith dynasty.

51. Ivory tray circular, broken in four, calf on edge; handle with lotus and three buds on each side of it, in relief. 5·9 long. xviiith dynasty.

52. Double circular dishes of ivory, handle lost. 3·6 long.

53. Handle of ivory toilet dish, formed by five lotus flowers and buds. 3·3 long.

54. Two conventional lotus flowers, 0·9 wide and broken.

55. Conventional lotus flower, 1·6 high.

56. Three pieces of high relief decoration, derived from conventional lotus. xxth dynasty?

57. Roughly carved lotus flower on long stem. 6·3 long. xiith dynasty. (See similar flowers in *El Arabeh*, xiv.)

58. Papyrus head, bored to fit on stem; 0·6 high. xixth dynasty?

59. Pomegranate, ivory stained red. Horn plug in base hole. 1·2 high. xxth dynasty?

(60.) Strip of ivory, with nine rosettes in sunk relief. 2·6 long. xviiith dynasty.

(61–2.) Two strips of bone with convolvulus trailer incised, filled with green colour. 3·2 long. xviiith dynasty.

63. Ivory inlay stained red.

(64.) Part of wooden lid of toilet vase, with lotus flower pattern. xviiith dynasty. (See other wood carvings in section on *Furniture* and *Woodwork*.)

94. *Artificial forms.*

(65.) Part of kohl tube in form of a column; hippopotamus ivory. 2·5 high. xviiith dynasty. (See others in section of *Toilet*.)

66. Globular vase, an ivory model. 1·1 wide. xiith dynasty?

67. Four-lobed lid of kohl tubes, with hinge pin and fastening. xviiith dynasty.

(68.) Vase with side projection pierced, clumsy work, much shattered. 4·3 high. xixth? dynasty.

69. Side of cup, of hippopotamus ivory. 4·4 high.

(70.) Parts of cup of same, retaining the fluted outside.

71. Flat oval plate of ivory with 4 holes for pegging on, and 45 holes plugged with ebony for ornament.

(72.) Pieces of ivory kohl tubes.

(73.) Bird's shank bone, plugged with wood below: needle case?

(74.) Two undetermined pieces of ivory, and one of bone.

(75.) Spacers of bone for necklaces, 1 of 9 holes, 10 of 10 holes, 2 of 11 holes. xviiith dynasty.

(76.) Six netting bones, made of ribs. xviiith dynasty.

(77.) Three bone pegs.

(78.) Knob of bone.

(79.) Pendants of flail, carved in wood.

(80.) Ivory and ebony slips for inlay in a box or chair. xviiith dynasty.

95. *Roman ivory carving.* Pl. xxxix.

81. Piece of bone panel with upper part of male figure.

82. Piece of circular box with kneeling Eros.

83. Piece of bone with upper part of crowned female figure.

84. Strip of bone with foliage pattern. 4·3 long.

85. Bone panel with palmetto and band of balls. vith cent.?

86. Rosette of ivory, flat back.

87. Piece of border with bird in scroll work.

88. Piece of border with stag running.

(89.) Upper part of cylindrical box, incised pattern of a dwarf, ten plants, and two birds. The dwarf is looking back upward, and holds an axe in his hand. ivth cent.?

90. Piece of deeply cut relief of vine scroll with grapes. vith cent.?

91. Panel of vine scroll, treated geometrically. Hippopotamus ivory. Mediaeval Arab?

92. Panel of bone with bird and two deer; coarse work. Mediaeval?

(93.) Small bone panel, partly drafted out.

94. Knife handle of bone with circle and spot ornament. Roman.

(95.) Handle of hippopotamus hide?

(96.) Wedge of bone, pierced for string.

97. Roundel of bone with scroll and three vine leaves. Roman.

(98.) Flat plate of bone with circles, coloured red and green.

99–100. Pieces of ivory with arched pattern around. Parts of chess men?

101. Piece of ivory tray with arched pattern around. vth cent.?

102. Ivory chess man, seated figure.

103. Ivory chess man.

96. *Wood carving.*

104. Hair pin with running dog at head.

105. Piece of panel with long cross. xiith cent.?

106. Seated figure blowing a pipe; another below with a drum.

107. Panel with geometrical foliage.

108. Panel with bird and branch.

109. Panel with geometrical foliage.

110. Similar, of large design.

111. Panel with bird and deer in foliage.

112. Panel with flamboyant scroll pattern.

113. Panel with girl dressed in long trousers and wide sleeves, seated on the ground blowing a pipe: foliage background.

114. Panel of geometrical pattern.

A large group of late Roman bone carving was brought by a workman from the mounds in Lake Menzaleh. This region was flooded in the time of Justinian, but the glass coin weights found there indicate that the sites were in use as late as El 'Aadid A.D. 1171. There is thus no precise date to the remains from there, ranging from the xiith cent. A.D. back to the iiird, and perhaps earlier. The quantity of fragments and duplicates makes it better to group these.

Four pieces and two scraps of carved bone with vine patterns. Roman.

Seven pieces of flat scroll border, in bone. Roman.

Thirteen hair pins with heads; thirty plain rods without heads.

Toggle of bone, for dress fastening.

Five very rude bone dolls.

Twenty spindle whorls of bone.

Twelve slips of open work in bone, for inlaying.

About ninety pieces of bone work, more or less carved.

About a hundred and thirty turned pegs of bone for mushrabiyeh work. Arab.

CHAPTER XII

FURNITURE AND WOODWORK.

Pl. xl.

Objects not in plates have a bracket (prefixed.

97. *Furniture.* 1. Wooden stool cut from a piece of trunk with three branches; from the precise divergence of them for legs they seem to have been trained into the required form. Seat 13 high, 11 wide; legs $14\frac{1}{2}$ long, 2 thick, Tarkhan, grave 415. Age of Narmer.

2. Stool cut from a single block, 10 wide, 3.7 high. Kahun. xiith dynasty.

(3–4. Legs of stools cut in a roll below. 14.4 and 6.5 high. Kahun. xiith dynasty.

A similar but simpler form is that of the model couch of the xiith dynasty from Hawara; see Funerary section. Published in *Labyrinth*, xxx.

(5. Curved leg of a stool, 14.4 long. Kahun. xiith dynasty.

6. Leg of a chair; tendon lines on heel marked out. 11.2 high. Gurob. xviiith dynasty.

7. Leg of a chair with part of false angle-piece; whitened. 19.3 high. xviiith dynasty.

(8. Turned leg of stool; mortise holes do not go through, but have had false inlays over them. 12.0 high. Gurob. xviiith dynasty.

9. Part of leg of cross stool; remains of horizontal-grain wood on long tenon below. 18.1 long. Gurob. xviiith dynasty.

(10. Leg of a sloping-seat stool. 10.2 long. Gurob. xviiith dynasty.

11. Pair of lion-headed legs of couch, painted. Roman.

12. A similar pair, rougher painting. Roman.

(13. Lion's feet of a similar pair. Illahun.

14. Pair of turned legs of a couch. Fayum. Roman.

(15–16. Turned legs of small stands. 8·4 and 5·4 long. Roman.

(17. Piece of foot board? Inlayed with squares of bone, decorated with circle and spot. Hollowed beneath, with ridge along edge.

(18. Forked branch, with a square hole at the forking, and a tenon at the end: probably part of a stand. 21·0 high. Gurob. xviiith dynasty.

(19-20. Side poles of bed frames, pierced with slots for webbing. Tarkhan. 1st dynasty.

(21. Circular top of a table, turned, 12·3 across. Three undercut mortise holes for legs have been broken, and three more mortise holes have been cut between them. Fayum. Roman.

(22. Part of end of a coffin, with deep cut mortising for roof boards. Meydum. ivth dynasty.

(23. Part of the corner-post of a coffin with mortising of side panels. Gurob. Ptolemaic.

(24. Pieces of coffins, showing tenon and planing. Hawara. Roman.

(25. Joint of a stool; mortise and tenon. Rifeh.

(26. Angle for joint, cut from straight-grain wood, with two mortises. Kahun. xiith dynasty.

(27. Large angle for joint, cut from trained bent grain wood. 8·2 × 5·1. Kahun. xiith dynasty.

(28. Small angle of bent grain, 2·5 × 1·9. Kahun. xiith dynasty.

(29. Slip of veneer from an angle piece. Kahun. xiith dynasty.

(30. End of coffin, with figure of Isis kneeling on the *nub* sign, incised and filled with dark green wax. See similar use of green wax inlay on the red granite sarcophagus of Ramessu III (Paris).

98. *Boxes and bowls.* 31. Side, top, and end, of box of sycomore, covered with papyrus on which are patterns in red, brown, green, and black. Lahun. xxiiird dynasty.

(32. Small drawer of hard wood.

33. Front of box with bronze lock, patterns of lines of circle-and-dot. Also piece of back and of lid. Roman.

(34. Box with curved sides, one cross division, cut in one block. Sliding lid with rabbet edge. Lock of bronze with two bolts pressed up by springs, one on each side of the key hole, pin for pipe-key. It is not apparent how both could be depressed at once by a key. In the box is a piece of a bronze plate with 3 holes, and a ring on a stem of iron. Roman.

(35. Curved-bottom box with three compartments, cut in one block. Grooves for lid, which is lost. Roman.

(36. Small lid for a box, 1·55 × 1·25. Gurob.

(37. Leather box, 6 × 5 × 3½ high, with 0·7 deep of fatty matter in it; top edge turned in 0·4; two holes on each side for suspension. This box for fat was made of leather because a wooden box would let the fat soak away. xiith dynasty?

(38. Piece of hippopotamus hide pierced roughly with two holes; 11 × 5 × 1·1 thick. Kahun. xiith dynasty.

(39. Two pieces of turned wood pan, with upright sides. 3·5 across, 2·0 high; pierced lug on bottom edge for hanging up. Kahun. xiith dynasty.

(40. Part of spheroidal bowl, with slight foot; 4·5 across, mouth 3·5 wide, 2·7 high, foot 2·0 wide. Kahun. xiith dynasty.

(41. Part of open bowl, with wide lug pierced on edge, fish incised on base; about 5·0 wide, 1·1 high. Kahun. xiith dynasty.

(42. Part of horn bowl, ribbed sides; about 4·2 across, 1·3 high. Kahun. xiith dynasty.

(43. Part of bowl or lid, circular curve; 4·1 across, 1·1 high. Kahun. xiith dynasty.

44. Pair of bowls with 3 divisions, cut in one block, △ mark on outsides. Of uncertain date and place.

(45. Turned lid, with knob handle; 3·0 across, 1·2 high. Kahun. xiith dynasty.

(46. Flat lid, thinning to the edge; central hole. 4·9 across, 0·3 high. Kahun. xiith dynasty.

(47. Flat lid, with central hole; 2·0 across, 0·4 thick. Kahun. xiith dynasty.

(48. Lid with recessed seat, hole at one side; 2·7 across, 0·5 high. Gurob. xviiith dynasty.

(49. Part of lid with 3 rows of petal pattern deeply incised; 4·7 across, 0·6 high, recessed loop hole under the middle. Gurob. xviiith dynasty.

(50. Part of ring stand of wood; 3·8 across. Kahun. xiith dynasty.

(51. Part of trumpet-shaped ring stand; about 6·0 wide. Kahun. xiith dynasty.

(52. Part of large ring stand; about 8·0 across. Kahun. xiith dynasty.

(53. Wooden dish with two handles, and lid with hinge piece and fastening piece. Turned, and lid ornamented with hexagonal compass patterns, not Egyptian in style. 4·3 across, 1·7 high. Ahnas. xviiith dynasty? Syrian?

(54. Egg-shaped wooden cup, with three feet, two bands of wavy lines in sunk relief round top. Swivel lid lost, internal projections for hinge and

fastening. Found with scarab of Amenhetep III. Kahun. xviiith dynasty.

(55. Part of tall cylindrical pot of wood; 5·0 high, 4·0 across. Incised design of calves, two lying down, one galloping, with clumps and sprays of plants; above and below a basket pattern border. Blue filling in lines. Gurob. xviiith dynasty.

(56. Part of a cylinder pot; 3·3 high, about 2·4 across. Incised design of band with galloping calf, zigzag line, band with fish; border patterns above and below. Gurob. xviiith dynasty.

(57. Small pot cut in wood; 2·0 across, mouth 0·7 wide, 1·4 high. Source? xiith dynasty?

(58—9. Turned wooden bottles, in one piece. 7·0 high, 2·7 across; 4·3 high, 2·1 across. The necks are only 0·52 and 0·45 wide; yet the inside is turned out leaving only about 0·04 thickness for the sides. Wushym. Roman.

99. *Woodwork.* 60. Panel with group of papyrus incised and inlayed with red and blue. 3·0 × 2·2. Gurob. xviiith dynasty.

(61. Piece of box, with three red bands, on each of which are three circles of white spots around a blue centre; usual barred border. 4·3 × 2·4. xixth dynasty?

(62. Bunch of grapes carved in wood and coloured blue. 3·0 long. Gurob. xixth dynasty.

(63. *Kherp* end, 3·4 flat part, 1·5 papyrus head, high.

(64. Semicircular fan handle, 5·8 across, with holes for 27 feathers. Kahun. xiith dynasty.

(65. Piece of similar, in ivory stained brown; about 4·0 across; holes for about 25 feathers. Kahun. xiith dynasty.

(66. Fan handle on papyrus head; 3·0 wide; holes for 11 feathers. xixth dynasty?

(67. Fan handle on papyrus head; slit for insertion; one side broken away. 3·0 wide, 9·5 high. Inscribed "(Fan) bearer every day to Amen, Pakherti." xixth dynasty.

(68. Wooden panel, round headed; like those inscribed by Amenhetep I. 3·3 × 2·7. xviiith dynasty.

(69. Flat wood outline of dish on stand holding two bouquets, and with two papyrus flowers tied round the stem. Painted in red, green, blue, and black. Part of decorative furniture. xixth dynasty?

(70. Hand wand, very short; with head of Hathor flanked by uraei on the back of the hand. 6·6 long. xixth dynasty?

(71. Loop and stem of *onkh*, and cross piece of another; from furniture open work. Kahun. xiith dynasty.

(72. Loop of palm fibre, bound with string in zigzag pattern. Use unknown. Roman or Coptic.

73—4. Wooden objects, hollowed out in circle and along bar. Hole through centre of circles in 74, none in 73. Nailed on at each end, with one bronze nail remaining. On the circle, lotus leaf pattern on both; on 73 around the pattern a band of signs on each side. The signs comprise Maot-neb-ra cartouche (Amenhetep III) *nesut, ne, ur, neter*, and combinations unknown in hieroglyphs. These are certainly of xviiith—xixth dynasty as 74 was found at Gurob, and another was in a tomb group of the xviiith dynasty at Abydos (*El Amrah*, li). They seem as if engraved by foreigners partly using Egyptian signs. See pl. xl. xviiith dynasty.

(75. Model boat, hollowed out of one block, 20·6 long. Flat end partly broken. One thwart, not passing through side.

(76. Leather seed tray for a bird's perch. 4·5 long, 3·0 high. Kahun. xiith dynasty.

77. Wooden *khaker* ornament. 18·8 high. Ramesseum. xxth dynasty?

(78. Paddle of an oar, from a funeral boat? 4·4 long. Kahun. xiith dynasty.

(79. Well formed wooden object, possibly model of a lute. Kahun. xiith dynasty.

80. Two clappers (?) and two turned rods. Wushym. Roman.

(The following are not illustrated.)

(81. Walking stick, grave 819. Tarkhan. 41·0 long.

82. Walking stick, Tarkhan, 32·2 long, broken.

83. Walking stick, Tarkhan, club end. 38·7 long.

84. Walking stick, Tarkhan, grave 2017, xith dynasty. 47·6 long.

85. Walking stick, 38·7 long; bound with string for 5 inches at upper end.

86. Walking stick of tamarisk, 49·2 long, 1·5 thick. Rifeh. xiith dynasty.

87. Walking stick, 48·5 long. Gurob.

88. Walking stick of thorn?, 45·0 long. Gurob?

89. Walking stick, covered with 5 rows of bracts. 33·0 long, broken. Gurob?

90. Uas sceptre, stem from Lahun, head from Thebes.

91—2. Two plain rods of similar light wood.

93. Double scoop, end to end. 19·8 long, 2·0 wide.

94. Scoop or dish of wood. 12·8 × 4·1. Vandyke pattern on a stem incised outside.

95. Scoop. 14·7 × 4·0.

96. Model window in wall, from house model, 10 × 7·9, window 3·1 × 3·1. Gizeh.

97. Model of grid window, 3·8 × 2·3, broken.

98. Pair of doors from a shrine with two bolts. 5·6 high, 4·9 wide.

99. Knife handle, with slot for iron blade, rusted in. Kahun. xxiiird dynasty?

100. Handle of borer? Kahun.

101. Handle or stand?

102. Top of staff or handle, square socket. Ebony.

103. Hook for shaduf with rope attached. Roman?

104. Small hook, similar.

105. Large hook for camel girth. Wushym. Roman.

106. Large hook for camel girth, with spur to hang goods on. Wushym. Roman.

107. Wood loop, with rope attached. Roman.

108. Wood loop, small. Roman?

109–10. Wood loop. Kahun. Roman?

111. Wood loop, with rope attached. Gurob. xviiith dynasty?

112. Wood loop. Hawara. Roman?

113. Wood loop, covered with thread. Roman.

114. Rounded wooden block, 11·5 × 6·2 × 3·1, with square hole through it 4·5 × 2·5.

115. Wooden projection, 4·0 × 2·4 × 0·8, with square hole through it 0·8 × 0·8. Kahun.

116. Wooden projection, 5·0 × 3·7 rounded, with hole 2·4 × 2·1, for tether? Gurob.

117. Wooden peg used by builders of the pyramid of Hawara, found between the bricks. 4·0 long. xiith dynasty.

118. Peg with enlarged head. Kahun. xiith dynasty.

119. Stout peg. Kahun. xiith dynasty.

120. Square peg with knob on one side. Kahun. Roman?

121. Finely made peg. By work and condition, of xiith dynasty?

122. Set of eight pegs, made exactly as 117, probably xiith dynasty.

123. Six odd pegs. Fayum. Roman?

124. Peg with hook top. Roman?

125. Peg lashed to cross bar. Fayum. Roman.

126. Pawl of a saqieh wheel of *sont* wood. Roman?

127. Knob handle of a box. Gurob. xviiith dynasty.

128. Uraeus, well carved with tail up the back to top of disc. Suspension hole.

129. Uraeus, roughly blocked out. Peg below. Roman?

130. Wooden link, pierced with two slots, 11·5 long, 2·8 across; slots 1·4 × 0·4. Kahun. xiith dynasty.

131–7. Cylindrical blocks with rounded top, and notch out of side. They always have a flat base so as to stand upright. The surfaces worn are on the base of the notch in 131–2, and less in 133. The inner angle of the notch is not worn, so they have not been used to hold a running rope or cord: 131–2 are too large to be grasped round by the hand. 133 shows wear about the tip. 131–2 have been much used as mallets to beat on a peg, but this may not belong to their proper use. On the back of 133 is a large △ mark. Kahun. xiith dynasty. These have lately been identified as jacks to support heddle rods. (*Ancient Egypt*, 1922, p. 71.)

138–9. Rounded cones, use unknown. Kahun, xiith dynasty.

140. Unfinished stamp? Kahun. xiith dynasty.

141. Unknown tool. Roman?

(Not in cases.)

142. Plank of 1st dynasty wooden house, 79·5 × 15 to 17 × 1·2 thick. Tarkhan. 1st dynasty.

143. Box, stuccoed. 15·6 × 8·8 × 10·5 high. Kahun. xiith dynasty.

144. Lid of box, 9·5 × 8·5. Kahun. xiith dynasty.

145–9. Raw hide lashings of tools. Kahun. xiith dynasty.

150. Plait of white leather.

151. Strip of cow hide. Kahun. xiith dynasty.

152. Strips of hippopotamus hide. Kahun. xiith dynasty.

100. *Basketry.*

153. Oval basket and lid, with string of blue beads. xiith dynasty.

154. Oval lid. Gurob. xviiith dynasty.

155. Oval basket with patterns in red and black, like modern Nubian work. Gurob. xviiith dynasty.

156. Circular lid, with loop of ancient string. xiith–xviiith dynasty.

157. Pair of flat bag-baskets; 5 long, 4 deep, 1·3 wide. Seeds inside. Thebes. xviiith dynasty?

158–(9. Saucer-baskets, crossing sides; 8 wide, 1·3 high. Roman.

160. Saucer-basket, close woven; 8 wide, 1½ high. Roman.

161. Cylindrical basket and lid; 3½ wide, 3 high, Hawara. Roman (and similar lid).

162. Cylindrical basket and deep cover, flat, thin, elastic work. Red and white. 4 wide, 4 high. Roman.

163. Part of conical basket, same make. About 8 wide, 5 high. Roman. (See GAYET, *Exp. Nec. d'Antinoe*, xvii, 2, for similar form.)

(164. Small lid, same work; 2·3 across.

(165. Cup basket, same work, flattened; 4·7 wide. 7·0 high. Roman.

(166. Flat frail basket; 12½ wide flat, 8 high. Roman.

167. Another, with three shells on the edge; 6½ wide flat, 3 high. Hawara. Roman.

168. Another; 11½ wide flat, 6½ high. Hawara. Roman.

(169. Another, with loophandles, and loops round the top for fastening; 14 wide, 11 high. Roman.

170. Square lid of papyrus box, stitched with thread; 7·6×7·0. Kafr Ammar. xxiiird dynasty.

171. Piece of papyrus box.

172. Stiff circular basket, hexagonal plait; 13 wide, 7 high. Roman.

173. Another; 8 wide, 5½ high. Roman.

174. Another; 9 wide, 5·2 high. Roman.

(175. Very open, cross sides, collapsed; 5 wide, 4½ high. Roman.

(176. Another, less open; 4 wide, 5 high. Roman.

177. Conical basket with slanting uprights, no cross band; 4½ wide, 2½ high.

Brushes.

178. Flat brush of split reed; 18 long, 11 wide. Gurob. xviiith dynasty.

179–84 (185–7. Nine small brushes, for white-washing, &c. 3 to 10½ long. Mostly from Hawara. Roman.

CHAPTER XIII
METAL FITTINGS.
Pls. xliii–xlvi.

101. *Lead.*

1. Four lotus flowers cast in closed mould, flat on back.

2. Fifteen net sinkers. Amarna. xviiith dynasty.

3. Ring, figure of Osiris.

(4. Ring, plain.

(5. Kohl stick.

(6. Necklace spacer, 6 holes.

7–8. Two nails: a minute hole through the head of each.

9. Model tub, with a ring handle in one piece on each side, and wavy pattern; cast in a mould in two halves.

(10. Net sinker, as 2. Gurob. xviiith dynasty.

(11. Four net sinkers of folded sheet lead. Gurob.

(12. Net sinker of sheet lead coiled. Gurob.

(13. Earring, and runlet of lead.

14. Model dish with two heads; underneath, a quadruple acanthus pattern round a circle.

15. Model tray with three discs, spotted and radiate, (bread?), grapes, wine cup, two lotus flowers, haunch, and bird. Memphis.

16. Model tray with two cupids and crane, panther and wild boar, gryphon chasing a stag, two cupids on dolphins, acanthus on handles. Memphis.

17. Model tray, with vine pattern.

(18. Model tray, dolphin in a vine border.

19. Model tray, plain, fluted sides.

These leaden models of trays or dishes, 14–19, seem to have been patterns for silversmiths to submit to their patrons, for orders. Another of the finest work is in *Memphis* III, xxxiii.

20. Imitation fastening, to stitch on girdle?

21. Strainer with punched holes. Amarna. Roman.

(22. Plain disc of sheet lead, 3·76×3·47. Lahun.

(23. Cast sheet lead, 5·5×1·8, formerly nailed through.

(24. Leaden ball, with bronze loop. 770 grains, possibly a weight. Memphis.

102. *Bronze.*

25. Cartouche stamp with *uzat* eye. Memphis, as following to 43.

26–7. Cast beaks of hawks, for attachment to wooden figures.

28. Pair of tubular attachments, made of sheet metal.

29–30. Sockets for inlaid eyes of animals.

31. Ear, for attachment to wooden statue.

32. Arm, with dovetail to attach to statuette.

33. Hair of crown of head, to attach to statuette.

34. Nail.

35. Pieces of sheet bronze wreath.

36. Buckle.

37. Leaf ornament from furniture.

(38. Three little bells, to attach to dress?

(39. Model situla.

(40. Coin of Carthage. *Obv.* Lion walking l., disc above. *Rev.* Horse trotting to l, emblem of Tanith in front.

(41. Coin of a Ptolemy, ΔI before eagle. The copper has been entirely removed by atomic changes, and only white oxide of tin remains.

(42. Two rivet plates.

43. Long curl of hair from a statue, made by bending over sheet metal, and then impressing it.

44. Cross of sheet bronze, rivetted, with three chains, for hanging censer? With the following, down to 52 B from towns in Lake Menzaleh.

(45. Another cross and chains, and a third cross.

46. Small mirror, cast *cire perdue* with design on back.

47. Open work, cast in bronze, and portions of a similar piece.

48. Pelta ornament, with studs at back to fasten to leather.

49. Cast ornament.

50. Double seven-pointed disc, from horse's bit?

51–2. Ornamental nails.

Coins of Ptolemies, Diocletian, Maximian, Crispus, Constantius, Valentinian, and Arabic glass weights of El Hakim, Ez Zahir, and El 'Aadid, 996–1171 A.D. These date the Menzaleh group.

13 bronze Arabic weights.

24 bronze kohl sticks.

Part of Roman mirror case

Leg of a statuette.

Balance beam.

52 B. Various rings and fragments of bronzework, all from Menzaleh.

53–5. Three ornamental attachments. Oxyrhynkhos. Roman.

56. Folding balance beam. Oxyrhynkhos. Roman.

103. *Furniture fittings.*

57. Bronze hinge corner of door; charcoal within it. Memphis.

58. Smaller hinge corner.

59. Hinge corner, with ring for holding hingepin. Memphis.

60. Large hinge corner. Memphis.

(61. Pair of large hinge corners, 8 inches along the side. Memphis.

62. Bottom shoe for a door with hinge pin, Memphis, and front corner for same door.

63. Bronze tube ending in a square shank, core still in it.

64. Frog foot of a cista.

65. Foliated foot of a cista.

66. Hinge.

67. Two halves of hinges. Memphis.

68–9. Two pairs of hinges, nails in place. Memphis.

70. Bronze cast over plaster core. Memphis.

71. Bronze vase, copied from furniture forms.

72. Bronze dish on foot.

73. Bronze pot on three legs.

74. Bronze tap; deeply encrusted in part, but without any proof of Roman age.

75. Part of a central flow tap.

76. Pieces of open work *zed* ornament.

77. Triangular frame with winged Medusa heads, and dragons at the corners.

78. Nine flatted rings, and four rounded rings, attachments for carrying furniture(?). Shurafa.

79. Four crossing sockets and a hook, for holding a cord on a trellis screen(?).

80. Corner piece for a couch, sides 7·0×5·3×4·0 high, with rest for a cross bar.

81. Corner piece for a couch, sides 6·5×5·7×3·5 high, with socket for a cross bar.

82. Four iron bars united by a cast bronze cross piece; part of a grating.

83. Hollow casting of a handle, to be attached to a large circle about two feet diameter.

84. Thin casting over ash core still in place; and two lesser pieces.

85–9. Caps for legs of furniture; 89, cast solid.

90. Hollow quadrant piece, for connection of furniture.

91–2. Vesica-shaped pieces, for junctions of lattice work (?).

93. Junction piece for corner post and two flat bars; moulding on top.

94–5. Pair of corner pieces for a cabinet, square upright, and two horizontal bars on edge. Memphis.

96. Pair of base pieces for same, to join upright with side bars and flooring. Memphis.

97. Large attachment plate, and hollow wide projection, ending in a hinge. Memphis.

(98. Part of large bronze bolt, 8½ long originally. Memphis.

(99–100. Two large bronze tubes cast, 15·8 long, 2·5 wide tapering to 1·5; the second broken.

101. Palm capital, heavy casting closed at top. Memphis. xxvith dynasty?

102. Capital, partly filled with lead; closed at top. Memphis. Roman.

103. Twisted column, ash core still in casting. Roman.

(104. Beard from a statue, to be inlaid. Memphis, as also on to 122.

(105. Bell.

(106. Hawk head, plaster inside the bronze.

(107. Short pestle, 2·5 long.

(108. Hair pin.

(109. Handle with turned ornament.

(110. Conventional lotus, hollow at back.

111. Conventional palmetto.

112. Square altar with ribbed cone. Quft.

113. Satyr head from corner of furniture.

114. Cupid head on pendant.

(115. Cat catching bird, upon socket, for carrying pole (?).

(116. Lion head on end of club.

(117. Gryphon (?) foot of stand.

(118. Fish, flat sheet.

119. Papyrus head, solid casting, with bar to attach to furniture.

120. Pair of handles, with two lions seizing ram.

121. Ribbed ring handle, and another smaller.

122. Snail on 8-lobed foot. Apparently a paper weight, no attachment. Memphis.

(123. Massive bronze handle of a crater.

(124. Thin square handle with rings, from a box.

125. Pair of heavy bronze pegs, round heads, peg half cut away flat.

126. Leg of a table or stand, 20·3 high; upper part broken. Fayum.

127. Leg of a stand, with part of a circle 17 inches wide.

128. Lion leg of a circular stand.

129. Lion leg of a square stand.

130. Loop handle, with small ring on the top; ends of papyrus form.

131. Handle from a bowl, with papyrus ends.

(132. Attachment from a bowl with two rings for drop handle.

133. Handle with palmetto ends, silver.

(133 A. Similar, of bronze. Memphis.

(134. Dipper with twisted handles, and a second handle.

(135. Handle of dipper ending in duck's head. Gurob. Roman.

(136. Hinges of mirror case. Memphis.

(137. Horse, open work, on iron base.

(138-9. Fire trimmers, hand on end. 139 from Memphis. See *Tools and W.* 118-20.

(140-9. Ten bronze figures from Memphis. King kneeling, Mummy, Min, Nebhat, Horus (2), Thoth (2), Cat, Jackal couchant.

CHAPTER XIV

GAMES.

104. In attempting to understand ancient games, it is needful to remember the very various types which are familiar in modern games. There are three main classes,—(A) depending largely on chance (as card games, backgammon, and dominoes), (B) on skill of hand (as billiards, tennis, or cricket) or (C) on skill of head (as chess and draughts); it is only the latter class—or board games—that we deal with here.

The principle of winning in board games may be either by taking off the enemy, or by gaining a prescribed position without removing any pieces. The third mode of winning, by occupying the game until at fault (as in billiards or cricket), scarcely enters into board games. The taking of pieces of the enemy may be effected by occupying the position of his piece (as in chess, or the taking a blot in back-gammon); or by jumping over him (as in draughts), or by enclosing him between two pieces, one on each side (as in sīga). The games of position, without taking off the enemy, are halma and bagatelle, also partially in backgammon and the opening moves in sīga. All of these different principles of play must be kept in mind, in tracing the methods of ancient games.

105. The most usual game was that called *Sent*, played on a board of 3×10 squares, using six pieces by each of the two players. Two stages of the game are shown at Beni Hasan, best copied by CAILLIAUD, *Arts et Métiers*, pl. 41 A. In the first stage, the six pieces of one kind alternate with six of the other kind. In the second stage marked *aseb*, "consummated," presumably the end of the game, each player has all his pieces at his own end of the board. No pieces are ever represented set apart as if captured. The game seems to have been one of position, beginning mixed, and then segregrating. This resembles English backgammon, where pieces are set in mixed order, and then separated into the table of each player. In the scene at Saqqareh only the first mixed stage is shown. The players say, "I make a three in *sent*"; and reply, "Carrying of two threes in *sent*." In another instance, there is the inscription "Playing six" (*Rev. Arch.*, 1865, p. 61). These references to high moves being three and six must be connected with the squares being in three rows; such a move of three was an advance of a whole row, and points to the single moves being across the board, while a lucky move enabled the piece to be put one or two rows forward. How the moves were regulated is shown by two knuckle bones found with a set of the xixth dynasty (QUIBELL, *Excavations at Saqqara*, 1907–8, lviii). A knuckle bone carved in ivory was found at Meydum with an alabaster dish of the xviiith or xixth dynasty (*Labyrinth*, p. 27, xvii, 15–6). This carving in ivory proves that the other bones were not casually left with the game. For the throw to be 3 or 6 as a maximum, presumably the two wide faces counted, and either of the edges. This would give 1, 2, or 3; and the two bones together would give 6.

The game must have consisted, therefore, in obstructing the adversary. It may be conjectured that a direct block between two men could only be got over by throwing two to jump over, or perhaps only by throwing three so as to pass direct into a fresh row. The principle of the count of the bones differed from that of the Greek *astragali* or Roman *talus*. In Egypt, the much earlier date of the bones shows that the invention there was quite clear of classical influence.

The earliest form of the game is shown in the tomb of Hesy (QUIBELL, *Excavations at Saqqara*, 1911–2, pl. xi). There, the playing pieces are seven on each side, of the form usual in the early dyn-

asties; between them are four throwing sticks, imitations of strips of bark, carved in ivory, for determining the throw. These strips are well known in the 1st dynasty, and will be described in the Archaic catalogue. The four throwing sticks continued to the xixth dynasty, as found with the Leyden game board (*Aeg. Mon. Leyden*, figs. 274, 277, *Desc. Raison.*, p. 109). The use of four sticks, for casting lots by number, seems to have a source in common with the four arrows used for divination in early China, and the divining by the arrows practised by Semites (Ezek: 21, 21; *Encyc. Biblica, Divination*). It may be conjectured that this system originated in Elam or Mesopotamia, and spread thence in both directions. That the four arrows in China and Japan descend in unbroken line into the four suits of cards, has been proved by STEWART CULIN (*Catalogue of Games... in U. S. National Museum*).

The system of marks on the boards is uniform in its nature, only differing in detail. The marks always read upright when the length of the board is horizontal. From the drawings, it is clear that the players sat at either end of the board. Looking at the board with the marks upright, the numbering of the squares begins from the bottom right hand (6 examples) or the top left hand (2). The numbering always proceeds along the length and, as the counting was across the breadth of the board, the numbers are those of the rows and not of the single squares. The signs on the first five squares are in the following order:—

Hesy	I			IIII	
Senusert II		II	III	X	*nefer*
Kahun		II	III	X	*nefer*
Univ. C.		II	III	X	*nefer*
Leyden		2 seated men	3 seated men	*mu*	*neferu*
Paris		2 seated men	*bau* birds	*mu*	*neferu*
Cairo	Ra	*neterui*	*bau*	*mu*	*neferu*
Univ. C.	Falcon	*neterui*	*neteru*	*mu*	*sa*
Univ. C.	Falcon	*yui*	*yu*	boat	*mes*
	Ra on *nub*			on *mu*	

The *yui* and *yu* are 2, and 3, reed leaves on legs, *mes* is the owl and bent *s*. Loose squares of inlay marked with two seated men, boat on *mu*, and *bau* were found at Abydos (*El Amrah*, xlix); and squares with X, *mu*, and *neferu* (*El Amrah*, li). There are also two fragments here, catalogued below, which do not advance the question.

The only signs of counting at the other end of the rows are the *dua* star on the last place, and the ten sign at the end of the first row, and at the beginning of the second row (QUIBELL, *Tomb of Hesy*, xi).

The pieces used by the players only differed as two uniform sets, without any mark of different values. Each set was of six pieces; the distinction of sets was by being conical or with a top knob; or by being conical and reel shaped.

The boards here are as follow:—

1. Slab of limestone; 3×10 squares roughly scored. From the temenos of the tomb of Senusert II, Abydos. xiith dynasty.

2. Slab of limestone; 3×10 squares roughly cut. Marks II, III, X, *nefer*. Memphis. (The next object is a model watering tank, of no concern here.)

3. Slab of slate; 3×10 squares, engraved with double lines; notched dummy handle at one end. Marks; falcon, *neterui, neteru, mu* (2 water lines), and *sa*. The forms of *neter* and *sa* are archaic, but the board is evidently of the xxvith–xxxth dynasty, by comparison with the following. On the reverse are 3×11 circles, which will be noticed later.

4. A slab of steatite similarly divided, but on both sides. At the end is a handle of two lotus flowers joined. The dividing lines are triple. Marks; falcon on *nub*, Ra above; two reed leaves on legs; three such; boat on double water line; owl *m*, crook *s*. End broken off through the eighth square.

5. Fragment of similar board of blue paste, with first two rows: triple lines of division. Marks; falcon on *nub*, two *neters* facing. 3, 4 and 5 were bought together.

6. Fragment of similar board, of very absorbent blue paste. Marks; falcon on tall perch, eye above; reed leaf on legs, *aper* clothing, *th*; sky raining, *th*.

Other boards for different games will be noted below.

106. *Playing pieces.*

Setting aside the pieces which certainly belong to other games, we note here those which may be for *sent*. The ivory pieces of the 1st dynasty will be dealt with in the Archaic section. The numbers with a loop prefixed are not in the plate.

Conic, ogival.

7. Opaque red glass, conic with six curved sides. Roman?

8. Opaque green glass, similar form. Roman.

9. Variegated glass, conic, purple, blue, green, yellow, and white. Roman.

Rosettes.

10. White glaze with brown lines. xviiith dynasty.
(11–2. Ivory; octafoil rosettes in sunk relief. From inlaying? xviiith dynasty.

Domes.

13–4 (15–25. Dull green glazed; low dome. xixth dynasty?
(26–7. Glass, clear yellowish, opaque violet; low dome. xviiith dynasty?
(28. Indigo glaze; low dome. xviiith dynasty.
29–30. Smooth grey-green glaze; low dome. xxviith dynasty?
31–(32. Green glaze, gone brown, seated dog of yellow glaze inlay. xixth dynasty?
(33–4. Jackal couchant, violet with green inlay, green with blue inlay. xviiith dynasty.

Reels.

35 (36–7. Indigo black and blue mottled paste (?), violet and white mottled paste. xviiith dynasty.
38 (39–41. With wide edges. Blue glaze (3). Clear yellowish glass. xviiith dynasty.
42 (43–4. Narrow edges. Green glazed schist; schist, glaze lost; violet glaze. Gurob. xviiith dynasty.
(45–6. Biconic with sharp waist; blue glaze, violet glaze. xviiith dynasty.
(47. Alabaster, rounded form, ear stud? xviiith dynasty.

Light-house type.

48–51 (52–6. Fine blue green glaze, a set of 9 bought together. xviiith dynasty?
(57–62. Similar, rather rougher. Green glaze.
63–65 (66. Shorter type set of 4 bought with 48–56. Green glaze.
(67–73. Similar, rather rougher. Green glaze.
(74–88. Flatter forms. Green and blue glaze.
89–90. Flattest forms.

Conic, pointed heads.

91–92. Alabaster.
93–(94. Green glazed schist. xviiith dynasty.
95–(96. Green glazed schist. xviiith dynasty.
97–(98. Green glazed schist and indigo glaze. Gurob. xviiith dynasty.
99–100. Blue glaze, black glaze.
101–(2. Violet glaze, xviiith dynasty; blue glaze with black spiral. Kahun. xiith dynasty.
103. Blue glaze.
104–(5. Blue paste; blue glaze, gone white and brown.
106–7. Light blue glaze, gone white, rough.
108–(9. Blue glaze; violet glaze. xviiith dynasty.

110 (111–2. Blue glaze.

113 (114–7. Blue glaze, gone white.

118. Flower-shaped pendant, perhaps for playing; green glaze.

119–21. Ebony.

122. Clay. Kahun. xiith dynasty.

With pin holes for separate heads.

(123–4. Indigo and full blue glaze.

Conical.

125. Green quartzose mottled, ogival.

126. White quartz, similar.

127. White milky glass.

128. Dark blue glass.

(127–32. Similar forms, violet glaze (2), black glaze, limestone.

133–(4. Very hard white limestone; hard white limestone. Gurob. xviiith dynasty.

(135–6. More bulgy forms, crystal, yellow and blue glass, gone white.

137–8. Crystal and obsidian. Quft.

Rounded top, cone.

139–41 (142–5. Clay painted red. Rifeh, cemetery S. xvth dynasty?

(146–8. Clay painted red, larger sizes up to 2·5 wide, 1·8 high. xiith dynasty?

149. More domed, crystal; so cut as to form a contact magnifier, enlarging $2\frac{1}{2}$ times. Quft.

Tall cones.

150–1. Green glaze, rounded top.

152. Ivory, ogival sides. Quft.

153. Red jasper, ogival side.

154. Blue glaze, gone white.

(155. Blue glaze.

156. Light blue glaze.

157. Calcite.

158. Limestone.

Animal forms.

159. Ram's head; blue glaze, gone white. xxvith dynasty?

160. Dog's head; blue glaze. xiith dynasty.

161. Dog's head; blue glaze, hollow up middle.

162. Dog's head; grey steatite.

163. Dog's head; durite.

164. Dog's head upon reel form; schist glazed green.

165. Horse's head with mane; green glaze.

166. Cat's head; blue glaze.

167. Lion's head; blue glaze, gone white; on base 8 radii.

168. Couchant cat; grey-green glaze.

169. Bes head; green glaze.

170. Bes head; blue, gone white.

171. Bes seated holding drum; blue glaze, faded.

172. Baboon head; glaze gone brown.

173. Baboon seated; bronze. Probably a playing piece, by the wide circular base.

(174. Ebony, like the calcite 155, but with two ears projecting at the top.

The materials of these game pieces are: glazed pottery 115, glazed schist 9, glass 9, clay 11, stones 16, ivory 3, ebony 4, bronze 1, total 168. The knuckle bones are not placed here, as they are of Roman age, and probably belong to a different game.

In Graeco-Roman sites, discs of pottery, chipped round, and sometimes ground, commonly occur. They were doubtless made for gaming pieces.

Regarding the age of the game, the earliest proof of it is the sign *men*, which is a 3×10 board in plan, with a row of pieces along the top edge. This sign is first seen about the age of Mena (*Royal Tombs* II, xiv, 100), but only roughly divided into 2×5, owing to the small scale. The earliest example of the division of the sign in 3×10 is at the close of the iiird dynasty (*Medum*, xix, top left). The earliest figure of a board 3×10 is of the early iiird dynasty in the tomb of Hesy (QUIBELL, *Excavations at Saqqara*, 1911–2, xi). The latest that is dated is of the xxvith dynasty, roughly scored on the bottoms of plates at Defeneh (*Tanis* II, 74). The history of the game probably exceeded these limits both ways. There are but few examples in museums; beside the four (and fragments) in University College, described above, there are two or three in Paris, two in Cairo, one each in British Museum, Leyden, Berlin, Manchester (from Kahun) and New York: probably there are others unrecorded. The efficient publications are in Leyden Catalogue, ccxliv; PRISSE, *Art* (New York), QUIBELL, *Excavations at Saqqara* 1907–8, lviii, lix, and DARESSY, *Ostraka* (Cairo Cat.), xxxi, 25183. These, and some other specimens, are copied in *Proc. Soc. Bib. A.*, 1902, 341–8.

107. *Square board games.*

The Game of Twenty Squares.

Another game board is placed on the reverse of the 3×10 box, on the examples in Cairo, Leyden, and New York. It has 3×4 squares at one end, with the middle row prolonged for 8 squares further. On the Cairo example, down the middle row is inscribed on the 4th square, "There is nothing," on the 8th "I have carried away," on the 12th the name of the owner, *Kho.* The 4th was apparently a forfeit, and the 8th a square where the adversary was captured. The 4th, 8th and 12th squares are likewise coloured differently to others on the Paris board (DEVERIA, *Mémoires,* 11, 86). There is no sign as to how the play extended over the group and the line of squares. From the ends differing in arrangement, the game was probably played by two players moving in the same direction. The pieces used were the same as for *sent.* Birch guessed that this is the game of *thau (Trans. Soc. Lit.,* ix, 269), and that this means "robbers"; it might equally well mean "boys" or "captains" or "prefects."

The Game of Forty-two and Pool (175).

One instance of a board (175) of 3×14 holes with a pool, was found on a rough block of limestone at Memphis (xlvii, 175). The lines are not regular, but it seems probable that it was played like *sent,* but with a longer range between players. The pool suggests that pieces were taken, in this game. The holes are so small that the pieces were probably beans, or little chips of pottery.

The Game of Eighteen Squares.

This is the earliest board-game known, being found in a grave of about S.D. 42; as there was with it an animal figure comb, it can hardly be later, and a silver bead makes it unlikely to be earlier. The board of mud is divided in 3×6 squares, and with it are 9 conical draughtsmen and two larger (AYRTON, *El Mahasna,* xvii).

The Game of Fifty-eight Holes (176).

Boards of various materials for this game have been found at Kahun (xiith dynasty), Thebes, Sedment (ixth dynasty), Gezer, and Susa; there are also two others at Cairo, and one formed as a frog, in the Louvre. (See all in *Sedment,* 7, xxii.) The Theban board has 5 pegs with jackals' heads and 5 with dogs' heads, showing that 5 belonged to each player; as the pieces differed in shape they were intended to be intermixed on the board. The holes are symmetrically arranged, and the board has some resemblance to a human figure. The holes are divided into groups, each 5th hole being marked. Going up one side at the 10th hole is a cross passage to the 25th hole in the descending middle row. There is also a line linking the 27th and 29th holes. These suggest that on reaching these holes there was a jump forward or backward. The linking lines of 10th to 25th seem as if derived from a form where those holes came close together, as in the Cairo and Gezer boards, and the Louvre frog. Some boards have a pool at the 20th hole, top middle place. See further in *Sedment,* p. 7, xxii.

The Game of Forty-two Squares (177).

This is shown by a Roman terracotta, divided into 6×7 squares. On these squares, 17 low domed pieces are placed (xlviii, 177). Of these, 12 would go on one colour of chequers, and 5 on another. It seems, then, unlikely that there was a chequer system here, and there is no difference visible on the squares. The odd number of pieces suggests that some were taken, and that it was a capture game. Fayum.

The Game of Thirty-three Holes (backs of 3, 4, 5, 6).

On the backs of four late *sent* boards there are 3×11 circles, the centre circle filled with a 6 or 8 leaved rosette (see pl. xlviii). It was probably played with the same pieces and knuckle bones as the game of *sent.*

The Game of Twenty Holes (178).

This is a small slab of limestone with three rows of holes, 7, 6, and 7. They are about large enough to hold small peas. The end hole of each row has a little channel joining it to one shallow compartment at the end. From Memphis. 1913.

The Game of Forty Pieces (179–97).

A set of 20 cones of red breccia and 19 cones of alabaster was bought in Egypt. They obviously belong together, being exactly alike in form and work. Presumably, one of the alabaster has been lost, and there were twenty on each side; but, as one of the breccia is much larger than the rest, it is possible that the set is complete, 19 on each side and one larger. No board has been found for moving so large a company. This ends the games on a squared board. The following are only played on a line.

108. *The spiral Game of Henu* (198—215).

This was played on a spiral board, the spiral ending in a serpent's head in the middle, and its tail outside. Such is figured in the tomb of Hesy, with about 545 divisions between the head and tail. A similar serpent in limestone, of the early dynasties has 72 divisions between the head and tail (*Amulets*, xlvii, 96 f.; Univ. Coll., Archaic section). Playing on a spiral board, with the name of *henu*, is figured on a vth dynasty tomb at Saqqareh (WILK., *M. and C.*, fig. 323 = LEPS., *D.*, ii, 61). This latter shows balls being used, 10 in all, by the two players. The subject is much complicated by the outfit shown in the tomb of Hesy. There are 6 white, 6 red, and 6 black balls, on each side, also 3 dogs and 3 lions. The balls might be played in a circular groove, and stop at different divisions, but the lions and dogs are far too large to play on such divisions. Further, there were actual ivory lions found in the Royal Tombs; they were about 3 inches long, greatly worn by rubbing on the base, and by fingering on the sides where picked up. How the lions and dogs were used, then, is quite obscure. As there is nothing to throw a number by,—either bark-strips or knuckle bones,—it looks as if the balls gave a number to play the lions and dogs, or *vice versa*. Possibly the balls were filliped round the spiral, losing the move if a ball touched an adversary, and the dogs hunted the lion according to the numbers thrown. But there is no board shown, on which to move the animals; and, on the limestone serpent no ball could travel the groove, owing to cross cuts, and the groove not continuing at the ends. A set of four lions, a hare, and many balls, was found at Ballas, with other gaming pieces (*Naqada*, p. 14, pl. vii). Probably connected with this game are 13 rough balls of red breccia (198—210), and 5 fine balls of hard limestone (211—15). See also the Archaic catalogue to be published later.

The Game with Ten Bricks (216—25).

Another game, also shown in the tomb of Hesy, was played with pieces like small bricks, 5 black, 5 white, on a long strip board divided alternately into 16 yellow and 16 brown spaces. A set of 10 such bricks, here, is made up of eight of red breccia and two of grey and white marble. The mode of playing is unknown. In the set found at Ballas, there were 16 bricks in pairs, 6 pairs of limestone, 1 pair thinner of fine pink-veined limestone, 1 pair of bone (*Naqada*, p. 14).

109. *Siga*.

In addition to the portable game boards, of ten different arrangements just described, there is the national game of Egypt at present, called sīga. The only evidence for this being ancient is in some groups of holes for this game being roughly cut on the almost upright face of the masonry of the pyramid of Sneferu at Meydum. It would be impossible to play the game on such a face, and presumably the holes must have been cut while the blocks were lying on the ground before building. We have, then, to balance the improbability of these being the only ancient examples of the game, against the improbability of such holes being cut in the steep face for no purpose by the Arab Egyptians, when destroying the outer casing. It seems more likely that sīga was known anciently, and passed out of use after the pyramid age. The Meydum squares were accepted as ancient by VIRCHOW and REISS (*Verh. d. Berl. Anthrop. Ges.*, 16 Nov. 1889).

The game of sīga consists of two stages, the placing on the board, and after that is complete, the taking of the adversary's men. The placing is by far the more intricate part; the men are taken by B moving, so that a piece of A is between two pieces of B; then B has the right of removing A's piece and substituting one of the two of B. If this move again traps another of A's pieces, B can take that likewise. Thus a long run of taking is possible, as it is at draughts. Hence, in placing the men, the object is to arrange long courses of taking moves, and to defeat such courses by placing pieces in obstructive positions. The moving is one square at a time, in any direction except diagonally.

The board is a square of an odd number of holes: 5×5, 7×7, or 9×9, the usual being 7×7.

The centre square is to be left vacant; the first move, after placing the men, being into the centre. In the placing, A begins by putting a man next to the centre, B does likewise; A and B thus fill up the four squares joining the centre. They continue alternately to place men until the board is filled, striving to create long runs of taking off for the second stage, and to break up those of the adversary. This takes a great amount of foresight and imagination, and sīga is one of the most exacting games known for such abilities. After the men are placed, the first move is into the central square; that move may not enclose a man, in which case the adversary moves alternately, until the board begins to be cleared by trapping enemy pieces. The bad feature of the game is that it is so liable to be drawn, by each player creating a barrier, behind which they have only their own men, and can continue to move these without any chance of attack. To plan a barrier is one of the motives in placing the men.

110. *Graeco-Roman game pieces* (226–91).

226. Bone disc with bearded head. On the flat back, V Є, 5 in Latin and Greek notation. Probably an admission ticket.

227. Astragalus or knuckle bone, in grey steatite. In relief on one of the large faces, a male and female figure are carved, the throw termed "Venus."

228–9. Astragali of grey steatite, the smaller carefully carved.

230. Talus, or long die of bone; marks, 1, opposite 6 (3 each end), 2, opposite 5 (2, 1, 2).

231. Talus of bone, similar, but smaller.

232. Talus of bone, similar, but 6 marked as 2, 2, 2. For variants of these, see DEVERIA, *Mémoires* II, pl. v.

Cubical dice.

233. Hard brown limestone; on each face, the hieroglyphic name of a god. Osiris, Horus, Isis, Nebhat around, on the top Hathor, on the base Hor-hudet. Fairly good work, though probably Ptolemaic.

234–58. Bone dice. All follow the normal numbering, opposites being 6 and 1, 5 and 2, 4 and 3: except No. 234 with 5 opposite 4 and 3 opposite 2. 255–6 were from Naukratis. Side of cube 0·26 to 0·75. (255–8 not in plate.)

259. Ebony die.

260. White glazed pottery, with violet circles.

261–(2. Bone, rounded forms, like the previous.

263. Bronze, solid.

264. Limestone, much worn. From near Defeneh.

265. Pottery die, impressed before baking. Opposites 6, 5; 4, 3; 2, 1.

266. Bronze, hollow.

267. Bone, much rounded.

268. Limestone, rounded.

269. White marble. Opposites 6, 5; 4, 2; 3, 1.

270. Grey limestone.

271–3. White marble. 272 opposites 6, 3; 5, 2; 4, 1. 273. 6, 4; 5, 1; 3, 2.

274. Alabaster. Opposites 6, 1; 5, 4; 3, 2.

275–83. Grey steatite. 275 opposites 6, 5; 4, 2; 3, 1. 277 opposites 6, 2; 5, 1; 4, 3. 279 opposites 6, 5; 4, 3; 2, 1. 282 opposites 6, 5; 4, 2; 3, 1.

284. Wood. Opposites 9, 6; 5, 3; 4, 2.

(285–6. Plain cubes of white marble and of blue paste.

287. Grey steatite, pentagonal dodecahedron, with Greek numerals, A to I, I A, I B. N. 1–5, 7–12, 50.

288. Grey steatite, eikosihedron, Greek numerals, A, B, Γ, Δ, E around one pole; Z, H, Θ, I, K, Λ, M, N, Ξ, O, around equator; Π, P, C, T, Y around other pole, i.e. 1–9, 10–80, 100–400; but the non-alphabetic 6, and 90 are omitted.

289. Piece of blue stone ware, glazed outside; eikosihedron; remaining letters Z, H, ... Ξ, O, Π, P; about 3·2 wide when complete.

290. Grey steatite, eikosihedron, with same lettering as 288.

291. Limestone, six-sided pyramids, joined with belt of triangles. Letters written in ink. Beginning round equator, A, B, Γ, Δ, E, Z, H, Θ, I, K, Λ, M; round lower pole, N, Ξ, O, Π, P, C; round upper pole, T, Y, Φ, X, Ψ, Ω. As to the age of these, the lettering has advanced to the forms C and Ω but still retains the square E. They might be assigned to the 1st cent. A.D.

111. *Music* (292–315).

Bells.

292. Bronze flatted bell; with part of iron fastening for tongue. For cattle. 3·5 high.

293. Bronze flatted bell; with part of iron fastening for tongue. For cattle. 5·7 high.

294. Bronze bell, with part of iron tongue. 2·1 high.

295–(6. Pair of bronze bells, no tongues. Wushym. 2·5 high.

297. Bronze bell with loose ring, tongue broken out. 2·0 high.

298. Square bronze bell, loop inside for tongue. Lion face (?) in relief on one side. 1·9 high.

299. Bronze bell in form of Bes head, crowned with feathers. Part of ring for tongue inside. 2·9 high.

(299 A. Bronze bell with head of Bes. 1·3 high.

300. Bronze bell, with heads of baboon, dog, and ram, and an animal on the top. 1·4 high.

301–2. Bronze bells for sheep, with slit to insert a ball. This form gives a much lower note for its size—about middle B and C—than the open bells.

303. Toy bell of bronze; handle in form of Bes. 1·5 high.

304. Toy bell of bronze; ram's head before loop handle. 1·1 high.

305. Toy bell of bronze, with ring and part of tongue. 0·8 high.

See also child's bracelets with small bells, under *Toilet*.

306–(7. Pair of bronze cymbals. Tomb in mound east of Naukratis. Roman.

308–(9. Two bronze cymbals, partly broken.

Such cymbals were attached to long springy handles, so as to clatter when shaken. (PRICE, *Sale Catalogue*, xiv, 437). Two pairs were lately found, mounted, at Lahun; one is in this collection.

310. Pan pipes, of reed, with knob at the bottom of each. Fastened by a strip of palm-stick on each side, with string and resin. Depths (choked), 2·16, 1·82, 1·71, 1·56, 1·45, 1·28: the last reed broken away at the top. Roman.

311. Pair of reed pipes, similar holes; mouthpieces lost. Spaces 1·14 to 1·24, practically equal. Gurob. viith cent. A.D.?

Modern Egyptian *zumara* pipes are placed with these, for comparison.

312. Limestone; two figures seated, one blowing a pipe, the other beating a drum. Greek period.

313. Limestone; female figure holding a three-stringed lyre. Greek period.

314. Limestone, seated figure holding a five-stringed lute. Roman.

315. Neck of harp, both ends broken; has had at least five pegs, of which three remain. Those found at Saqqara have 17 and 18 pegs, see QUIBELL, *Excavations at Saqqara*, 1906–7, xxxiii. xixth dynasty.

112. *Wands for dancing* (316–20). Pl. li.

Dancers are represented holding wands in the hand, to mark time in the dance, see the section 91 on Hand Wands, under Ivories.

316–(7. Portions of two such ivory wands with hands, from Kahun, agree with the dating to the xiith dynasty.

318. Part of wooden wand with inscription "Hu son of the *kas* of Urthekau." This connection of Hu, the god of taste, with Urthekau, the goddess of magic, is unnoticed by Lanzone. Gurob. xviiith dynasty.

319. Part of a hand wand of wood, with four bands of incised pattern, and lotus at the end. Hand broken. Gurob. xviiith dynasty.

320. Hand wand, of wood.

CHAPTER XV
TOYS.
Pls. l to lv.

113. *Tip cat and tops.*

321–(4. Sticks for playing tip cat, with the middle thinned so as to give a better blow. Kahun. xiith dynasty.

325–(7. Sticks tapering to the end, for tip cat. 325 has on the middle of it the signs C X, apparently incised with a flint. Kahun. xiith dynasty.

328–35. Tip cats, 3·2 to 7·3 long. Kahun. xiith dynasty.

(336–8. Tip cats, probably from Kahun, unmarked.

(339. Tip cat from grave 677. Tarkhan.

340–52. Wooden tops, 1·0 to 3·5 high. Kahun. xiith dynasty.

(353. Double top, pointed at each end. Kahun. xiith dynasty.

(354–7. Wooden tops, unmarked, probably Kahun.

(358. Wooden top. Gurob. xviiith dynasty?

359. Lathe-turned wooden top. Hawara. Roman.

360. Lathe-turned wooden top, drum-shaped, with small peg. Roman.

114. *Balls.*

361. Wooden ball, 1·3 diam. Kahun. xiith dynasty.

362–3. White leather balls, in 12 gores. Thebes. Spoilt by damp.

364. Red leather ball, in 6 gores.

365. Ball made of strips of papyrus, probably to be covered.

366. Glazed pottery ball, 4 green, 4 black meridians; with thread hole for hanging up; perhaps from room decoration.

367. Green glazed pottery ball, imitation fruit (?) from foundation deposit. (See *Koptos*, xv, 62.)

115. *Rattles.*

368. Rattle of brown pottery, with animal head on the handle: three pellets of pottery in the inside. Thebes. xiith dynasty?

369. Rattle of red pottery with white spots; five pellets of black pottery in the inside. Thebes. xviiith dynasty? (See *El Arabah*, xvii, E 255, Amenhetep II.)

116. *Limestone figures.*

370. Boy crawling on the ground. xiith dynasty.

(371. Part of figure of girl, tumbling; from knees to chest. xiith dynasty.

372. Rude head on forked legs; similar figures of peg form occur in the tomb of Pasar (*Gizeh and Rifeh*, xxiii, 50). xixth dynasty.

373. Figure of conic form.

374. Two boys wrestling, roughly cut. Kahun. xiith dynasty.

375. Baboon seated, playing a lute. xviiith dynasty.

376. Baboon standing, playing a lute; blue and red colouring. xviiith dynasty.

377. Baboon and young one. xviiith dynasty. (See other figures, under Statuettes.)

(378. Rude carving of a loaded boat.

117. *Dolls.*

379–82. Pieces of flat thin board cut to a human outline, without legs. Black, and sometimes red, patterning is marked on them, in various bands of crossing lines and vandykes, always ending with a large delta below. One of these is from Rifeh, grave 98, and therefore of the xiith–xviiith dynasties. Another was found in a tomb early in the xiith dynasty (*Ramesseum*, iii, 9). When complete, these dolls have long masses of hair, made up of from 2 to 5 threads with little lumps of mud rolled round them. See GARSTANG, *Burial Customs*; *Aeg. Mon. Leyden*, ccxliii, 493 apparently a later style than usual. There are two lots of this hair, here,

ending in a loop for attachment, one lot attached to the edge of a doubled piece of linen, and a quantity loose. Beside that from Rifeh, one was found and two were bought at Thebes, and one was found at Beni Hasan. Thus they belong to Upper Egypt. It is noticeable that breasts are never marked on these, though they seem to represent adults.

383–5. Another type of wooden doll had jointed arms and legs. There is some attempt at modelling of the figure, and a definite head and face. In all three there is a hole in the middle of the back; in one this comes through to the front: there are traces of resin in it, as if something had been attached. Nos. 383, 385 were found at Kahun (pl. viii, 15, 16). xiith dynasty.

386–9. Limestone dolls; with heavy wig, in two side masses, and a plaited tail at the back; ending at the knees. Such figures are dated early in the xiith dynasty (*Ramesseum*, iii, 10, 13), and to the xiith or xiiith (*El Arabah*, xvii, 5, p. 10). 388, only head and shoulders remain. 389, head lost, girdle marked on waist at back by three crosses.

390–1. Lower parts of two blue glazed figures, similarly ending at the knees; with girdle, bracelets, and tatu patterns on the thighs. That these figures, 365–73, were for toys is shown by a similar wooden figure (see Funerary section) found with a model couch in the grave of a girl, thus removing these from the class of concubine figures. Moreover, both of these glazed figures are from the town of Kahun, and not funerary. xiith dynasty.

392–3. Dolls of rag and thread. xiith dynasty.

Pottery dolls are of four classes, before the late Roman group. (1) Those with bell-shaped wigs on each side of the face, slight breasts, and very steatopygous, of drab pottery. (2) Those with an infant on the back. (3) Those with a shelf behind the head pierced for hanging hair; all these classes have the hands at the sides. (4) Massive flat forms of extreme coarseness, with the hands below the breasts.

Class I. 394–5 (6–7). Drab pottery dolls with bell-wigs; double girdle line of dots; and wide ring of dots round navel, and on each haunch. Two heads similar.

Class II. 398–401. Drab pottery dolls with infants; 398 with small infant hanging on at shoulders, and supported by woman's hands turned behind, slight spots round navel. 399 with larger infant astride of the hips, and holding on the shoulders; the woman's hair is modelled in seven long locks around the head. 400-1, two busts from dolls, with hair in long locks.

402. Rude head with oblong gorget on throat, in 3 × 8 divisions, 5 dots above, 6 below.

403. Piece of pottery modelling of three thick masses of hair, from a broken figure.

(404. Torso of doll, with punching of small circles on delta and haunch.

(405. Very flat negroid head, in brown pottery, with large ring earrings.

Class III. 406-13. Dolls with shelving head, double neck ring, and girdle line. The neck rings are spotted 407, barred 408-9, plain 410-13. No dots round navel, two plain spots on haunches. Brown and drab pottery.

(414-9. Pieces; 414 without neck rings, others uncertain.

(420-2. Similar, but no girdle. 420 red pottery from Nubt. 421-2 drab fragments. As to the date of these, very few have been recorded in groups. Of class I, there were two in a cemetery ranging from xiith to xviiith dynasty (*Diospolis*, xxvi, Y 216, 320, p. 53), and one in a cemetery of the xiiith to xviith dynasty (*Cemeteries of Abydos* II, xiv, 1, Z. 1). The form of the wig is a fair guide to the period, as the wide bell shape is often found on the statuettes of the xiith dynasty. Class II is probably slightly later.

Class II or III, with and without girdle, occurred in a cemetery of the xith dynasty, which ended before the xiith (*Qurneh*, xxxi, 6, 7, p. 2). With girdle, it occurred in a fine tomb fully of the xiith dynasty (*Diospolis*, xxvi, W 72, pp. 43-4); also at Abydos with a stele of the xiith (*El Arabah*, xvii, E 312, p. 46), and in a cemetery of the xiiith to xviith (*Cemeteries of Abydos* II, xiv, 1, R 59). Similarly, the type is found with objects of the xviiith dynasty (*El Amrah*, xlviii, D 29), and at Deir el Bahri, with the head of class III, it is asserted to be "exclusively of the xviiith dynasty" (*Temple xith dynasty* III, xxiv, p. 25). The type of head shelving backward is well known on early xviiith dynasty statuettes. It seems, then, that these figures begin with the bell-wigs in the xiith, or probably the xith, dynasty; those of following ages are headless, and cannot be fixed in type; and then in the xviiith dynasty the shelving head appears. Two fragments show that the legs, and halves of the body, were modelled separately and stuck together while soft.

423. A somewhat similar figure, with the back ledge for hanging the hair; this was made by moulding in one piece, the arms being united with the body. Such figures were placed on couches in the grave as concubines, and whether they arose from the doll figures is not known. For others of this type, see Funerary section, and *Ancient Egypt*, 1917, 77.

(424. A triangular-shaped fragment of the legs of a doll, very wide at the top, and coming to a point below, was found at Harageh, grave 111, with an alabaster vase certainly of the xiith dynasty.)

425-32. Class IV. Massive flat forms of extreme coarseness, with the hands below the breasts. The hair is in three sections, sides and back, in 425; in others, the back section is omitted. The breasts are slight, the delta is very large and heavily marked, the feet end in a point. No. 426 was found at Quft, but the halves may not be of the same figure. 430 was found in the N.W. corner of the Ramesseum, the 3rd gallery from the W. end. The head is much dwarfed and debased. (431 is from Thebes. At Diospolis such a figure was found in cemetery N, but not dated, *Diospolis*, xxvi.) No such figures are known from recorded graves which give a date. None have been found in Roman sites, or Defeneh or Naukratis, amid the quantity of rough pottery of those sites: nor were there any among the pottery figures offered at Deir el Bahri in the xviiith dynasty. The origin of these figures seems to be certainly the Babylonian Ashtoret figures. There are four ages of oriental influence, the button using people in the vith, the Hyksos, the xxiind dynasty of the "man of Susa," and the Persian age. Of these, the xxiind dynasty seems most likely, both by the fabric, and by the style of the figure from the Ramesseum.

433-6. Another class of rude statuettes of drab pottery seems to belong to the same age as above; similar rough pottery figures were found at Tell Yehudiyeh of about the xxth-xxiiird dynasties (*Hyksos and Isr. Cities*, xix D). 433-4 are standing with the arms raised, 435 is part of a horseman, pl. lv. (436 is a seated figure with the knees drawn up to the body.

437. Another very rude figure was found at Rifeh, grave 156, with pottery of the ixth-xth dynasties (*Gizeh and Rifeh*, xiii A, 23).

438. Horse's head in limestone, pierced below to fit a peg. Perhaps a toy or gaming piece. xviiith dynasty? Pl. li.

439. Flying pigeon; light blue glaze. xxvith dynasty? Pl. li.

440. Bird with upturned head; brown pottery. pl. lii.

118. *Mud toys made by children.*
Kahun. xiith dynasty.

441. Standing female figure, clothed to feet (head shapeless, not in pl.).

442. Standing swathed figure, roughly incised down the front with hieratic, "Tep-ta born of Neferith." Source unknown.

443. Brick-shaped figure, head lost, incised with breasts, necklace, navel, and delta.

444-5. Two block figures, one with thread and mud hair, one headless. Grains of corn inserted for eyes and vulva.

446. Brick-shaped figure, pinched-out nose and spots around for face, dots for girdle.

447. Brick-shaped figure, with incised nose and eyes, dots around; divided square of dots on back, for the hair.

448. Figure of similar style, with dots round face, and for navel? (pl. lii). White clay. Source unknown.

449. Brick figure, nose and eyes made by one pinch.

(450. Conical figure, pinched face, blue bead eyes.

451. Female figure walking, headless.

452. Male figure, one hand raised.

453. Standing figure, pinched face, hair and necklace marked by small circles.

(454-6. Portions of standing figures.

457. Brick-shaped figure, no head, prick lines.

458-(9. Brick figure, no head, cut eyes, traces of thread hair, pricked necklace, navel and girdle; also portion similar?

460-(1. Brick figure, head lost, breasts and pricked detail; also portion similar.

462. Pyramidal figure, two navel spots with ring of dots, two haunch spots similar, girdle line of pricks. Quft.

463-(4. Pig's (?) head, with blue bead eyes, whitened, with black around eyes.

465. Peg-shaped figure, nose, eyes impressed, long hair lines around head.

466. Jackal head?

467. Human figure?

468-9. Model vases.

470. Brick, incised, *hem khepu*; splinter through it for connecting to other parts.

471. Brick with rough hieratic signs on each surface.

472. Brick with notched ribs on it (hair?).

473. Brick with incised pricks, wrapped in linen, with a dab of clay outside.

474. Brick with ring and crescent in relief.

475-8. Male figure and three female. Riqqeh. xiith dynasty.

479. Mummy in a sarcophagus. Kahun. xiith dynasty.

480-1. Pigs.

482. Sheep.

483-4. Water birds (moor hens?) without legs, hole through middle. Buff clay.

485-6. Lizards.

487-92. Crocodiles.

493-6. Unknown.

497. Turtle? Harageh. xiith dynasty.

498-500. Pigs.

501-3. Pigs?

504. 505-(12. Sheep.

513-4. Boats.

515. Disc with finger punch, surrounded by two circles of pricks.

516-(22). 523-4. Similar, with one circle of pricks.

525. Disc with cross in rings, marked by pricks.

526. Disc pricked.

527. Disc with eight projections.

(528. Various portions of unknown objects in mud.

529. Mud balls containing organic matter, with signs scored on the outside.

(For similar figures of hippopotamus and cattle, now made in Nyasaland, see *Verh. d. Berl. Anthrop. Ges.*, 1900, p. 532.)

119. *Roman Toys.*

530. Doll of pottery, painted white, with traces of pink, and black hair and eyes. This, and the following numbers to 569, were found in a single grave of a child, iiird cent. A.D. For some details, see *Hawara*, xix.

531. Pottery sphinx.

532. Pieces of oval box; painted on a yellow ground with pink flowers and green birds.

533-4. Green glass bottles.

535-7. White glass bottles.

538. Alabaster vase.

539–42. (43–44. Spindles.

545. String of glazed pottery beads, white, blue, butt, brown, and black.

546. Taper holder of wood, colour-washed.

547. Handle? of plaited rush work.

548–50. Small pottery jugs and crater; reddish buff with manganese patches.

551. Wooden box with sliding lid.

552–3. Two sandals of rush work.

554. Model table of wood, one leg lost.

555. Model bedstead of split palm stick.

556. Basket.

557. Turned box and lid in form of a pomegranate.

(558.) Similar lid.

(559–60.) Two smaller wooden pots.

561. Turned amphora-shaped wooden pot and lid.

562. Turned wooden box.

563. Wooden box with sliding lid.

564. Sandal of twisted fibre.

(565–6.) Wooden combs.

(567.) Part of doll, of rushes covered with linen and thread.

(568.) Pottery stand.

(569.) 3 wide and 2 narrow slips of palm stick, 4·78 to 4·83 inches long.

Another group from a grave is the following, 570–83 (*Hawara*, xx, 12–22).

570. Doll of rushes covered with cloth; face modelled, red thread for lips, nipples, navel and groin: natural hair attached. Separate tunic.

571. Convex mirror of tinned copper in wooden case, with brass strip handle. Case and lid turned inside.

572. Basket.

573–6. White glass bottles (574 is not stated in the original list).

577. Opaque blue glass bottle.

578. Clear dark blue glass bottle.

579. Brass model cymbal.

580. Woven brass chain and hook.

(581.) Ribbed melon bead of blue glazed pottery.

(582.) White glass spindle whorl.

583. Various pieces of doll's clothing, red, green, blue, and white.

(584–5. Pottery pug-dogs with collar and three bullae. (See *Terracotta figures* for other animals, &c.)

586. Wooden bird, probably on wheels originally; hole in beak for string.

587–(9. Wooden horses, originally as next.

590. Wooden horse on wheels.

591. Bone figure in Phrygian cap, carved alike on both sides.

592. Bone doll, late Roman.

593. Bone doll, without features. Coptic.

594–6. Bone dolls.

597–9. Larger bone dolls, cut from a whole leg bone.

600. Wooden *onkh*-shaped doll.

601. Wooden doll with cross lines and circles.

602. Wooden doll, from Lahun.

603. Pottery figure, raised ornament. Byzantine.

604. Head of relief figure, painted. Byzantine.

605. Pottery head, red with white facing.

606–7. Very rude pottery figures, 607 with child at breast.

CHAPTER XVI

WRITING.

120. The earliest form of scribe's outfit that we know is that figured in full detail upon the wooden panels of Ra-hesy, best published by J. E. QUIBELL in *The Tomb of Hesy*, pls. xxix–xxxii. In those examples there are three objects always together; (A) a long cylindrical case to hold the writing reeds, probably made from a large reed, bound around with cord to prevent it splitting, and with a cap on the top to close it; (B) a palette with two pans on it, each of which (on two panels) has an object filling half of each pan; perhaps this represents a half-used cake of paint; (C) what looks like a small bag with running cord around the top edge, suggested by the different shapes of it on pl. xxix; this apparently was to hold the little water flask for mixing the ink. This group is the origin of the usual sign for a scribe, and it affected the scribe's outfit down to Roman times (lviii, 50). In this sign on a sealing of Perabsen of the iind dynasty the water pot is globular (*Royal Tombs* II, xxi, 166). But the sign in the inscriptions of Rahesy always shows the puckered top of the bag.

In the vth dynasty the rectangular palette with round pans, each half full of ink, was still represented (*Saqqara Mastabas* I, xl, 93), and in the xiith dynasty in the tomb of Tehuti-hetep at El Bersheh, and that of Ameny at Beni Hasan.

What may be a variant of the water bottle in a bag is shown tied on the end of a reed case of Akhet-hetep (*Saqqara Mastabas* I, xiii); the long pointed form would agree with one of the long pointed alabaster vases of the vith dynasty in a bag, and this would be the best form to avoid spilling in carrying. Such were tied on to the palette, see the group of palettes of the vth dynasty in L. *Denk.* II, 47.

When we seek for the actual stone palettes they seem to be very rare. I have found only two, and there do not seem to be any others recorded or published. These two,—the larger in Cairo, the lesser in Manchester,—were found in a burial chamber of the mastaba at Gizeh of the time of king Zet, 1st dynasty; they are photographed in *Gizeh and Rifeh*, iii, and described on p. 5. They each had black colour in one pan, and red in the other, proving the purpose of the two pans. The sizes were 10·89 × 5·48, and 4·12 × 2·18 inches, both made of slate.

Three other examples made of slate have been bought, from unknown sites, pl. lvi, 1, 2, 3. Each of these has a hole through the flat base in the middle of one end, evidently for hanging it up, as it is shown hung in the scribe's outfit.

121. *Catalogue.* No. 1 is 7·36 × 3·50 to 3·60 inches; the pans 3·43 to 3·48 across. On one end are very faint hieroglyphs scratched, apparently *nesut, desher, da* (tall triangle), *she* (tank), and possibly the crossed arrows of Neit. A hole drilled at one end has broken out the edge; as also a similar hole at the other end; lastly a third drill hole remains next to one of these. There are traces of red paint around the bases of both pans. 1st dynasty.

2 is 4·44 × 2·34 inches; the pans 2·04 to 2·07 across. The pans do not stand up as high as in no. 1. A little patch of red colour remains in one pan, on the left side of the lower pan in the figure. A hole is drilled in one end; here, and in the earlier holes of no. 1, the hole is parallel to the length, and is met by another hole from the flat base. 1st dynasty.

3 is 3·27 × 2·04 inches; the pans are 1·32 to 1·38 across. A hole through one end is almost diagonal. There is no trace of colour remaining. 1st dynasty.

Comparing the dimensions of these palettes, they are usually twice as long as the width but not exactly so, and there is no repetition of dimensions, hence the size was probably made only for convenience.

4 is a single pan of alabaster, the base 1·66 to 1·80 across. It is probably of the early dynasties.

5. Slate palette with lid. Whether this was for ink or for kohl is not certain, but there seem to be traces of kohl below the lid. Size 4·28 × 3·12. The lid, with a handle, is of the same form as the ivory lids of kohl palettes found in 1st dynasty graves, see *Royal Tombs* II, xxxii (Mena age), via (Zer), *Gizeh and Rifeh*, iv (Zet). 1st–iind dynasty.

6. Brown basalt palette with hollow for a lid. 4·26 × 2·82. ivth dynasty?

7. Diorite ink slab with well to hold the ground ink. 3·38 × 2·12. ivth dynasty?

8. Slate palette, sloping below. 1·94 × 1·88. vith to xiith dynasty?

9. Chert palette with name of Zed-ka-ra, see *Scarabs*, ix, 5. 8. 3. The polishing of this is apparently faultlessly flat, and the intersections seem perfect. vth dynasty.

(10. Fragment of chert palette, 1·50 wide, similar stone but less fine work than 9. Quft. A similar palette was found at Abydos, at the vth dynasty level (*Abydos* II, xiv, 292).

11. Brown basalt palette, 7·9 × 4·7. Diorite muller, bought separately. xiith dynasty.

12. Black and blue-grey serpentine palette, 5·7 × 3·7. Basalt muller. xiith dynasty.

13. Brown basalt palette with cartouche border, 5·3 × 3·2. Basalt muller. xiith dynasty.

14. Black serpentine palette, with water well, 6·8 × 3·7; unusual depth, 1·6, with usual sloping sides beneath, reducing the base to 3·1 × 1·3. Basalt muller. xiith dynasty. None of these mullers were bought with the palettes.

(15. Black serpentine palette, 5·4 × 3·4. xiith dynasty. (15–8 not figured.)

(16. Diorite palette, 4·8 × 2·8. From Koptos. xiith dynasty.

(17. Black syenite palette, 4·9 × 3·1. xiith dynasty.

(18. Greenish serpentine palette, 4·4 × 2·7. xiith dynasty.

19. Quartzite and stone funeral model of palette, 2·5 × 1·7. Harageh. ixth–xth dynasty. The shallow palette with sloping sides below begins with the chert slabs of the vth; but it is usually found of black stone, common in the xiith dynasty. See *Dendereh*, xx; *Cemeteries of Abydos*, viii.

20. Crimson granular marble, 2·1 × 0·75.

21. Slate, 2·2 × 1·2. Koptos.

22. Black serpentine, 2·5 × 1·7. 20–2 are formed like ink slabs; they are too small for that use, and are deeply grooved by rubbing with a point. Being of soft stone they cannot be for sharpening, and the purpose is uncertain; possibly for crushing pellets of kohl.

(23. Slate palette, 3·9 × 2·6.

(24. Slate palette, 1·8 × 1·4. (23–4 not figured.) Ink, besides being ground up, was also kept ready liquified in ink pots.

25. Alabaster ink well, double; each well surrounded by a *shen* sign, the whole in a cartouche border, 5·1 × 3·1. Traces of red paint in upper, and of blue in lower well.

26. Blue-marble ink well or dish, with cartouche edging. ·1·8 × 1·1. By the stone, this is of the xiith dynasty.

27. Alabaster ink well (or kohl pot?) with undercut groove for sliding lid. 1·9 × 1·7. With two ridges below as feet. xiith dynasty?

28. Blue glaze pottery ink wells, in cartouche, 2·7 × 1·3. xixth dynasty?

29. Blue glazed cartouche ink well, 1·3 × 0·6. xxvith dynasty.

30. Blue and white glazed cartouche ink wells, 2·2 × 1·2. *Shen* sign around each well. xxviith dynasty.

31. Limestone ink wells, pierced suspension broken off right end. Colours,—red, black, black. Roughly written on base, *Hor taui*, with panelling below.

(32. Black obsidian burnisher? or possibly double finger amulet.

33. Brown chert burnisher, 2·66 long.

34. Light-brown chalcedony burnisher, 2·8 long.

35. Brown chert burnisher, 2·06 long. Flat below. Shells were used in early times to hold colour, probably for eye paint.

(36. Shell of *Spatha rubens* with powdered Chessylite. Meydum. iiird–ivth dynasty.

(37. Piece of hieroglyph of green paste. Meydum. iiird–ivth dynasty.

(38. Shell of *Spatha rubens* with blue frit paint.

(39. Cake of black soot ink. See cakes of black and of red ink, found with an axe of about the vith dynasty. *Gizeh and Rifeh*, xiii, no. 3, grave 194.

122. *Pen cases.*

There is here a good series of dated scribes' cases, from the ivth to the xixth dynasty. The only other early dated ones that I have seen were of the vth dynasty (*Deshasheh*, xxxiv, 11), one too much rotted to move (p. 34–5), the other since thrown away in a packing case at the Museum to which it was sent. Next after these is the palette of Khety, ixth dynasty, in Paris. These are all made in two layers, so as to hollow out easily the space for the reeds. Perhaps the earliest representation of the flat case for reeds with two colour pans is in the tomb of Ptah-hetep, vth dynasty (*Saqqara Mastabas*, ix, xiii).

40. Contemporary with the earliest examples named above is the case of "Khemten the royal purifying priest." 9·0 long. It shows a detail of the circumcision in the hieroglyph. Apparently no colour has been placed in the pans, and the rectangle is only a dummy of the opening for the reeds, so this was a funeral model. It is probably from the tomb of Khemten at Saqqara (*Mar. Mast.* D 50, of the middle of the vth dynasty.

41. Case made in two layers, like those of Deshasheh, with black and red colour pans. It was inscribed by scribe on both sides; on the front with a cartouche of Pepy I and two columns of hieratic; on the back with three cartouches of Pepy I, and signs between. Where the signs are clear the sense is not intelligible, and the back is very illegible. Length 17·55. vith dynasty.

42. Case with side slit, 12·0 long. Pans for black and red ink. On the back, hieratic ink inscription *Antef zd*, "Antef says." xith dynasty.

43. Case, with opening cut in front. 15·0 long, 2·34–2·44 wide, 1·20 to 1·25 thick, massive. Ink pans each surrounded by *shen*, red, white and black. The cracks in the wood are such that it would be physically impossible to cut the inscription after them; the antiquity of it is therefore certain. The name of the owner was probably on the cover of the reed space; the side inscriptions give the parentage. "Royal offering to Amen high of feathers, may he give his breaths, brightness in the earth, his outgoing and incoming in Kherneter, for the *ka* of his father Ta-am (name of a goddess not entered) over the desert, may she give things good and pure all offerings upon her table for the *ka* of his mother Auiu." Below are three figures with a table of offerings, named "her mother Mes," "Ta-am," "Lady of the house Tekh." Apparently Mes had a daughter Auiu who married Ta-am, and Tekh was either sister, or daughter of this marriage. 15·05 long. Bought at Thebes. Early xviiith dynasty.

44. Case with side slit. Six pans, used as three black and three red. On the slope of the reed opening is "For the *ka* of the praiser of the name of his god (the king), the great administrator of the lord of both lands, Huy." On the body are rows of ink dots placed as a tally of quantities delivered, 8 dots, 4, 5, 4, and 10. Length one cubit, 20·61, halved by the reed opening as 10·27 and 10·34. Found in a tomb at Gurob (*Kahun*, p. 36, xviii, 13). xviiith dynasty.

45. Case with front slip over the reed space, sliding in under-cut grooves. Two small square pans for black and red ink. On the front is inscribed finely in ink, "Hershef king of south and north." On the back is drawn the head and shoulder of a lion. Below it is a fine figure of Hershef, inscribed "Chapter of praising to thy *ka*, Hershef king of south and north, lord of Thet-Thet who raises his horns. Grant to cause to raise and establish the pillar of the festival of the lord of both lands." Thet-Thet was a place in the Fayum (BRUGSCH, *D. Geog.* 258). The raising the *zed* pillar was a great function in the *sed* festival. Length 14·1, exactly divided by the mouth of the opening. One reed remains with it. Found in a tomb at Gurob (*Kahun*, p. 36, xxiv, 5). xixth dynasty.

46. Case with five pans and three small ink holes. Colours,—orange, yellow, blue, red and black, with white in the little holes. On one side of the opening is *Neb ta*, incised. The cover of the reed space is a sliding lid tapering in breadth, and under-cut. Length 15·6. The stump of a pen of palm fibre was in this. xviiith dynasty?

(47. Case without pans. The cover of the reed space slid like the previous, but is lost. Traces of hieratic writing on the middle space. Length 18·0 inches. xixth dynasty?

48. Case with two pans, with black and red ink. The sides and back are in one piece, and the front is a separate slip, pinned on with eight dowels, the joint being mitre-cut. Length 11·65 and 11·63, the Roman foot: outside 1·30×0·96, inside 0·83×0·30. At the top is one hole straight through, and another running in from the edge and met by a hole from the end. Thus there were two suspensions, perhaps one for carrying, the other for the water pot. From this being exactly the Roman foot, it is dated to Roman times in accord with the obviously late style of it. Other pen-cases are on the basis of cubit lengths.

49. Olive wood case, apparently a modern imitation, different from the ancient examples in the open tray for reeds, and perfectly fresh state of the wood.

On the basis of these dated examples, and others that are published, we can summarise the forms. The double-layer type is from the vth dynasty (*Deshasheh*) vith (no. 41), and ixth (Khety). The side slit for cutting the space for reeds is of the xiith (no. 42; GARSTANG, *Burial Customs*, p. 77), and rather later (*El Amrah*, xliii); on to the xviiith (Huy, no. 44); and Bologna, of Tehutmes III. The loose lid is of the early xviiith (no. 43). Amenhetep I (Price, 2853 a) and Tehutmes III (*El Amrah*, xl, 9). The sliding lid does not seem to be earlier than the close of the xviiith dynasty; see 45–7; QUIBELL, *Excavations at Sakkarah*, 1906–7, xxxvi, 1; Leyden (*Cat.* xcv 288, xcvi 299) of Akhenaten; Turin, of Amenneb. In later times a hole was cut up from the end, and the pans were rectangular, sloping down from one edge, of xxvith–xxviiith dynasty, *Abydos* II, xv, 15.

Regarding the number of holes, two was usual, for black and red ink; these date from the vth dynasty (*Deshasheh*), vith (no. 41), xiith (no. 42; *Burial Customs*, p. 77), later (*El Amrah*, xliii), xviiith (Leyden xcv, 287; Tehutmes III, Bologna and *El Amrah*, xl; and Akhenaten, Leyden xcvi, 299), xixth (45, QUIBELL, *Excavations at Sakkarah*, 1906–7, xxxvi, 1; Leyden xcvi, 302, 308; Turin, Amen-neb) and Roman (48). Three holes are on 43 of xviiith, and *Abydos* II, xv, 15 of xxvith–viiith dynasty. Five holes on 46 of xixth, and Leyden xcv, 288. Six holes on no. 44, xviiith dynasty. Ten holes on one of Ani, xviiith dynasty at Turin. Eleven holes on the Turin case of Pen-rannut under Ramessu II.

Funerary cases are sometimes made of stone, alabaster or glazed schist, as a fragment of the scribe Sen-nefer (*Scarabs*, xxv, 24).

123. *Roman cases and pens.*

50. Bronze case for reed pens and ink pot. The case was over 8 inches long, 1·0 wide. The ink pot is 1·5 wide, 2·0 high, with a cap lid, conical, having a small hole in the top for the reed. The lower end as here shown probably went uppermost, the chain serving to secure the cap of the tube from being lost. From a pit grave at Saft el Henneh (Goshen). (*Hyksos and Isr. Cities*, p. 40, xxxvii B.) Roman age.

51. Reed for holding pens (?). The knot has not been pierced. Gurob.

52. Wooden case, with a hinge cut in the wood. At the end is a leaden pan, with a mass of fibre and black ink, as still used in Egypt. In the case are two short reed pens. On the lid is a band of zigzag pattern along the middle. Length 7·3. Coptic or Arabic.

53. Parchment cover from the foot of a scribe's case, as in the Cairo Museum. Incised with cross on steps and + ЄN TOYTШ NIKA.

54–8. Reed pens. 54 from Lahun, 58 from Wushym, others from Hawara. Roman.

59. Wooden counting board. Marks *nefer*, 1, 2, 3, 4, 5, 6, 7, 8, 9 spots; ten sign; ten with 1, 2, 3, 4, 5, 6, 7, 8, 9 spots; two ten signs; two tens and 5 spots; 3, 4, 5, 6, 7, 8, 9, ten signs; hundred sign. Thus it reads 1–19, 25, 30 to 90, 100. The spaces are not equal. This is made from a piece of old furniture, with nine dowel pins remaining at one end. From Kahun (*Illahun*, viii, 17). xiith dynasty.

124. *Writing tablets.*

In describing the tablets, the texts upon them will be briefly noted, leaving the discussion of such in detail to be dealt with under Inscriptions.

In the early dynasties, writing upon flakes of flint (*Gizeh and Rifeh*, iii A), or of limestone (*Meydum*, xiv, 1), was usual, and the use of limestone continued till Coptic times. Pottery ostraka began to be used similarly in later times, and became the usual material for receipts and letters in the Roman age. None of these materials were prepared for repeated use, as permanent tablets. In the representations of scribes the papyrus roll almost always appears, but in the vth dynasty there seems to be a tablet used, if we may judge by the way it is handled (L. *Denk.*, ii, 49). The first conclusive example of using a tablet is in the scene of the Amu at Beni Hasan (L. *Denk.*, ii, 131, 133). Of the same age are the figures of scribes on boats, with a flat tablet under the arm (Univ. Coll.). There are two fragments of such tablets here, as follows.

(60. Piece of tablet with hard polished white stucco face. The wood 0·2 thick, and the stucco on each side 0·04 thick. It is too hard to scratch with the finger nail, and cuts steatite freely, but is scratched by calcite. It is probably fixed with albumen.

61. Corner of a similar tablet from Kahun. xiith dynasty.

(62. Half of a tablet, 0·65 thick, stucco 0·03 thick, 12·0 wide. The white stucco is painted brown, and is laid on a basis of linen. Four lines of hieratic on one side and five lines on the other. From Thebes. xviiith dynasty.

(63. Corner of a similar tablet, 9 × 4 inches remaining. Thebes. xviiith dynasty.

64. Fragment of a Greek tablet, 12·0 high, 0·5 thick. It has a grey wash over it, which held the writing, and it was cleaned by washing off this grey base. On one side are 16 crowded lines in 4 inches; on the other 15 spaced lines of writing in 7 inches.

65. Groups of tablets hinged together appear to be of Roman introduction in Egypt. No. 65 is the cover of such a group 8·03 × 5·81 × 0·44 thick; recess 6·60 × 4·40. The outside is thinly stuccoed and painted with the three forms of Thoth,—with human body and ibis head, standing with sceptre; as an ibis on a shrine, a vulture before it; as a baboon seated holding a branch, with a falcon before it. Colours,—black, green, and greenish blue. Three hinge holes.

66. Complete set of five tablets, three double-sided, and two with outer plain faces. 7·14 × 6·14, recess 5·9 × 5·0. One has been broken and mended anciently by thin brass strips pinned on to each side. The wax has been removed before burial. Leather thongs for hinges added recently.

67–(69. Tablets with red wax one side and black on the other. One black side is uninscribed. Two pairs of threading holes. 3·4 wide.

70–(73. Tablets with black wax on both sides, inscribed. From the threading holes being exactly as on the previous, and the breadth also alike, it seems that all these seven tablets are of one set. It contains notes of domestic and travelling accounts and loans, of the third century B.C., referring to Ptolemais. I have to thank Mr. H. I. BELL for kindly examining these, and the following.

74. Plain wood cover of set of tablets; 5·94 × 3·83, recess 5·06 × 3·10. Inscribed with six lines of Latin inside, and ten and eight lines outside. Two hinge holes, and a tying hole. This is the second half of an affidavit by a soldier's son, under Hadrian, at Apollonopolis Magna.

(75. Part of a cover, 8·0 wide, recess 7·18. From Wushym.

(76. A cover; 4·23 × 3·43; black wax. Three pairs of threading holes, with internal recesses for

the knots. A central boss served to touch the next tablet and prevent the wax sticking. A recess 0·46 wide along the narrow side was probably for the stylus. Plain cross sealing hole.

77. A cover of similar construction, but 4·34 × 3·82. Floreate cross sealing hole.

(78. A cover, 3·33 × 2·11; with two pairs of thread holes. Traces of black wax. Wushym.

(79. Piece of double tablet, 6·60 wide. Remains of black wax. Wushym.

(80. Piece of cover, 3·30 wide. Remains of black wax. Cross sealing hole. Wushym.

(81. Piece of double tablet, 4·64 wide. Black wax. Three pairs of hinge holes.

(82. Piece of double tablet, 2·80 wide. Remains of black wax. Wushym.

(83. Cover, 3·53 × 2·92. Black wax. Two pairs of hinge holes, with recess for knots. Cross sealing hole. Wushym.

(84. Piece of cover, 4·07 wide. Black wax, Wushym.

(85. Piece of cover, 7·50 wide, recess 5·32 wide, unusually broad contact border. Black wax, with traces of Latin, and parts of 9 lines of Latin written on the plain wood outside. Two plain single holes for hinge. On a perfect example of a birth certificate, the outer writing is a duplicate for ready reference.

(86. Fragment of cover, 6·79 wide, recess 5·38, with broad border. Traces of 16 lines of Latin written on the plain wood outside. Plain black wax inside.

(87. Piece of cover, 5·65 wide, recess 4·40. Double sunk panel on the outside for the address. Two successive pairs of hinge holes.

(88. Thick cover, 6·0 × 3·20, recess 4·85 × 2·14. Traces of black wax. Two pairs of hinge holes. Wushym.

(89—91. Small plain slip covers, with two pairs of hinge holes, 2·65 × 1·87, 2·65 × 1·80, 1·76 × 1·48. Wushym.

(92. Cover with recess not waxed, but distempered, 10·5 × 5·0, recess 9·1 × 4·0. Two original hinge holes, coming out in edge; also three later rough holes. Inscribed inside with table of fractions, of 15ths and 16ths. Roughly cut on the outside "Phoibamn Daueït." Fully published by Sir HERBERT THOMPSON in *Ancient Egypt*, 1914, 52—4. Byzantine.

93. Shoulder blade of ox, trimmed down for writing, with 19 lines of names and sums of accounts. This is an example of the use of blade bones, on which the Quran is said to have been written.

94. Limestone block squared for drawing. The lines average 0·550 apart in the length, and 0·541 in the width, with an average error of 0·01. Memphis. xxvith dynasty?

125. *Examples of writing.*

The earliest example in the collection is in the early dynastic section, of the time of king Zet. It is a flint flake, 3·9 × 2·2; one face is the outer skin, on which is ink writing of numerals; these are ·88, 320, 40, 60, and 40. As this comes from a brick mastaba, it is probably a tally of bricks. The numbers being multiples of 20 (except 88), suggests that 20 was a donkey-load, which of that small size of bricks would be likely. This comes from the same grave as two slate palettes with raised pans, *Gizeh and Rifeh*, p. 5. 1st dynasty.

(95. Piece of waste limestone with accounts of the building of the pyramid of Meydum. Found in the pyramid waste used to fill up mastaba 17. iiird dynasty.

96. Mummy bandage inscribed for "the keeper of the palace gate Un-nefer son of Sebek-hetep the elder; life, health, strength."

97. Mummy bandage inscribed in "year 15, *sa* cloth . . . new year festival day 4." This and no. 96 had been on mummies of the xiith dynasty, later torn to pieces, and re-used to stuff Roman mummies at Hawara. *Roman Portraits*, p. 22. xiith dynasty. Other, and later, bandage inscriptions are in the Funerary section.

98. Pottery saucer, with ink-written inscription, partly incised. Kahun. xiith dynasty.

(99. Fragments of veneered coffin, inscribed. vith–xiith dynasty.

(100. Rough piece of wood with hieratic scrawls. xiith dynasty.

(101. Small piece of wood with hieratic. xiith dynasty.

(102. Part of drab pottery jar, with 11 lines of hieratic list. Tell Amarna. xviiith dynasty.

103. Wooden side of box (?) with incised inscription of Amenhetep II, "The good god, Ra-oa-kheperu, beloved by Amen, when he stretched the measuring line upon the temple of the West, *Ra-oa-kheperu-seshep-onkh*." The same inscription is on the foundation vases of this temple, (*Rec.* xvi, 30), and this is doubtless from the foundation

deposit of the funeral temple. Thebes. xviiith dynasty.

(104. Hieratic inscription on limestone.

(105–7. Hieratic datings on jars from the Ramesseum.

(108. Drawing of a peasant. Ramesseum.

(109. Painted papyrus, with figures of the Uzat, Sekhmet, Amen, sons of Horus, Set, Neit, Khnumu, and Isis. Of remarkably delicate drawing; by the figure of Set, probably early in the xixth dynasty.

(110. Drawing on wood of Sebek in human form, seated, with crocodile head, crowned. Gurob. xixth dynasty.

(111. Wooden dowel (?) with inscription of "the temple of Ra-user-maot, mery Amen (Ramessu III) set up west of the great lake," the Fayum. Gurob. xxth dynasty. The same inscription in a vertical column on the back.

(112. Wood, ink-written, "Sebek shedti god (falcon) in . . ." Gurob. xxth dynasty?

(113. Slip of wood covered with linen and stucco. Inscribed in blue, "Khebsenuf, the Osiris Urnure," from funeral furniture. Gurob. xixth dynasty?

(114. Limestone flake with a cartouche inkwritten, combined out of the two names of Ramessu VI. xxth dynasty.

115. Small square of limestone with two figures of men walking. On back *Ra·khet . . . . . khet·su,* rudely written. xixth dynasty?

(116. Small square of limestone with patterns. xixth dynasty?

117. Fragment of alabaster with female figure kneeling before two tables of offerings. *Mut-tem maot kheru.* On the back a *shen* sign incised. Perhaps a part of a funeral model of a scribe's case. xixth dynasty.

126. *Inscriptions on pottery vases.* Pl. lviii.

118. Piece of base of jar. Incised, ". . . born of Senef, his son *mer nut, that . . .*" (vizier). Source unknown, perhaps from the Royal Tombs at Abydos, as are all the following.

(119–21. Cartouches of Usarken I, ink-written.

(122. Cartouches of Usarken II, written in white.

(123. Cartouches of Usarken II, written in black, lower part only.

(124. Parts of illegible cartouches, in black.

(125. Incised scene of Osiris seated, "Asar lord of Ta-zeser"; adored by a kneeling figure, "Adoration of Osiris, may he give life, health and strength

for the *ka* of the divine father, the scribe of the troops, Unnefer."

(126. Top of scene of Osiris, and the "Divine father over the recruits."

(127. Scene of "Osiris lord of Rustau," adored by the "Divine father Osiris, scribe of the troops, Unnefer."

(128. Head of the "overseer of the recruits, Unnefer."

(129–32. Fragments of similar scenes.

133. Inscription beneath a scene, "Guardian of the dwelling of Osiris . . . I establish for thee thy heart upon the place . . . leader of the south and north . . ."

(134. Incised while wet, "Divine father, Osiris, Yeby, in Abydos."

(135–6. Parts of above inscription incised.

(137. Demotic ink inscription on jar. Dendereh.

127. *Inscriptions on wood and metal.*

(138. Carpenter's memorandum of 10 cubits, on a dowel. Ptolemaic?

(139. Adoration to Thoth, hieratic on wooden label. 12 lines, on reverse 5 lines. Abydos.

(140. Piece of brown pottery pan, with demotic writing.

(141. Demotic inscription on cloth of a mummy cover, "Ypy the man of the Fayum son of Huy." Four caricatures, and the Greek letters *Apa*, have been added by children. Hawara. Roman (*Roman Portraits,* sect. 48).

(142. Mummy label of wood, incised, CAYIC, "Sapsis."

143. Mummy label of wood, incised, ѠPOC ETѠN Δ "Horus 4 years."

(144. Mummy label of wood, written, EYΔE-MONIA KOMANOY, "Eudaimonia daughter of Komanos." Two well known men in Egypt were named Komanos. Reverse, 4 lines of cursive Greek.

(145. Wooden label of mummy of Diodoros of Arsinoe, an official of the market of the cloak sellers (*Roman Portraits,* p. 22). Hawara.

(146. Wooden board roughly inscribed with an epitaph.

(For other mummy labels see the Funerary section.)

(147. Piece of a framed board, covered with grey wash. Rudely inscribed with 11 lines of Greek.

(148. Fragment of incised inscription in bronze. . . EICI . . . . . KPAT . . . . A? Δ, end.

149. Incised inscription on pottery. ...**ABΔ** · **IOVIꞶM** ... (*Roman Portraits*, p. 22). Hawara. Roman.

150. Sketch in ink on wood, of royal falcon trampling on a serpent. Roman.

(151. Painting in white on black ground, on wood. Flowers? in two circles. Roman.

(152. Figure of a saint, drawn in ink on wood. Coptic.

153. Fragment of Arabic board with ends of 7 lines of writing. Wushym. Arab.

(154. Arabic receipt on papyrus, 917 A.D. "$1\frac{1}{6}$ dinar. Register 5. In the name of God, &c. Paid and delivered by al-Rabi'ah b. Gabriel one dinar and one sixth, good weight, in the month Phamenoth ... for the *kharaj* due from him for the year, year 304. This finishes the account due from him. (Written by .....) son of Abu Mūsā the collector." Translated by Prof. Margoliouth.

(155. Another receipt of the same period. Sealed with a Roman seal of a horseman.

CHAPTER XVII

STAMPS.

Pl. lx.

128. *Hieroglyphic seals* begin to appear in the xiith dynasty, and form the earliest class of flat stamps.

156. Limestone seal with figure of a man, *onkh zetta* "living eternally." xiith dynasty.

157. Limestone seal with nefer, and possibly a plan of a building. xiith dynasty.

158. Limestone seal with loop pattern, water line, lotus flower between *onkh* and bird, *ka nefer* below. xiith dynasty.

159. Limestone seal. "Desert of Qebti." Koptos. Handle not pierced.

160. Limestone seal with indistinct signs.

161. Limestone stamp. "Rennut the excellent, mistress of food." *ka* is here used in the sense of food.

162. Wooden stamp. "The excellent Rennut mistress of abundant food."

163. Wooden stamp, double. A god standing (Ptah?) broken away. "Rennut mistress of food." Gurob. xixth dynasty.

164. Wooden stamp. "With Amen Ra is plenty, the lord of food."

165. Limestone stamp. "Wine of the western river" (Canopic branch). From the temple of Tehutmes IV at Thebes (*Six Temples*, p. 21, iii, 23). xviiith dynasty.

166. Limestone stamp. "Men-nefer-ra beloved of Upuati of both lands."

167. Limestone stamp of "The divine adoress of Amen," one of the priest queens of the xxvth dynasty.

168. Tehuti and Rennut each in a cartouche. Limestone.

169. "Anup-ami-ut," Anubis in the bandages, or in the Oasis. Limestone. xxvith dynasty?

170. Two hawks (of Koptos?), *neterui nefer* between, lotus at side, *neb* below. Steatite.

171. "Amen-nen-Rennut." Bronze. xxvith dyn.

172. "Sebek shedti." Wood. Gurob. xixth dynasty?

173–8. "Temple of Amen." 173, 6, 7, 8 of bronze. 174–5 of green glaze. 176 has ram's head and disc on handle, 178 has ram-headed Amen seated, as a handle.

179. "Zed-ka-ra, neb ......" Of Shabataka? Limestone.

180. "The devoted, Nesikhonsu." Limestone.

181. "Mentu lord of the city"? Wood.

182. Cow's head of Hathor, serpent of the goddess beneath. Bronze. xxxth dynasty?

183. "The good god lord of both lands, lord of action, Tehuti, lord, great god, lord of Ani." Bronze. xxvith dynasty?

184. "Ymhetep the great, son of Ptah south of his fortress." Bronze. xxvith dynasty?

185. "May the god live. Peduher son of Ymhetep." Limestone. xxvith dynasty?

186. "Rennut of Hero-opolis give life to multitudes." Green glaze.

187. Limestone stamp, uncertain rendering. xxvith dynasty.

188. Pottery finger ring, roughly made, with goose in relief-outline for stamping.

189. Libyan and Asiatic captives bound to a stake, relief on pottery stamp (top pl. lx).

190. Wooden mould of crocodile and two fishes. Gurob. xixth dynasty?

191. Bronze open work, cast *cire perdue*, perhaps for inlay. Ram's head aegis crowned with sun.

192. Bronze brand, aegis of Horus-Ra. Tubular handle. xixth dynasty?

193. Crocodile or uraeus between wavy lines; pyramidal back, pierced. Wood. Roman?

194. Mould for casting a Semitic tablet. Slate.

129. *Roman age.* 195. Mould for casting medallion of Augustus (?). Black steatite.

196. Stamp APRE; pyramidal back pierced. Black steatite. Roman.

197. Stamp with male head; knob handle. Wood. Roman.

198. Stamp with uraeus; knob handle. Wood. Roman.

199. CAPAΠIAC HPAKΛEI; in centre ACT KTH (ἄστεος κτῆσις "city property"). Knob handle. Wood. Roman. Pl. lxi.

200. ΦIΛAΣTH?, or ΦIΛAΣ, TΞ = 360. Uraeus in centre. Knob handle, pierced; piece of palm fibre rope through it. Wood. Roman.

201. Swastika, + + A ⲱ in spaces. Knob handle, pierced. Wood. Gurob. Christian.

202. Foliated cross in relief. Ridge handle, pierced. Wood.

203. EΛOΓIA KYPIOY, cross in centre. Knob handle. Wood. Christian. Stamp for the bread of the Agapē.

204. O AΓIOC AΠA ΠAXⲱMI "saint Pachomios," cross in centre. Rough square handle pierced. Inscription direct. Wood. Coptic.

205. Monogram of Є AΠA MAXAIPH "Unto Apa Makhairē." Reverse, monogram of Є AΠA ΠAXⲱMH "Unto Apa Pakhōmē." Wooden stamp for cakes in honour of the saints.

206. Monogram of ANTⲱNIOY, Saint Anthony, IC XC = IHCOYC XPICTOC. Reverse, monogram of ΓЄⲱPΓIOY, Saint George, around an upright and diagonal cross (P formed by the O on the stem). Wooden stamp, as previous.

207. ΦOIBAMIA; ridge handle, pierced. Wood.

208. AVEΞ for AΛEΞ, Alexander; ridge handle pierced. Wood.

209. AMAZⲱI between crosses, Amazoi. "To Amazō," Artemis of Ephesos. Square handle, low, with diagonal cross. Wood. Christian.

210. ЄVΦOPIA, "abundance." Reverse ⲨATOC. Wood.

211. BIKTⲱP, Victor, Swastika. Small square handle, pierced. Wood.

212. BACIΛЄ(IOC) "Of the king," stamp for royal property. Small square handle, pierced, B on it. Wood. Christian.

213. BOA. Reverse BOYC. Wood.

214. Three joined circles. Square handle, pierced. Wood.

215. KAICAPO(Y) "Of Caesar." Well made loop handle. Wood. IInd cent. Pl. lxii. Such large, well cut, lettering is seen on stamps with the name of Trajan (*Fayum Towns*, xvi).

216. ⲐEⲱXAPIC AMHN "Theokharis, truly." Well cut rounded loop handle on back, XMΓ = 643. Wood. Christian.

217. Uraeus and ΠA. Ridge handle, pierced. Wood.

(218. A, two key patterns, emblem in middle, hand at end. Rounded loop handle on back. Wood.

219. ΠAHCIC. Hand. Paesis occurs on papyri and among martyrs. Rounded loop handle. Wood.

220. OPC(EYC). Hand. Perhaps Orsanos, Orses, or some other Horus name. Back, see photograph above, ridge handle, pierced. Wood.

221. Fret pattern and hand. Ridge handle, pierced. Wood.

222. Cross pattern, reverse, interlaced triangles; on a stem handle. Wood.

223. EVANⲐЄⲱ, "I prosper well," or "Triumph to God," and monogram of NIKⲱⲐEOY, "Of Nikotheos." Reverse monogram of ΠPⲱTEOY "Of Proteas." Wood.

224. Pottery stamp; five-rayed star; back indistinct. Pl. lxi.

225. Pottery stamp, with interlaced triangles in relief; loop handle on back.

226. Roundel of pottery with branched cross in relief. Koptos.

227. Wooden stamp I̅C̅ X̅C̅ NIKA; ridge handle broken off. Wood.

228. + IC XC NIKA. Shallow square handle on back. Wood.

229. I̅C̅ X̅C̅ NIKA three times repeated, and six various patterns. Reverse, square handle, pierced, with the same inscription. The K is in relief, in all cases, the rest incised. This formula appears on coins of John Zimisces 961–75, but was in use from A.D. 751 onward. Wood. This was probably intended for impressing Eulogial or Eucharistic bread. Pl. lxii.

230. Scroll between crosses. Also a cross on the end. Ridge handle, pierced, with loop of palm fibre rope. Wood.

130. *Arabic.* 231. Wooden stamp, "'Alai el Dyn" (Greatness of the Faith). No handle. Wood.

232. Wooden stamp, "Hasan abu Mtagār." Ridge handle pierced.

233. Arabic wooden stamp. Pl. lxi.

234. Pottery, roughly incised wet. "Allah." Reverse, "Billah"? Long reel of pottery.

235. Pottery, moulded "Ibn Kah"; pyramidal back with ridge, stamped trefoil patterns.

236. Wooden stamp, handle on back worn with use. The face inscription is an invocation, beginning "Oh, blessing of the Ten, help us in this juncture...!" On the back is an inscription at right angles to the face, "Hasan effendi has bequeathed the place of work of the mu'allim el nagar (or the carpenter) on the 18th Rabi awwal year 1255" = 1839 A.D. It seems to have been for sealing a large mud seal on the door of premises.

The following objects are not illustrated, as they are mostly published elsewhere.

131. *Clay sealings.* The use of the smaller stamps was probably for sealing jars of wine and provisions, as the frequent references to Rennut indicate. The large stamps of Roman and Arab period were probably for farm purposes, such as sealing up doors of granaries, and stamping on piles of flour to prevent theft. The hand which appears on four of these stamps is descended from the habit of marking with the hand, before the use of stamps, as continues to be done now in Egypt. The following are examples of the use of stamps. Those of the early dynasties are with the Proto-dynastic section, and are already published; whole bricks are in the Architectural section.

237–44. Jar sealings from the stores of the temple of Sety I at Qurneh, see *Qurneh*, pl. xlvi, p. 13.

237. "Oil of the glorious temple of Sety in the house of Amen." Conical, white plaster.

238. "Wine of the glorious temple of Sety in the house of Amen." Flat, black mud.

239. "Men-maot-Ra, oil of ....." Bun-shaped, white plaster.

240. "Palace of Men-maot-Ra, excellent wine from upon the west." Flat, black mud.

241. "Men-maot-Ra, honey of the palace on the west of Thebes." Bun-shaped, white plaster.

242. "Wine of ..... of Uti." Flat, black mud.

243. "Oil of the house of Bantanta." Conical, white plaster.

244. "Fresh oil of ducks." Conical, white plaster.

Thus the conical forms are all from oil, and the flat forms from wine jars.

245. Plaster sealing with cartouches of Ramessu III. Tell el Yehudiyeh.

246. Pottery impress of stamp of Ramessu III. "*Onkh Hor Ka nekht oa Suteniu, Onkh Să ra neb taui User maot ra mer Amen, nesut bati neb khou Ramessu heq An.*" The *onkh să ra* title is very unusual. Thebes.

247. Plaster sealing in a jar neck. ΚΕCΤΟΥ.... ΝѠΡΒΑΝΟΥ ΠΤΟΛΕΜΑΙΟΥ, the last four letters inside the circle, retrograde. Uraeus in centre. Koptos.

248. Plaster sealing, ink written ΔΙΟ...Β.

249. Mud and straw sealing ...CΚΟΛΗΟ in line. Circular stamp monogram of ΠΑCΕΑC? Byzantine.

250. Mud sealing. ... ΝΟΤΕ... ΑΕ .... in line. Circular stamp with cross. Byzantine.

251. Mud sealing, illegible; showing vine leaf plugging of jar neck. Byzantine.

252. Mud sealing; ΘΕΟΥΧ..... around a cross. Byzantine.

253–4. Mud sealings; ΕΚΛΗCΙΑ around a cross. Byzantine.

255. Stamp with large cross, Α, Ѡ, in lower corners. Mud.

256. Stamp with *orante*, arms raised, cross below each. Mud.

257. Jar sealing with signs scored on it ϹΧ.

258. Ball of mud with nine impressions of seal with galloping horse, *nefer* below.

259. Cake of dried dung, with the *onkh* cross impressed.

See other Byzantine stamps in *Tombs of the Courtiers*, xlviii.

---

260. Roll of plain papyrus; the interior of the Revenue Papyrus. Ptolemaic.

132. *Slips of stick for measures.* 261–80. Slips of palm stick with divisions and inscriptions. The writing refers to dimensions "Breadth of the belt" "Length of the back" "Back" "Left length of the inside" "Depth of the inside" "Breadth of the CVBC." Also personal names are given, Termuthis, Pelēsoukhos, Diōn, Anōlēnes. On four there is, within 5 inches of the end, a uraeus with disc on the head, the top toward the end; one of these has two uraei and a *ha* plant below.

There are three scales of division occasionally found; three single spaces averaging 1·287, probably a sixteenth of a cubit of 20·6, marked ΜΟΥΝΜ; three scales of division averaging 2·39 inches; one scale in red 24·2 long in 25 spaces, each divided in quarters. This is the Greek double foot, decimally divided, and 2·39, before named, is $2\frac{1}{2}$ such divisions.

The difficulties in dealing with these are:— (1) whether the lengths are intended between the lines, or (2) from a line to the butt, or (3) to the line before or after the writing. (4) What was the object measured? By the "belt" it was a figure of some kind; ΖѠΝ(η) and ΖѠϹ(τηρ) are both used. The *left* length of the inside is noticeable. Both of these seem to bar the measuring for cartonnage head pieces. Each of the slips have been broken up in three or four pieces; yet these were tied up together, and not scattered. Found broken up in the wrappings of mummy crocodiles. Hawara.

281. Various plain slips of palm stick, with the previous.

133. *Painting.* (Not in plates.)

282. Limestone incised for inlaying coloured paste. Tomb of Atet, Meydum. iiird dynasty. As also others following, to 290.

283. Inlaying from face, in red, black, and white paste.

284. Case of fragments of inlaying, and odd pieces.

285. Fragments of coloured stucco.

286. Bull leg of a chair, on fragment of limestone sculpture showing surface dressing by metal scraper.

All the above pieces were found loose after smashing of the sculptures.

287–8. Pieces of stucco on mud plaster, scene of ducks over a pond.

289. Similar, legs of a deer, and an indistinguishable fragment.

290. Similar, hind leg and tail of a baboon descending a desert slope.

291. Piece of wooden coffin painted, showing the method of marking out spaces along a band by fine red dividing lines. Each space varies according to the sign to be placed in it, and a plain space is left between each two sign spaces. The sign spaces (each including the inter space) seem to be in proportion one to another; the goose, *hetep,* and mouth as 11 units, seated figure as 8, triangle *da* and *nesut* as 6, leg as 5. The unit varies from 0·1656 to 0·1764, mean 0·1712 m.d. 0·0034. $\frac{1}{80}$ of the foreign foot of 13·41 is 0·1675, which may be the source of this unit. It has no relation to the Egyptian cubit or digit. The height of the band 1·49 has no relation to the spaces. The sign spaces without inter space agree more nearly, being on a basis of 0·1570 m.d. 0·0015; but this unit is not a likely fraction of a known measure. Rifeh. xiith dynasty.

292. Piece of painted wood with head and shoulders of a man, named "Keeper of the house, Tehuti-hetep." xviiith dynasty.

293. A case of fragments of paintings on stucco, from fine scenes. Tell Amarna (and on to 296). xviiith dynasty.

294. A case of fragments of coarser scenes.

295. A case of fragments of floor and ceiling painting.

296. Nineteen fragments of painted pavement, and one piece of bands from wall.

297. Fragment of painted board, with wreath, eagle, &c.; possibly part of an imperial portrait, such as was placed in minor temples. Fayum. iiird cent. A.D.

298. Wax portrait from Hawara, published in *Roman Portraits,* vi, 40.

299. Another, in *Roman Portraits,* viii, DD.

300. Another, in *Roman Portraits,* ix, WW.

INDEX

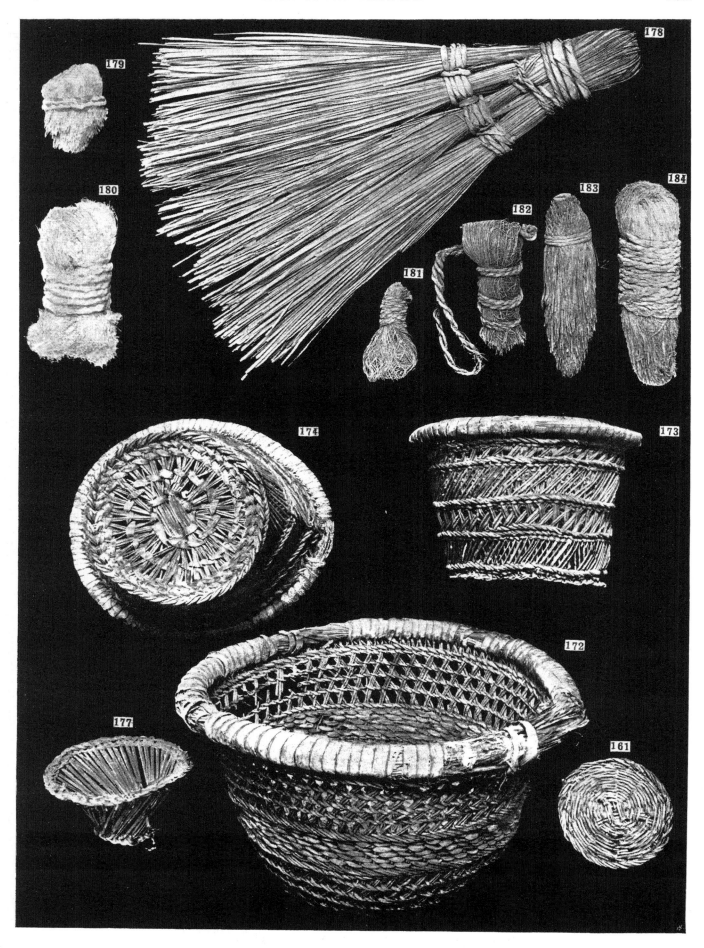

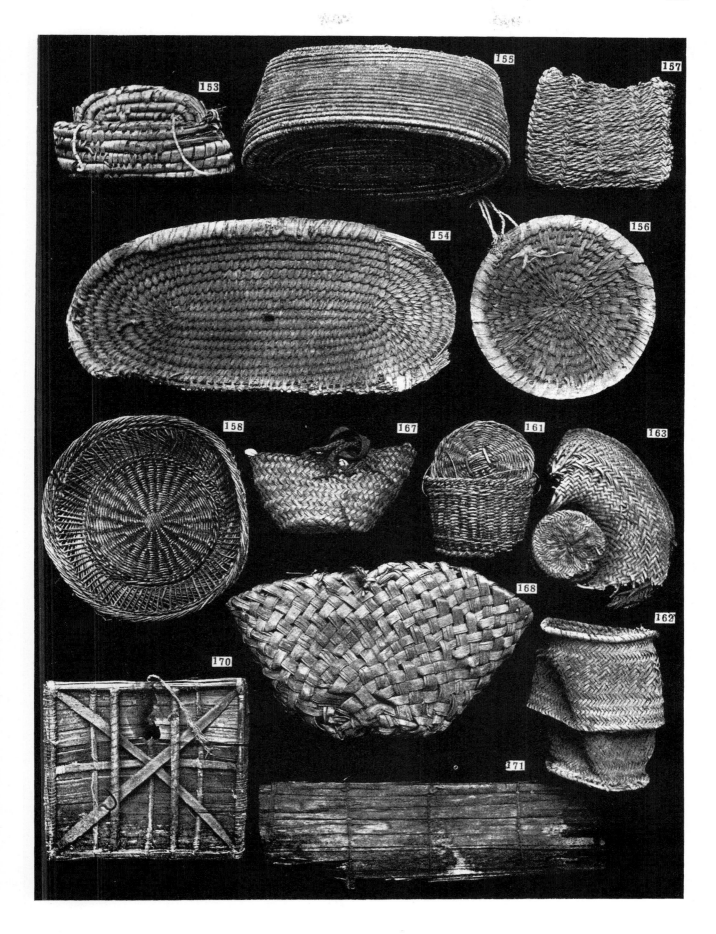

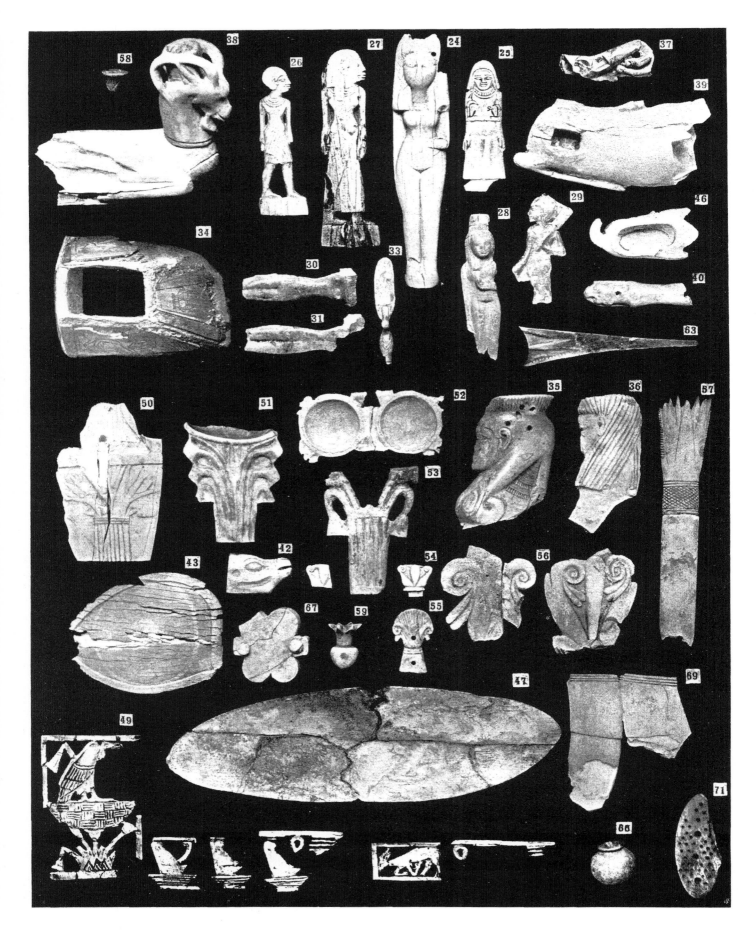

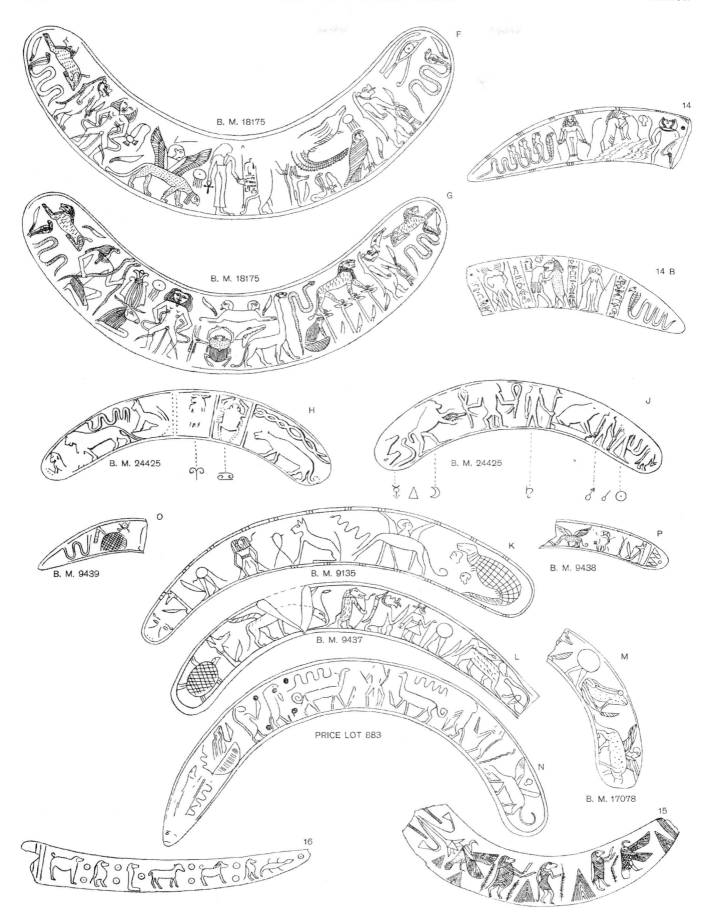

B. M. 18175

B. M. 18175

B. M. 24425

B. M. 24425

14

14 B

J

H

O

B. M. 9439

K

B. M. 9135

B. M. 9437

PRICE LOT 883

L

N

B. M. 17078

P

B. M. 9438

M

16

15

B. M. 9434

B. M. 38190

B. M. 9436

B. M. 6178

B. M. 24426

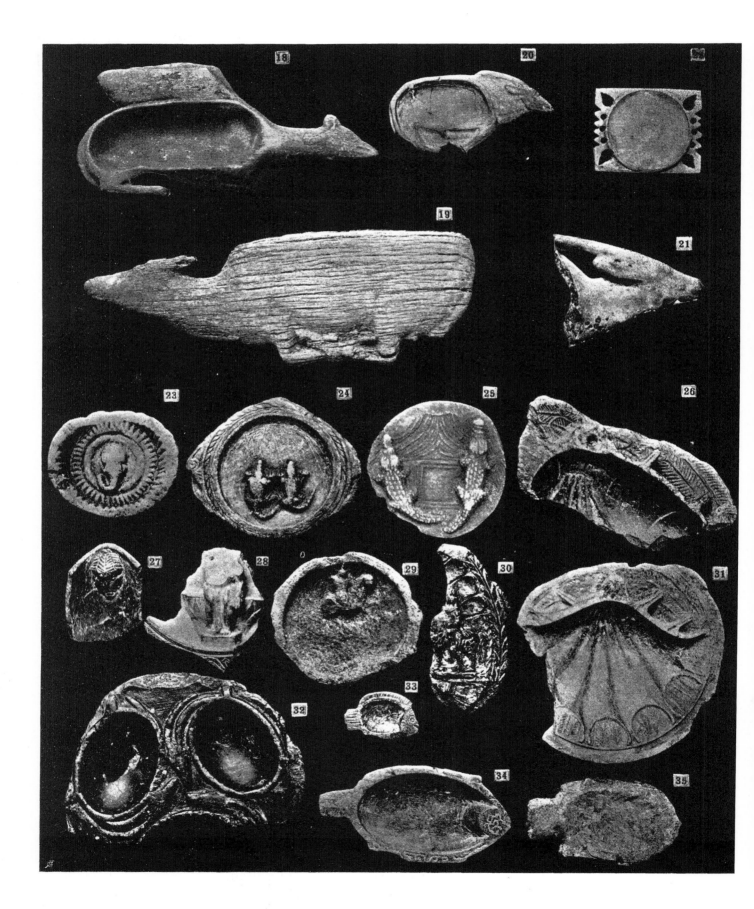

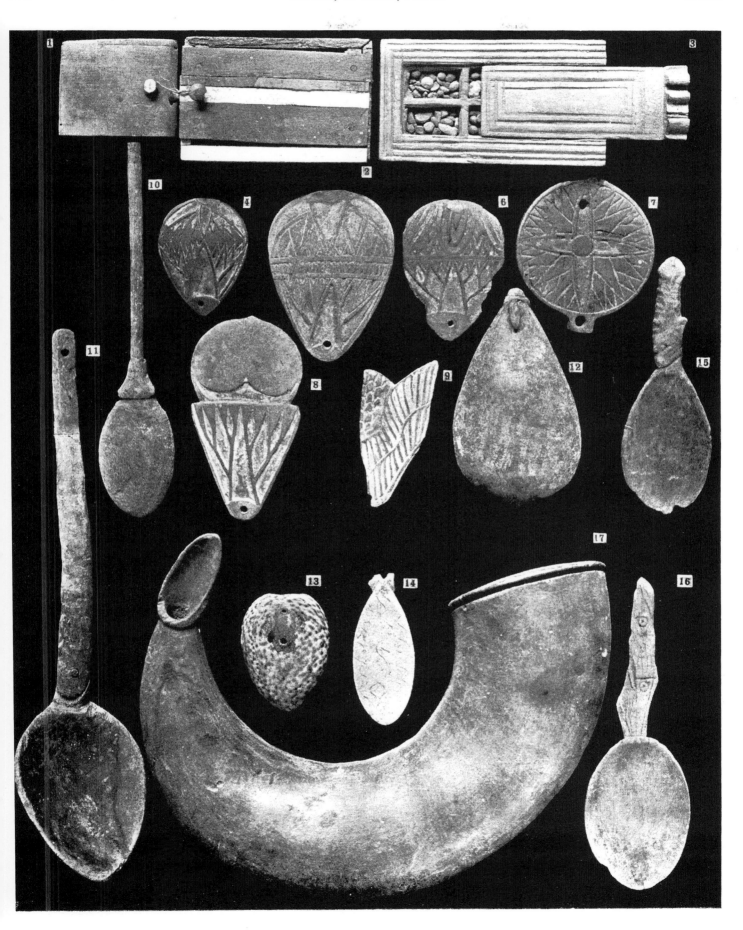

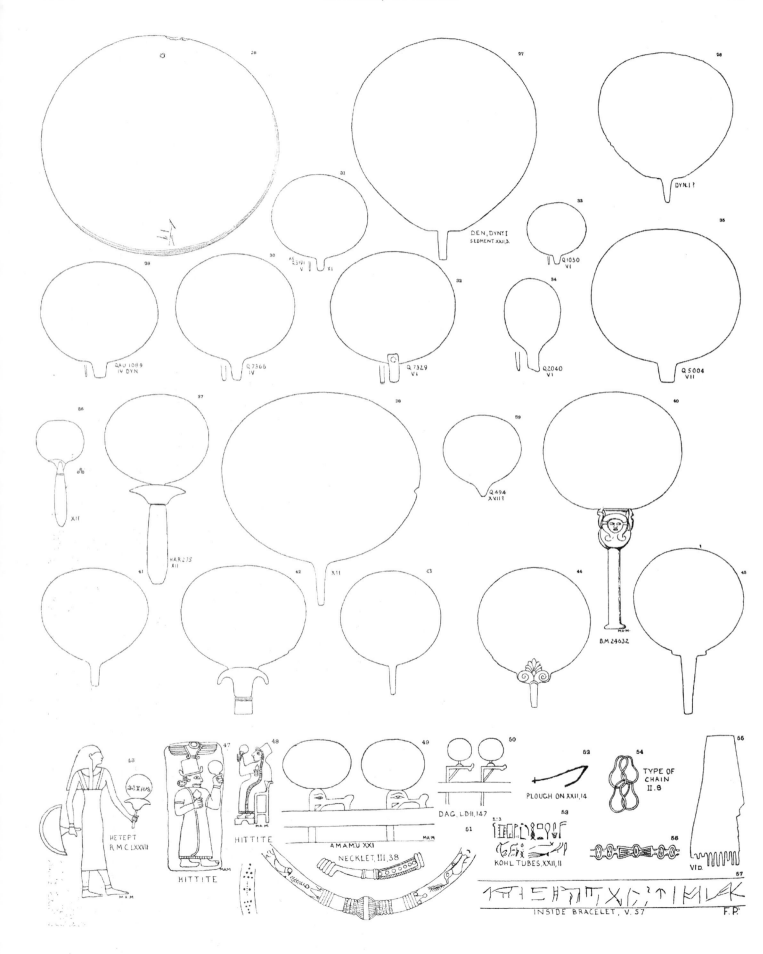

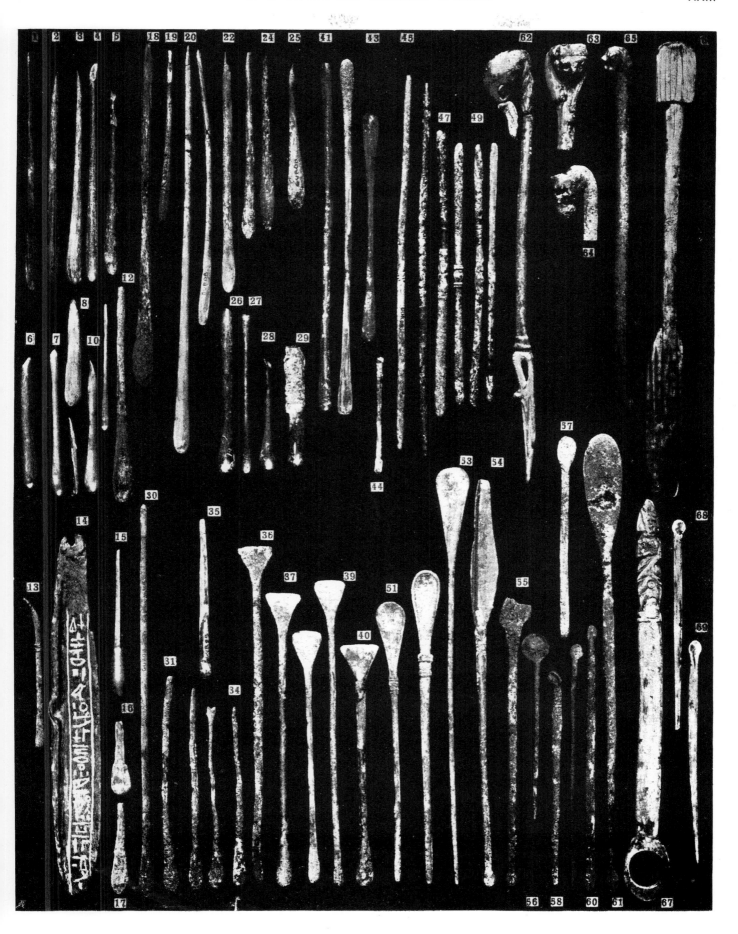

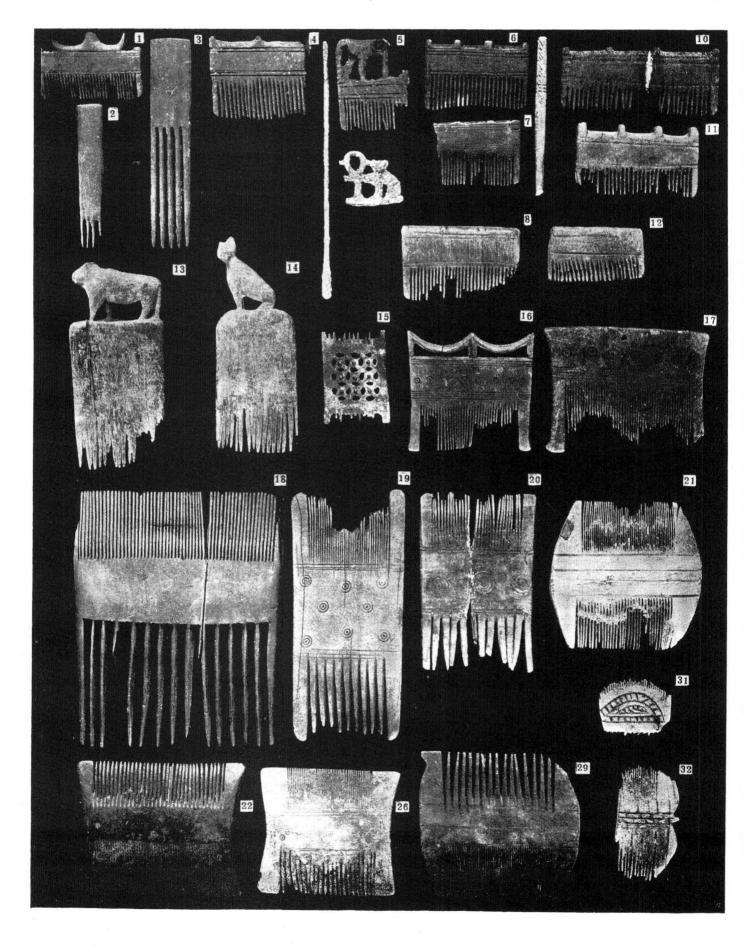

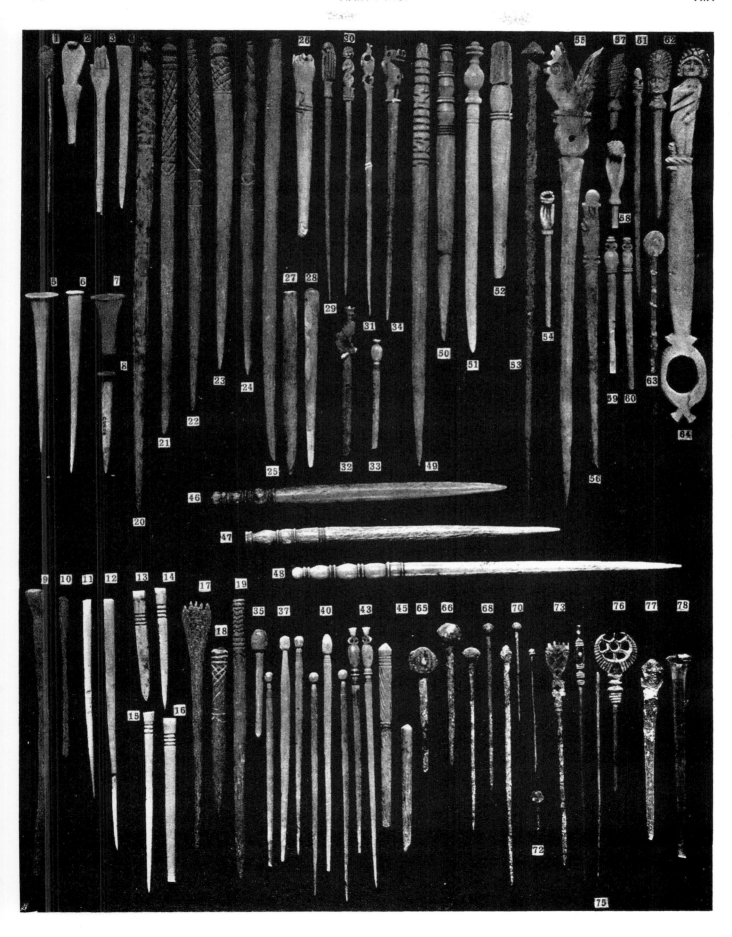

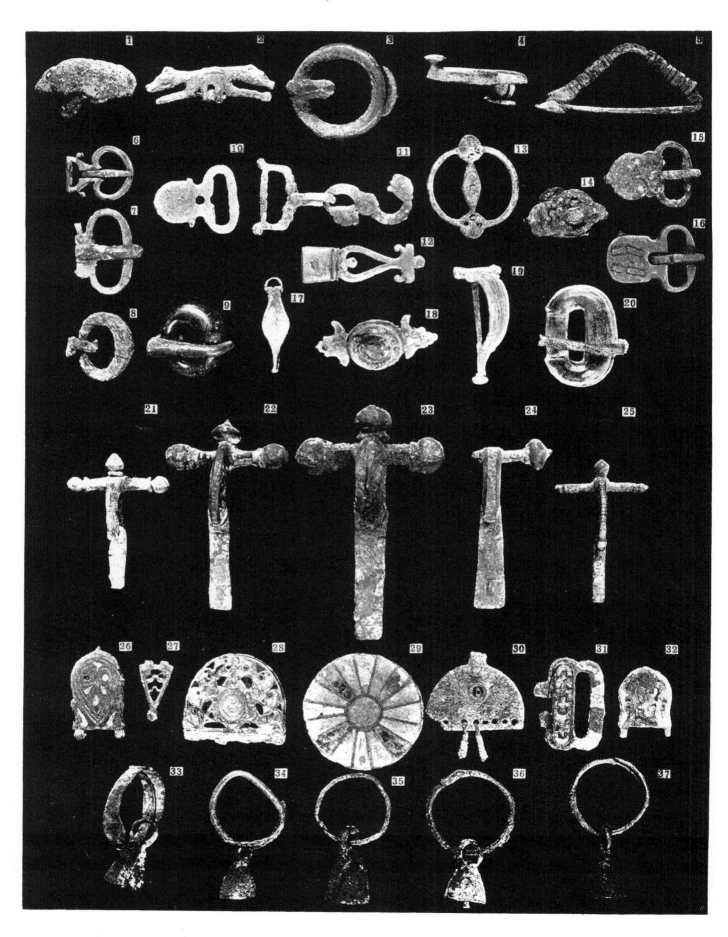

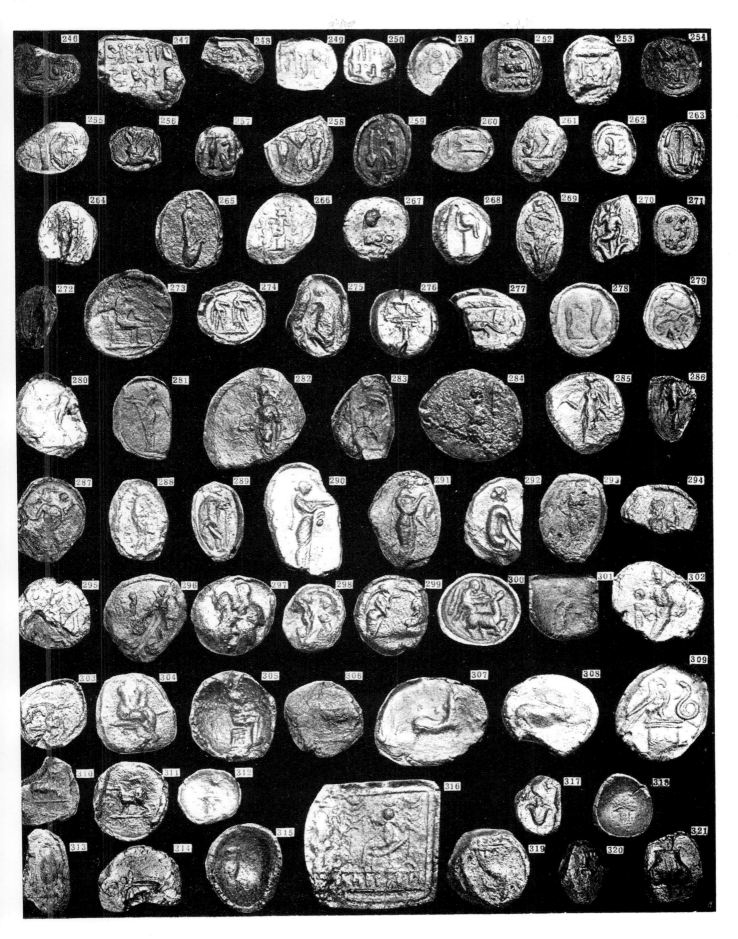

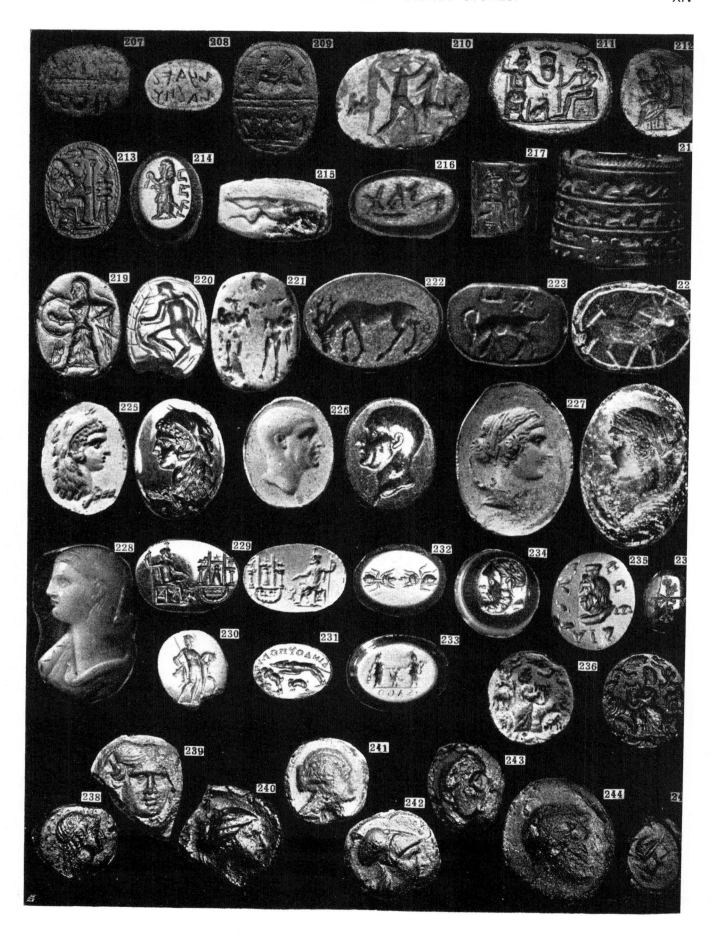

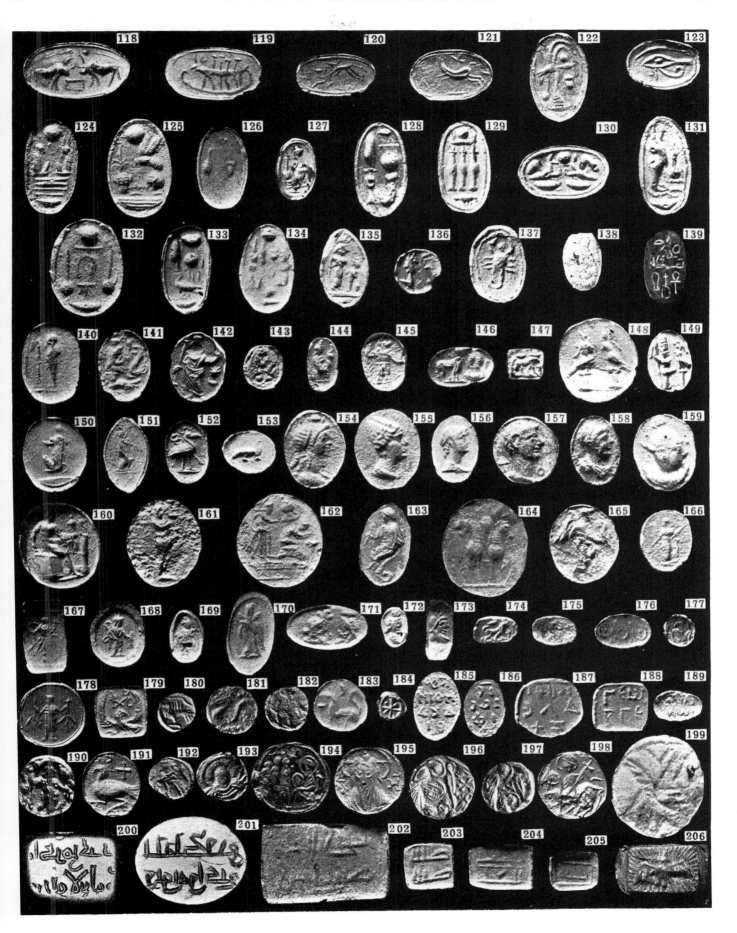

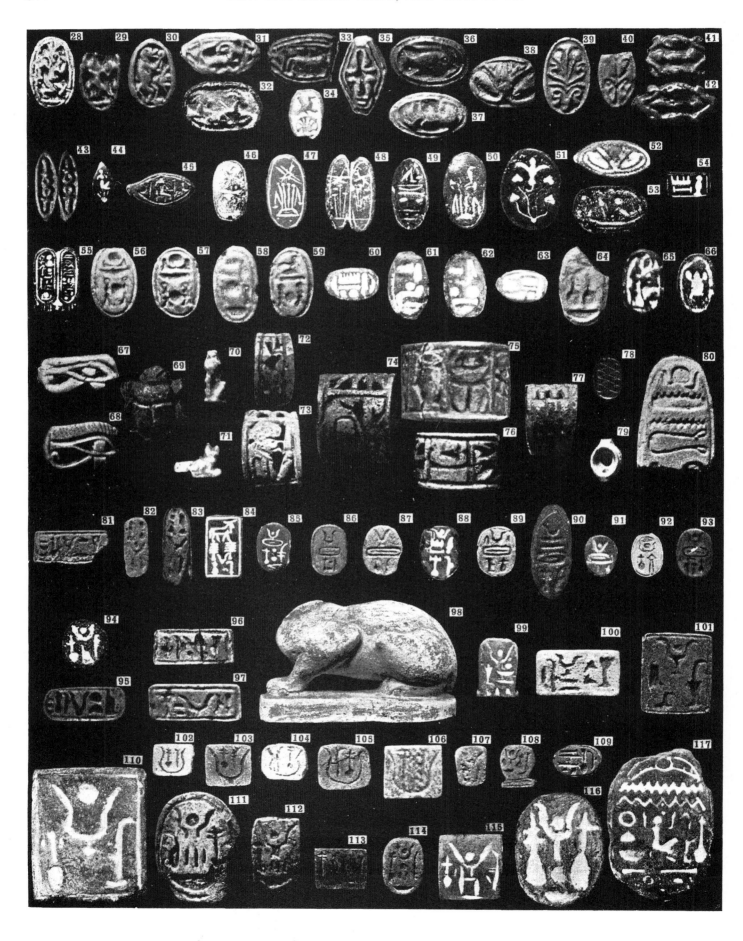

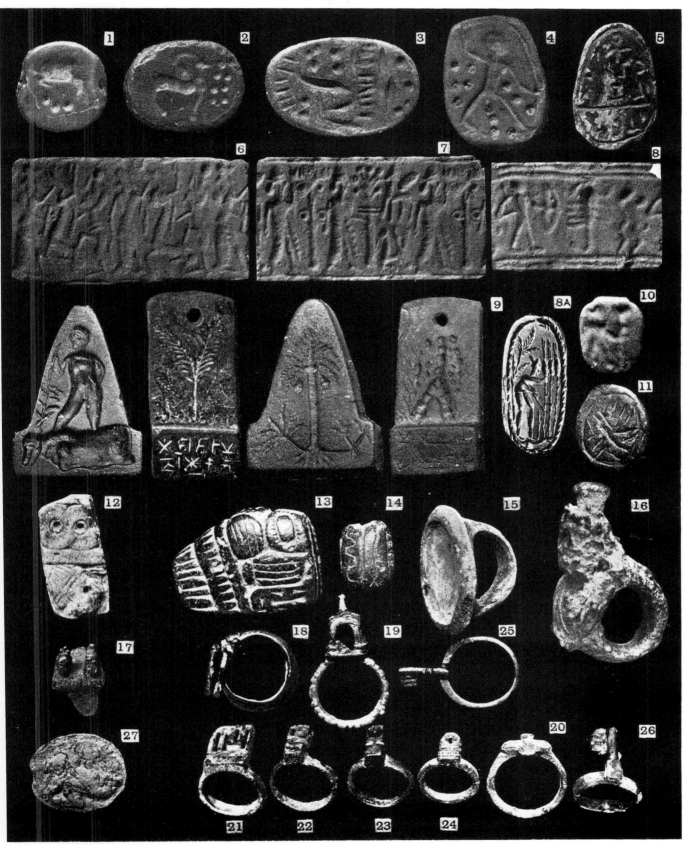

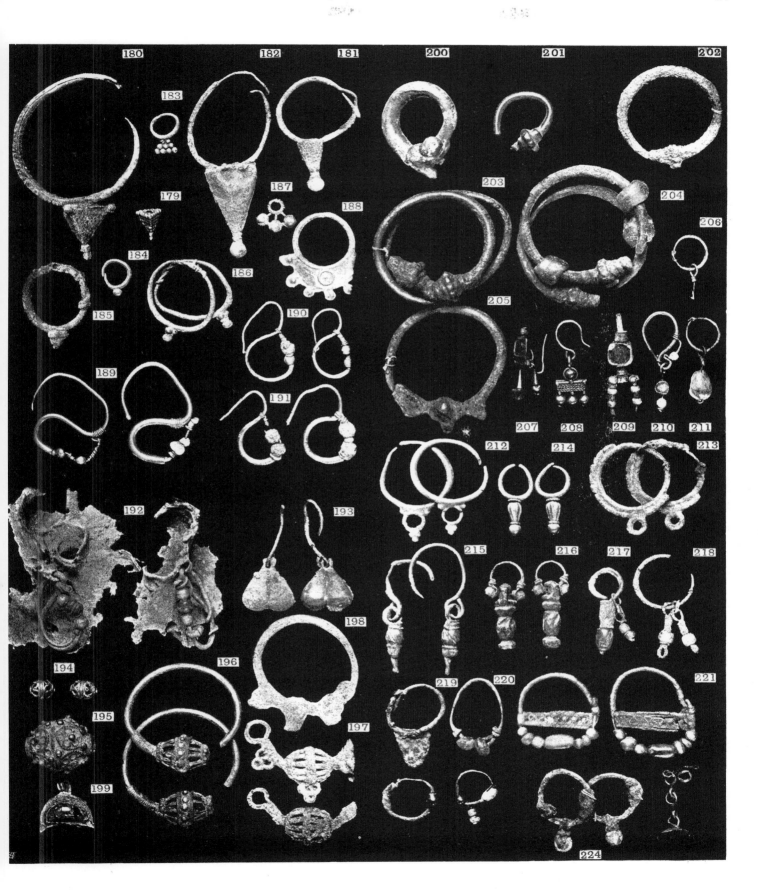

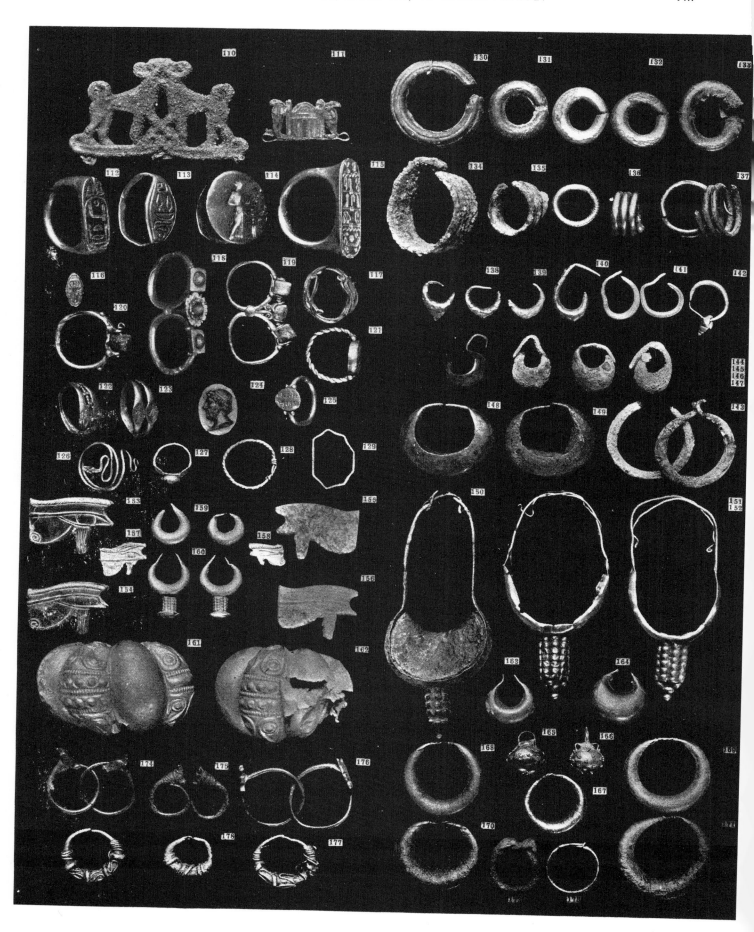

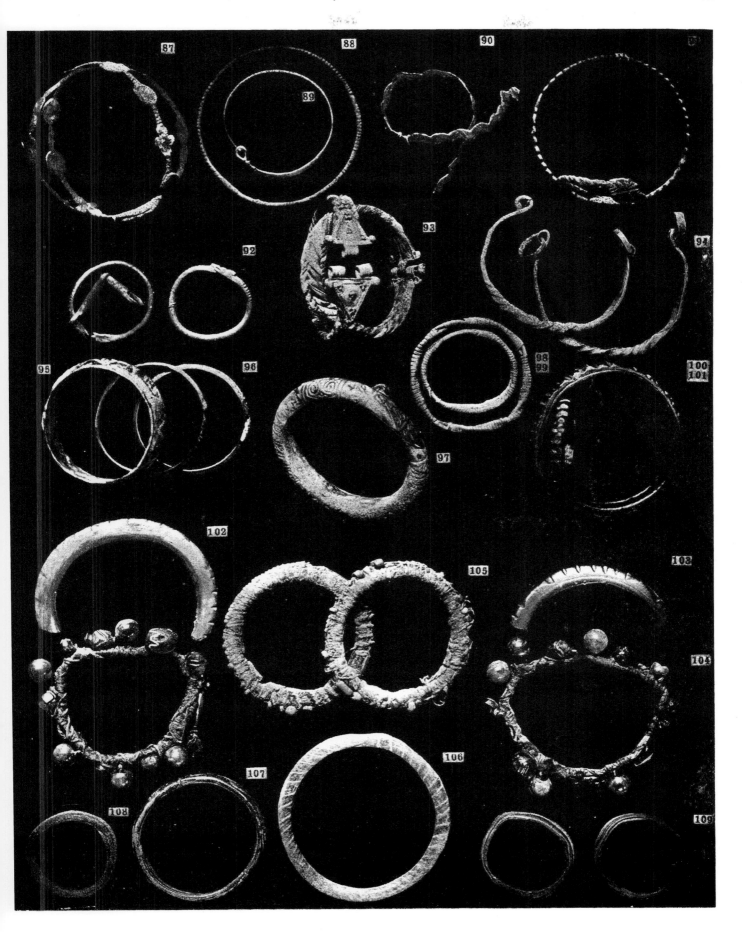

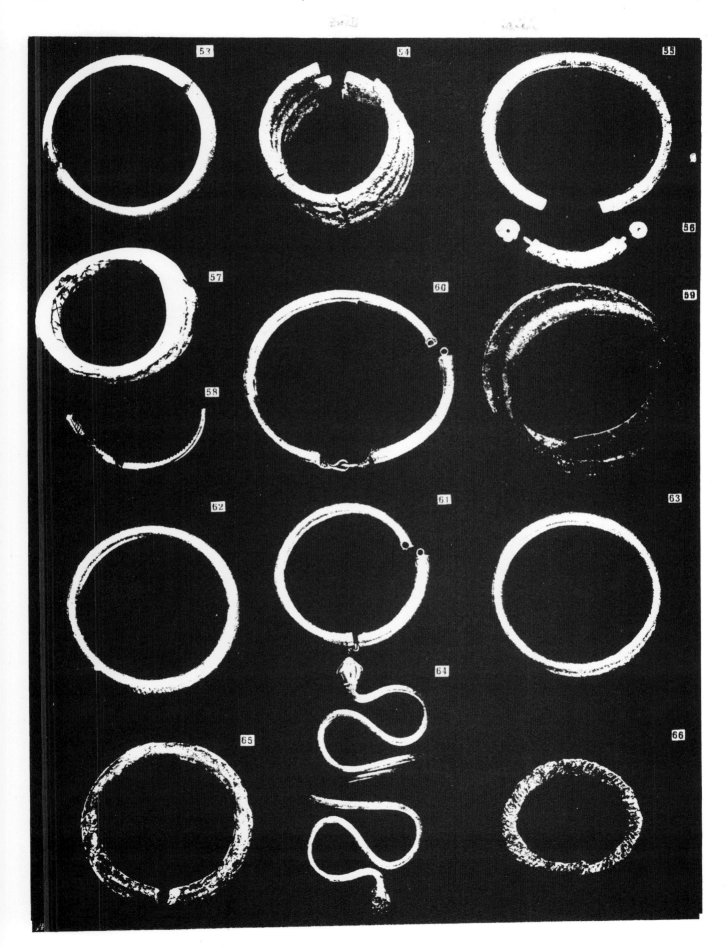

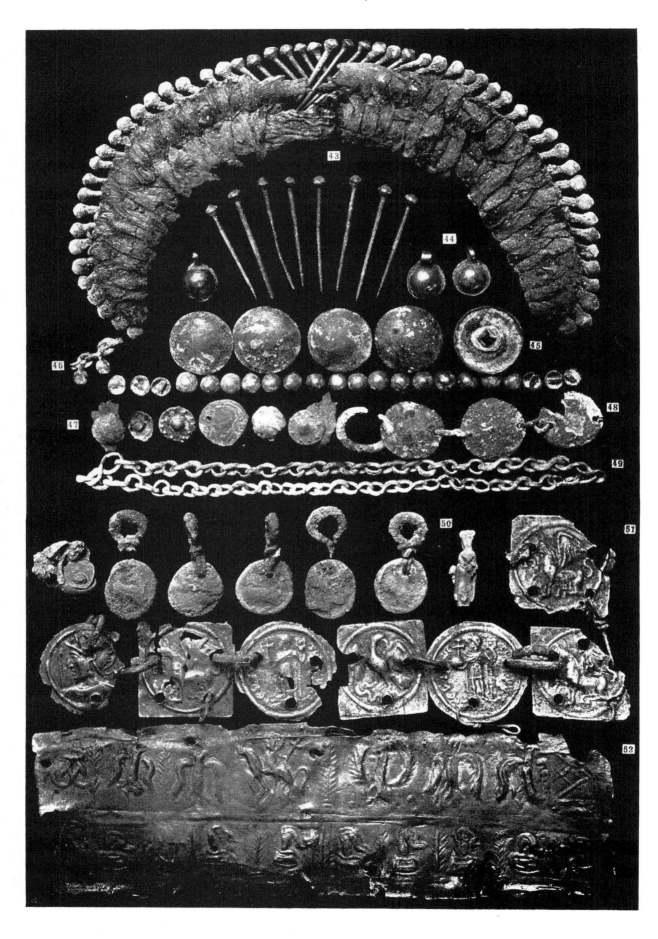

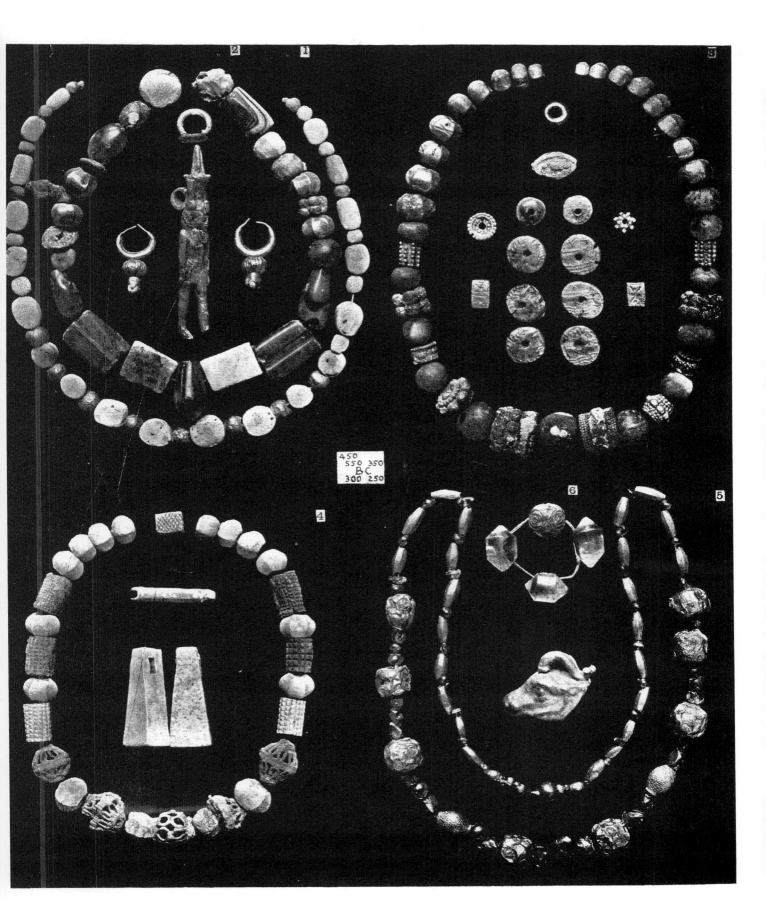

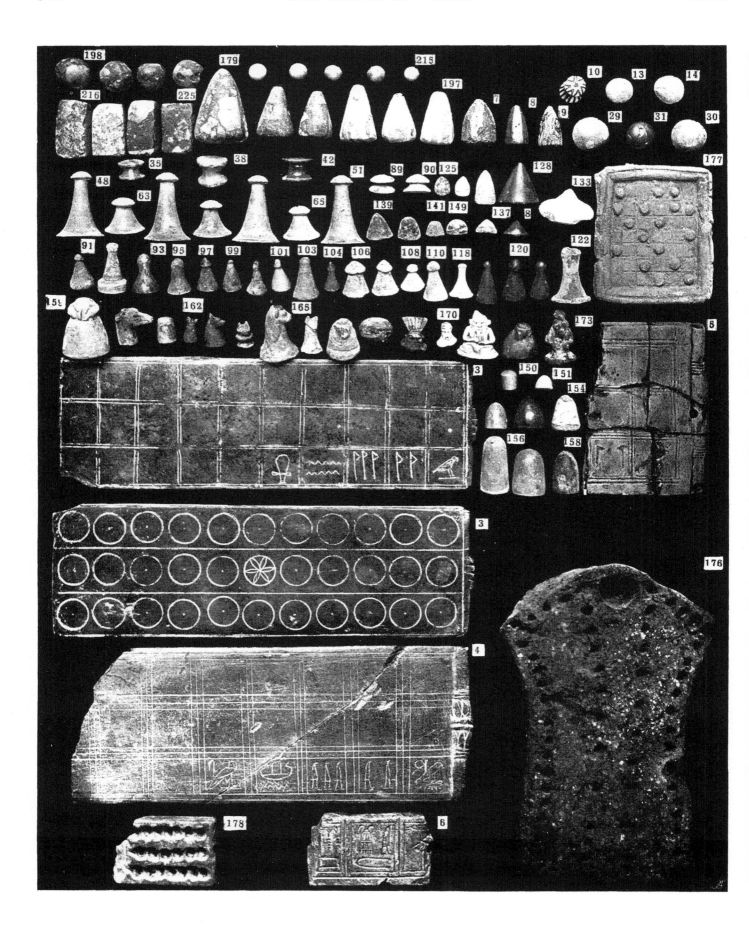

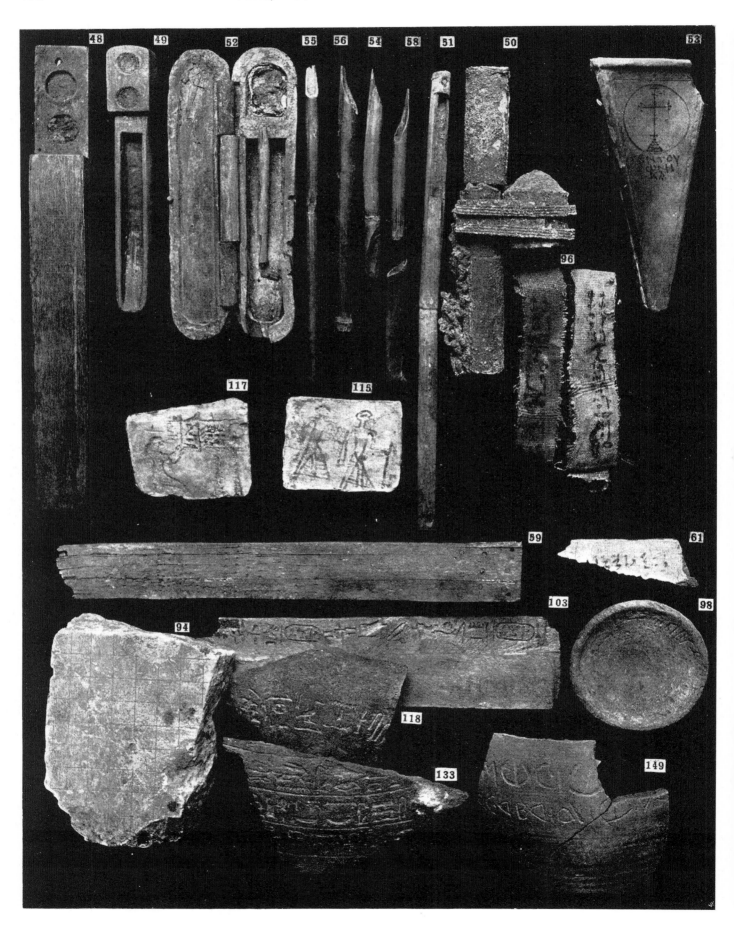